Routledge Revivals

The Collected Poems of Christopher Smart

First published in 1949, this book presents the collected works of eighteenth-century poet, Christopher Smart. Smart's character and his poetry are difficult to disentangle – both egocentric, given to exhibitionism, childish, oscillating between the extremes of self-belittlement and self-glorification. Few other poets, however, match him in directness of expression. It is the aim of this edition to present as complete a text as possible in the way that Smart himself would have seen it and, in giving some account of the poet's life, to link his poetry with it. The book will be of interest to students of eighteenth-century literature and history.

I0592941

The Collected Poems of Christopher Smart

Volume One

Edited by
Norman Callan

Routledge
Taylor & Francis Group

First published in 1949
by Routledge & Kegan Paul

This edition first published in 2017 by Routledge
2 Park Square, Milton Park, Abingdon, Oxon, OX14 4RN
and by Routledge
711 Third Avenue, New York, NY 10017

Routledge is an imprint of the Taylor & Francis Group, an informa business
Editorial Matter © 1949 Norman Callan

Publisher's Note
The publisher has gone to great lengths to ensure the quality of this reprint but points out that some imperfections in the original copies may be apparent.

Disclaimer
The publisher has made every effort to trace copyright holders and welcomes correspondence from those they have been unable to contact.

A Library of Congress record exists under LC control number: 50000063

ISBN 13: 978-1-138-22247-2 (hbk)
ISBN 13: 978-1-315-29481-0 (ebk)
ISBN 13: 978-1-138-22252-6 (pbk)

CHRISTOPHER SMART

By courtesy of the Editor of *The Library*

(From a painting now in the hall of Pembroke College, Cambridge)

THE
COLLECTED POEMS
OF
CHRISTOPHER SMART

edited, with an introduction
and critical comments
by
NORMAN CALLAN, M.A.

VOLUME ONE

ROUTLEDGE AND KEGAN PAUL LTD

First published in 1949
by Routledge and Kegan Paul Ltd
68-74 Carter Lane, London, E.C.4

Second impression 1967

To my Wife

Printed in Great Britain by Lowe & Brydone (Printers) Ltd, London

CONTENTS

CONTENTS

CONTENTS

MISCELLANEOUS POEMS

vii

CONTENTS

OCCASIONAL POEMS

CONTENTS

INTRODUCTION

INTRODUCTION

ATTRIBUTION AND TEXT

THIS edition contains all of Smart's poetry with the following exceptions:

> The Translation of Horace (1767)
> The Translation of Phaedrus (1765/6)
> The libretti of *Hannah* and *Abimelech*
> The Latin Poems

While the reasons for omitting these will, it is hoped, be obvious, a further caveat must be entered which is of a different kind. Smart wrote largely for the periodicals of his day, especially for the *Student*, the *Midwife* and the *Gentleman's Magazine*, and a great deal of his verse was printed either anonymously or over pseudonyms, of which he used a large number. We know he wrote as Mrs. Midnight, Mary Midnight, Mr. Lun, Zosimus Zephyr, Ferdinando Foot, Ebenezer Pentweazle, Nellie Pentweazle, Martinus Macularius, Quinbus Flestrin, the Female Student, and perhaps 'S',[1] and it may be that, like the Baker in Carroll's poem, he had other names as well. This makes the task of ascertaining the canon of Smart's poetry confusing, and the fact that many pieces are printed more than once does not lessen the difficulty. In view of this the claim for completeness may be a rash one, for there are perhaps poems lurking under other pseudonyms, or even under kr.own ones, which have yet to be discovered.

An edition of Smart is necessarily based on two main sources—(i) the collections Smart made of his

[1] For a list of pseudonyms, see Gray's *Bibliography*, mentioned later.

own verse, (ii) *The Poems of the Late Christopher Smart*, a collection made by the poet's nephew Christopher Hunter and published at Reading in 1791, twenty years after Smart's death. In addition there are Mr. W. F. Stead's text of *Jubilate Agno*, published as *Rejoice in the Lamb, a Song from Bedlam*, London, 1939, and various minor attributions.

(i) Smart's own publications are listed on p. xxxix.

(ii) Hunter has been taken to task for excluding *A Song to David*, but perhaps it is as well that he did so, for if its inclusion had meant the dropping of other, lesser poems, our knowledge of Smart's verse would have been the poorer. As it is, he is the only known source for a number of *Fables*, and for such poems as 'To Miss S—— P——e', 'Ode to Lady Harriot', and so on. His date and his family connexion with Smart would seem to make his acceptance of a poem reasonably trustworthy.

I have been unable to see the manuscript of *Jubilate Agno*, but Mr. Stead's text supplies a more than adequate substitute. For the method followed in reproducing this text see the note on p. 377.

In 1902 Mr. G. J. Gray published in vol. vi. of *Transactions of the Bibliographical Society*, 'A Bibliography of the Writings of Christopher Smart'. This remains for all practical purposes the definitive account of Smart's work, or at any rate of his poetry, the only important addition being the *Jubilate Agno*. Attempts to add to Gray's list have not proved very successful, based as they have necessarily been on internal evidence. The most ambitious of these attempts, the attribution of an anonymous *Benedicite Paraphrased* which appeared in the *Museum* (1746) to Smart, has now been shown to be inadmissible since the poem is elsewhere reprinted under the name of the Rev. James Merrick. The leaning of this edition is therefore towards caution, no poem being accepted without reasonably good external evidence for its attribution.[1] This has led to the exclusion of at least two pieces which may still be shown to be genuine, namely, the *Paraphrase of the Lord's Prayer* (*Gentleman's Magazine*, 1754) and the fable of the *Kite and the Doves* (*Universal Visiter*, 1756).

The text of the edition is based on printed copies, since, apart from *Jubilate Agno*, and one or two minor pieces such as the lines 'To Lyce' in the library of Pembroke College, no manuscript of Smart's poetry is known. The general principles followed have been (i) to present a text printed in Smart's lifetime wherever possible, (ii) where there are two such texts, to prefer the later one, (iii) to prefer Hunter's text to that of his successors Anderson and Chalmers, who follow Hunter's mistakes and add to them. Occasional departures have been made when either an earlier text or a posthumous one seemed preferable. In all cases the source of the text is indicated at the foot of the poem.

As far as possible it has been the aim of this edition to present a text as Smart would have seen it. He is reputed to have been careless about seeing his work through the press, but despite the rather condescending tone of his editors, their efforts to improve on him seem to me almost always wrong. Smart, for instance, describes the cock as the 'night-exploding' bird—an epithet which he got either from Lucretius or Milton. This may be unduly pedantic, but Hunter's emendation to 'night-exploring' is pure nonsense. Similarly in the line

And sorrow'd silence o'er th' untimely urn

which Hunter emends to 'Sorrowing in silence . . .', it seems to me more likely that Smart is coining a Latinism on Miltonic lines than that he meant to write what Hunter attributes to him. In fact, the more carefully

[1] Hunter's acceptance of a poem is regarded as such.

one reads Smart's text the more convinced one becomes that if what is to be presented is what Smart wrote, and not what somebody else thought he should have written, one must stick to the copy he himself allowed to be made public. No attempt, therefore, has been made to improve either Smart's spelling or his punctuation, neither of which is so out-of-the-way as to cause difficulty to the modern reader. A few corrections of obvious misprints (such as *land* for *laud*) have been made silently, but the occasions when anything more than this has been attempted have been signified in the notes. *Jubilate Agno*, the *Psalms*, the *Parables*, and the *Hymns for Children* have been printed from photostat copies of the respective editions: in other cases Hunter's text has been corrected by earlier editions wherever such existed. But many poems have had to be copied out first by hand and then in typescript, a process which does not make for accuracy, so that, in spite of care, some errors may have crept in. It is to be hoped that these are neither too numerous nor too seriously damaging.

A word should be said about the order of the poems. No strict chronological order has been possible, since we are not sure when most of the poems were written. Smart's own method of mixing poems of various kinds has considerable attractions, but in the end the difficulties it presented in an edition of this nature, and the overriding need for some kind of orderliness made it unworkable. The poems have been grouped under five heads, and within each section the order of publication has generally been followed. Exceptions have been made where a number of poems addressed to the same person indicate that they were written at about the same time, or where several poems fall together as a group not large enough to justify a section to itself.

Finally the Notes. Some readers will be disappointed at finding them so scanty. Where, however, the choice lay between a complete text and fuller annotation, the former was obviously preferable. Mostly I have restricted myself to biographical references which seemed important to an understanding of Smart's poetry, and for the greater portion of what Smart wrote this should be sufficient. The outstanding exception is of course *Jubilate Agno*, where nothing short of Mr. Stead's copiousness would have served any purpose in elucidating Smart's quaint erudition. I have therefore made no attempt to do this, using the notes as a clearing-house for biographical matter connected with other poems, and leaving the substance to speak for itself.

SMART'S LIFE

For one who has been called 'a forgotten poet' Smart has attracted a surprising amount of biographical attention. There are three full-length lives, several shorter sketches, and the list of detailed studies of portions or incidents in his life is formidable. The kind of life Smart lived forms a fatal attraction for the curioso of literature. There is the early romance with Anne Vane, well enough authenticated to be taken seriously, and sufficiently obscure to encourage speculation about its effect on the rest of the poet's life; a secret (or nearly secret) marriage; insanity and confinement, with the concealments inevitably attaching to such matters; and lastly, the fantastic intrigues of eighteenth-century Grub Street. From another point of view also it must be recognized that Smart was a notable if eccentric figure in his day. He could (and did) claim acquaintance with more than one aristocratic family, and his literary friendships included all the great of his time from Johnson downwards. A glance through the list of subscribers to his version of the Psalms is indication enough of the solicitude of his friends and of the interest his personality aroused.

Above all, it is this personality which has whetted the taste of the curious. For in view of the amount of material available, Smart remains a strangely shadowy figure, repulsive or attractive according to the temperament of the investigator, yet always enigmatic: and it is here that biography—or, not to put too fine a point on it, literary gossip—and literature touch. With the possible exception of Christopher Hunter, the poet's nephew, whose *Memoir* prefixed to the Reading edition of Smart's poems is a masterpiece of astute vagueness, no serious critic has been able to avoid presenting him in the light of a paradox—the paradox of a man who seems to have lived a sordid existence and yet produced one of the greatest religious lyrics in English poetry. The brief critical appendix to these volumes indicates the situation clearly enough. It seems impossible to avoid taking sides on the moral issue of the essential goodness or badness of Smart's nature, and inevitably this *parti pris* affects the literary judgement.

Common sense, therefore, as well as reasons of space, would seem to desiderate only the barest outline of such facts as are known of Smart's life. Some of these facts, especially dates, are controversial, and the reader who wishes to form his own judgement on such matters is referred to the body of literature which has grown up around Smart.[1]

Christopher Smart was born in 1722 at Shipbourne Fairlawn in Kent, where his father, Peter Smart, was steward to William, Viscount Vane, a younger member of the Barnard family whose seat was Raby Castle, near Durham. Smart's birth was premature, a fact which may account for his delicate constitution, and until the age of eleven he seems to have lived a sheltered life, acquiring most of his education from his father, a man of some culture.

---

[1] See 'Bibliography'.

When Smart was eleven his father died, and his mother transferred the family to Durham, where, says Hunter, 'he would have the advantages of a good school, change of air to strengthen a weakly frame, and the notice and protection of his father's relations'.

The Smart family had been associated with Durham for some generations. Dr. Peter Smart, the poet's grandfather, had been headmaster of Durham Grammar School, and it was at this school that Christopher now received the grounding in Latin and Greek which later won him considerable notice at Cambridge. The relations mentioned by Hunter may or may not have been the family of Lord Barnard. Smart was of course no connexion by blood, but he and his sister were received as members of the family at Raby Castle, and it is evident that he spent much of his time there.

One of his companions was Anne Vane, daughter of Henry Vane, who later succeeded to the Barnard title. Smart fell in love with her, and (if the story told by his daughter Mrs. Le Noir is true) the verses 'To Ethelinda' were written for her when he was thirteen. At about the same time the pair eloped together, but were quickly brought back again. Not much notice seems to have been taken of the affair, and Smart went on living at Raby Castle.

Those who are looking for a key to Smart's erratic career will find it readily in this early episode. Anne Vane grew up an attractive, witty woman, and his disappointed love may have given rise to some of Smart's later irresponsibilities. He mentions her more frequently than anyone else in *Jubilate Agno*, and Mr. W. F. Stead hazards the guess that she meant to him 'a great deal more than Mary Chaworth meant to Byron'. This is a possible interpretation, but without much stronger evidence it must remain a tentative hypothesis. Apart from the references in *Jubilate Agno*, Smart's only allusions to her are in the *Ode to Lord Barnard* and in the *Epithalamium*, which is usually assumed to have been written to celebrate Anne Vane's wedding in 1746.

When Smart was seventeen he went up to Pembroke Hall, Cambridge. He was enabled to do this by a yearly pension of forty pounds, granted to him by Anne Vane's maternal grandmother, Henrietta, Duchess of Cleveland, who had been impressed by the reports of Smart's abilities as a classical scholar.

Since Smart's sycophantic flattery of the aristocracy has come in for a good deal of strong condemnation, particularly in connexion with the *Ode to Lord Barnard*, it may be as well, without attempting to exculpate him, to point out that his debt to the Barnard family was considerable. At Raby Castle, whatever we may make of the business of Anne Vane, he must have had a cultural background more enlightened than any that his family's limited means could have provided. Moreover, besides the initial pension, which enabled him to go up to Cambridge, he may well have owed it to the kindness of Henry Vane, Anne's father, that this pension was continued after the death of the duchess, perhaps even as late as 1749 when he had got badly into debt. These facts, as well as other possible kindnesses of which we know nothing, while they do not excuse the hyperboles of the *Ode*, do at least give a ground for Smart's gratitude—a point which his critics have sometimes forgotten: and the same may be true of his addresses to the Delavals, another family with which Smart had connexions from his Cambridge days until the time of his death.

At Pembroke Smart quickly made a name. He was awarded a classics scholarship in 1743, and published a good deal of Latin verse, as well as an ode in honour

of the tercentenary of his college, and one celebrating
the return of George II from the War of the Austrian
Succession. In 1745 he was elected fellow, and there-
after held several college appointments. He acquired a
reputation, too, as a wit, which led him into drinking
and spending more than he could afford. One of our
chief sources for this aspect of Smart's life are the
letters which Thomas Gray wrote to his friend
Wharton. As one would expect, the scholarly, retiring
Gray disliked Smart's convivialities, and if the com-
ment that Gray 'walked as if he had fouled his small-
clothes, and looked as if he smelt it' is really Smart's
it would seem that the dislike was mutual. At this time
much of Smart's energies were taken up with the pro-
duction of his farce *The grateful Fair, or A Trip to
Cambridge*, and of this Gray wrote:

'... he is amusing himself with a comedy of his own
writing, which he makes all the boys of his acquaint-
ance act, and intends to borrow the Zodiack Room,
and have it performed publicly. Our friend Lawman,
the mad attorney, is his copyist; and truly the Author
is himself to the full as mad as he. His piece [he says] is
inimitable, true sterling wit and humour by God; and
he can't hear the Prologue without being ready to die
with laughter. He acts five parts himself, and is only
sorry, he can't do all the rest.'

The play, apart from the prologue and one soliloquy,
has not survived, but Smart's evident delight in it (and
there is no reason to assume that Gray has exaggerated
his remarks) is a clear indication that he was turning
from scholarly pursuits to tastes which were later to be
given full rein in the *Midwife* and the *Old Woman's
Oratory*. In the same letter Gray comments:

'... his vanity and faculty of lying ... are come to
their full maturity. All this must come to gaol or

bedlam, and that without any help, almost without
pity....'

Another of Smart's distractions was his position as
tutor to John Blake Delaval, a wild young man who
was sent down in 1746 for taking a certain Nell
Burnet to his rooms disguised as an officer. Gray gives
an acidly amusing account of Smart's appointment to
the tutorship, and of the discovery of the mis-
demeanour which led to the expulsion of his protégé;
and a year later he is prophesying the same fate for
Smart himself, saying that he 'must necessarily be
abîmé in a very short time, his debts daily increase'.
Finally, in 1747, Smart was arrested for debt at the
suit of a London tailor. Gray describes the efforts
which were made by the fellows of the college to clear
up his indebtedness (for about £350) and grudgingly
adds his own contribution, urging Wharton (success-
fully, it seems) to persuade Henry Vane to continue
Smart's pension, which was naturally in danger of
being stopped when Smart's behaviour became gener-
ally known.

Smart was for the time being rescued from his
creditors, but the long absences (presumably in Lon-
don) indicated by the college books, and everything
else we can learn, show that he was tiring of academic
life. Finally, he gave it up for London's Grub
Street.

This seems to have happened about 1749. He had
made friends in London before leaving Cambridge,
and his poetry had begun to appear in periodicals as
early as 1746. He went into partnership with John
Newbery, the enterprising bookseller and vendor of
quack medicines, writing for his two papers, the
Student and the *Midwife*, certainly editing the latter,
and perhaps the former as well. In these journals (they
are faint echoes of the *Spectator*) he wrote copious

prose and verse under an assortment of pseudonyms. He also published a collection of his own poems.

Out of his work on the *Midwife* there grew another enterprise. This was the Old Woman's Oratory. As we have seen, Smart had always had a hankering for theatricals, and this kind of performance seems to have suited his temperament. The show was put on first at a tavern, and then at the New Theatre, Haymarket, and, as far as can be judged, was a mixture of opera, buffoonery, and extravagant parody of Orator Henley's performances in the Clare Market.[1] A programme printed in the *London Daily Advertiser* for December 2nd, 1751, gives some idea of its nature:

'*Tomorrow the 3d inst. will be exhibited in the Great Room at the Castle Tavern in Pater-noster-Row*, A GRAND CONCERT of VOCAL and INSTRUMENTAL MUSICK, BY several EMINENT HANDS. At the same time will be Opened, and given gratis, THE OLD WOMAN'S ORATORY, OR, HENLEY IN PETTICOATS. To be conducted by Mrs. MIDNIGHT, Author of the MIDWIFE, And her FAMILY. N.B. There will be FOUR ORATIONS, After the First of which, Signior ANTONIO AMBROSIANO, from Naples, will perform A CONCERTO on the CREMONA STACCATO, Vulgarly called the SALT-BOX. After the Second, will be presented, A GREAT CREATURE, On a very Uncommon Instrument. After the Third, A Solo on the Viol d'Amore, and another Piece by the GREAT CREATURE. Then the Candles will be snuffed to soft Musick by Signior Claudio Molepitano, For his Diversion, being the First Time of any Gentleman's appearing in that Character. And the whole will conclude with an Oration by OLD TIME in Favour of *Matrimony*; a solo on the Violin-cello by CUPID *in*

---

[1] See notes to the *Hilliad*.

propria persona; and a Song to the Tune of the *Roast Beef of Old England*; to which all the good Company are desired to join in the Chorus.'

Smart was author of the script, producer, and perhaps took the part of Mrs. Midnight as well. He certainly acted in the show, though one reference to Master Smart 'who makes me laugh so heartily with his spoons and salt-box' suggests that his part was that of Signior Ambrosiano. In view of what Gray tells us of *A Trip to Cambridge* he may well have taken both parts.

Originally intended to advertise the *Midwife* the Oratory assumed more importance as time went on, so that the paper began to appear irregularly, and, when it did appear, to rely for copy more and more on the script of the Oratory. Finally the *Midwife* ceased publication in 1752. The Oratory continued for several years longer, though Smart's connexion with it ended sooner, perhaps when Mrs. Midnight took to substituting animal comedians for human ones.

All this activity, along with two literary quarrels, the first with William Kenrick, writer of the *Pasquinade*, the second with the charlatan Sir John Hill, against whom Smart wrote the first book of the *Hilliad*, kept Smart very much in the public eye. His verse was appearing in the *Monthly Magazine* and the *Gentleman's Magazine*, and he was also competing for the Seatonian Prize, for which purpose he had been allowed to keep his name on the college books. This prize, for a poem on the attributes of the Supreme Being, he won with such regularity (four times in five years) that it was a matter for comment when he failed to do so.

In 1753 Smart married Anna Maria Carnan, Newbery's step-daughter, and went with her to live at Canonbury House, Islington. From this time onwards his life is obscure. He seems to have suffered from several bouts of serious illness, and to have been so badly in want of money that he was forced into the hack-work of translating Horace into prose. In 1756 he and his friend Richard Rolt entered into a contract with the bookseller Richard Gardner to write for a periodical called the *Universal Visiter*, and to undertake no work of a similar kind for a term of ninety-nine years. The contract has been the subject of much debate, Johnson (who wrote several pieces to help Smart out) even suggesting that no one in his senses could have entered into it; but in point of fact the terms were in no way harsh, nor is there any sign that they were harshly applied.

In any case they had little effect on Smart, for in the same year his period of confinement for insanity had begun. Here again there is a dearth of fact, both as to the cause of his being shut up and the place of his confinement. It would appear that he was at first kept in a private house (possibly Newbery's), that he was subsequently transferred to a regular asylum (perhaps St. Luke's), that a further period of private confinement followed, and that he was once again shut up in a regular asylum (Bethlehem or elsewhere) until some time in 1763.

The causes of his malady we learn largely from casual comment, often either hostile or facetious. His two failings seem to have been a form of religious mania and chronic inebriety. Johnson's two statements on the matter are widely quoted, both as evidence of Smart's fundamental sanity and of the Doctor's goodness of heart:

'Madness frequently discovers itself merely by unnecessary deviation from the usual modes of the world. My poor friend Smart shewed the disturbance of his mind, by falling on his knees, and saying his prayers in the street, or in any other unusual place. Now although, rationally speaking, it is greater madness not to pray at all, than to pray as Smart did, I am afraid there are so many who do not pray, that their understanding is not called in question.'

And again:

'I did not think he ought to be shut up. His infirmities were not noxious to society. He insisted on people praying with him; and I'd as lief pray with Kit Smart as anyone else. Another charge was that he did not love clean linen; and I have no passion for it.'

But what Dr. Pottle has told us of Boswell's methods of reconstructing Johnson's conversation, together with the fact that elsewhere Johnson speaks slightingly of Smart, makes this evidence somewhat suspect. In the absence of more definite information opinions on the rights and wrongs of the case remain a matter of personal sympathy.

Curiously enough this evidence may be already in our hands. During his confinement Smart compiled the long poem *Jubilate Agno*, the manuscript of which remained unknown until it was edited by Mr. W. F. Stead in 1939. The poem is a storehouse of biographical material for Smart's life, and thanks to patient editing has already thrown light on the nature of Smart's confinement and its duration. But owing to its cryptic style and the intimate nature of the references, much of it still remains obscure. How much more this poem will tell us about Smart's life depends largely on how much research can be done on it; and this in turn depends on how far such research may seem worth while.

Apart from its own literary merits, *Jubilate Agno* serves yet another purpose in enabling us to trace the genesis of Smart's *Song to David*, which was published soon after his release in 1763. Whether *A Song to David* was actually written in confinement is not known, but clearly Smart had been meditating the subject all the time that he was writing the *Jubilate Agno*. This is also true of his version of the *Psalms*, published by subscription in 1765. Here again the actual date of writing is uncertain. Mr. Middleton Murry has suggested that the *Psalms* were versified before the *Song* was written, and it is true that in *Jubilate Agno* Smart does refer to his 'version of the Psalms'. It would seem likely, however, that a work of this extent covered a period of several years, and that the *Song* was published while the *Psalms* had yet to be completed.

After his release Smart did not return to his family, and though they made attempts to get in touch with him he seems to have rebuffed them. Clearly one of the causes of irritation in the Smart household was the poet's improvidence, and Newbery had made testamentary dispositions which prevented Smart from benefiting from anything his wife might inherit. These dispositions may have been wise, but Smart resented them: he no longer published with Newbery, and intercourse with his family seems to have come to an end. Newbery, however, was generous. He set aside the profits of Goldsmith's *Martial Review* for his son-in-law, and indeed it is a testimonial to the respect and liking in which Smart was held that all his friends lent their help when he was in trouble. Johnson, Garrick, Burney, Goldsmith, Rolt, even Mason and Gray came to his assistance in one way or another.

Smart lived for a while in a house overlooking St. James's Park. He worked industriously. Beside the *Song to David* and the *Psalms* he published two collections of his own poems, verse translations of Horace and Phaedrus, and a rendering of 'the parables of our Lord' done in 'familiar verse'. He also wrote

the libretti of two operas, *Hannah* and *Abimelech*.
Altogether he seems to have been contented at this
time. A pension of £50 a year had been secured for
him, and if (as seems likely) the Epistle to Dr. Nares
belongs to this period, he may have been quite well off.

However, Smart's 'oeconomy forsook him' again.
There are records of various pathetic begging letters to
his friends (among them one to his brother-in-law,
Thomas Carnan) dated from 1766 onwards, which
show him in great want; and in 1769 (or about then)
he was taken for debt to the King's Bench prison. His
friends, especially Dr. Burney, obtained for him the
liberty of the 'rules'. While in prison he wrote his last
book of poems, the *Hymns for the Amusement of
Children*, which was published by Carnan in 1770. He
died in 1771.

SMART'S POETRY

It is not an easy matter to dissociate the poetry
Smart wrote from the life he lived. This is due in some
measure to the sort of criticism which has been applied
to his work since Browning included him in *Parleyings
with Certain People*, but much more to Smart's own
nature. Like Donne and Milton, he is persistently ego-
centric, but whereas they show the ego at grips with
the great problems of humanity, Smart's ego seems
too often entangled in a pettifogging exhibitionism.
His tone is so personal that unless the reader is pre-
pared to make the effort to understand his personality
he is continually subject to a feeling of irritation at the
self-absorption everywhere apparent.

For a sympathetic approach to his poetry Smart's
psychological development is therefore of some im-
portance. He is one of those people who never out-
grow the inferiorities and assertiveness of childhood.
He oscillates between extremes of self-belittlement and
self-glorification; between

For I am a little fellow ...

and

... now the deed's
DETERMINED, DARED and DONE.

In his earlier poetry (this is particularly true of the
Seatonian poems) much of the reader's pleasure,
though by no means all, comes from the sudden transi-
tions from grandiloquence to simplicity; from a
passage of Miltonic 'elevation' such as that in *On the
Goodness* beginning

> *Without thy aid, without thy gladsome beams*
> *The tribes of woodland warblers wou'd remain*
> *Mute on the bending branches ...*

to

> *And though their throats coarse ruttling hurt the ear*
> *They mean it all for music ...*

In the later verse, the *Hymns for the Fasts and Festivals*
and the *Hymns for Children* particularly, it is the
second mood which predominates. Under the stress of
emotional suffering, Smart seems to have turned more
and more to his childhood; not only to the sights and
sounds of the Medway countryside but to the emo-
tional attitudes and the unquestioning acceptances of
that time. No observation is more true of Smart than
Mr. Stead's that for all his recondite learning he lacked
an analytical mind. In *Jubilate Agno*, and to some
extent in all the poetry which follows, he simplifies the
problem of relating learning to understanding by view-
ing everything, from Pliny's natural history to the
reformation of the calendar, in the light of a naïve
literalness, which, however irritating it may be philo-
sophically, often makes for moving poetry. His cat
Jeoffrey is the servant of the Lord, who tells him he is
a good cat, spinks and ouzels proclaim that they too

have a Saviour, the writing of an Ode to a successful
admiral is to be compared to the swiftness of the ship
'when Christ the seaman was on board'.

A directness of expression, which makes no distinc-
tion between analogy and identity, has been singled
out as the most noteworthy characteristic of Smart's
verse by critics from Browning to Mr. Middleton
Murry. Used too exclusively this approach, however
penetrating, leads to the ignoring of other good quali-
ties in his poetry, qualities which are equally the
product of childhood. Smart's childhood must have
been a period of unusual sensitivity, heightened, one
may suppose, by his early love for Anne Vane; and it
is at moments when he succeeds in re-creating the
intense perceptiveness of those years that his poetry
glows. Enough has been written of the *Song to David*
and the *Hymns* for anyone who has an acquaintance
with those poems to know where to look for such
moments: but elsewhere in his poetry they have not
been generally recognized. They are to be found
everywhere: in the *Fables*—

> *The dew and herbage all around*
> *Like pearls and emeralds on the ground,*
> *The uncultur'd flowers that rudely rise,*
> *Where smiling freedom art defies,*
> *The lark in transport towering high,*
> *The crimson curtains of the sky* ...

in the pastoral pieces:

> *Their scythes upon the adverse bank*
> *Glitter 'mongst th' entangled trees,*
> *Where the hazels form a rank,* '
> *And court'sy to the courting breeze* ...

even amid the *facetiae* of *The Pretty Barmaid*, in such
a line as

> *Markt little hemispheres with stars.*

Smart is a poet with the eye of a painter developed to an unusually high degree. He has the stereoscopic vision which makes the object leap to the eye, the painter's sense of physical texture, and his skill in 'composing' a picture:

> *Then came Sleep, serene and bland,*
> *Bearing a death watch in his hand;*
> *In fluid air around him swims*
> *A tribe grotesque of mimic dreams.*

He is a miniaturist rather than a painter of broad effects. One of his key words is 'little'—which takes us back once more to his childhood and to his sensitiveness about his small stature—and the careful reader will find his poetry full of minute arabesques, which owe something of their manner to Pope, who was another poet with a miniaturist's eye, but for the most part are so peculiar to Smart that it is not easy to compare them with anything else in English poetry.

This is Smart's strongest claim, and a more than sufficient one, for greater notice than he has hitherto received; but it is by no means the only one. There is, for instance, his versatility. He practised almost every 'kind' of poetry which a conventional age recognized as such, and gave to each his own personal inflexion. The 'Night Piece', for example, had acquired almost a genre of its own since Lady Winchilsea's time, yet the kind of fantasy evident in the quatrain just quoted (a quatrain which Hunter significantly omits) is to be found in no other piece of the same type that I know of. 'The Fair Recluse' affords a similar instance. This is a 'gothic' poem which derives from Pope's 'Unfortunate Lady' and perhaps from *Clarissa*, and most of it might have been written by any poet of the period: but there is one quatrain which is peculiarly Smart's own—

> *Say, must these tears for ever flow,*
> *Can I from patience learn content,*
> *While solitude still nurses woe,*
> *And leaves me leisure to repent?*

The tone of these not very striking lines is of some
importance in understanding Smart's poetry. It looks
back to the earlier 'Eagle Confin'd' and forward to the
Psalms. From his early Cambridge days Smart un-
doubtedly suffered from a feeling—later all too unhap-
pily actualized—that he was being persecuted, and it is
this sense of a personal situation which gives his verse
a cryptic emphasis whenever the subject affords an
opportunity. Another instance is to be found in
'Reason and Imagination'. By accepted canons of
criticism this sort of thing should not happen: poetry
is supposed to be a release from emotion, and I am not
concerned to justify Smart's habit of identifying him-
self with a 'persecution situation' whenever he can.
What I do wish to emphasize is that when he 'trans-
lates' from Psalm xc

> *O be thou placable by pray'r,*
> *And stand between us and despair,*
> *How long wilt thou postpone?*
> *To these our off'rings as they burn,*
> *Do thou propitiate thy return,*
> *And let our tears atone.*

the poetry is what it is because Smart sees his own
position and that of persecuted Israel as one and the
same.

The clearest illustration, however, of the 'difference'
of Smart's poetry from that of his contemporaries is to
be seen in the *Fables*. Again, they are poems of a
recognized 'kind': the *Monthly Review* compared them
generously with the *Fables* of Gay and Moore. Yet,
though Gay was certainly one of Smart's heroes

(Smart regarded himself as the inheritor of the tradition of the Scriblerus Club in the war on dullness), the comparison is not really helpful. For one thing, Smart identifies himself invariably with the underdog; but it is more important to notice that the *Fables* do not depend for their effect on any neat point or moral so much as on the way the allegorical figures, 'nature', the bees, the mandrake, 'imagination', and so on, develop a personality of their own. This pictorial individuality more often than not overlays the moral and turns the poem into a fantasy quite unlike Gay's witty cautions.

What may be called the grandiose characteristic of Smart's style also arose from his personality. It is true that the use of Miltonic blank verse whenever the grand manner seemed to be required by the subject had become almost obligatory by the middle of the century, and that the *Hop Garden* and the Seatonian poems owe something to *Cider* and the *Seasons* as well as to *Paradise Lost*; but there was an element in Smart's nature compounded about equally of bravado and an infinite capacity for astonishment which showed itself in other things besides his handling of the technicalities of inversion and periphrasis. It is to be found in the early pindaric ode 'To the King', in the naïve outbursts of patriotism in *Jubilate Agno* and *General Draper*, in the *Psalms*, and even in such a passage as this from the *Hymns*:

> *I speak for all—for them that fly,*
> *And for the race that swim;*
> *For all that dwell in moist and dry,*
> *Beasts, reptiles, flow'rs and gems to vie*
> *When gratitude begins her hymn.*

Most clearly of all it is to be seen in *A Song to David*. In this poem Smart succeeded completely, for perhaps the only time, in harmonizing the extremes of his temperament, bravado and gentleness, erudition and simplicity, the immense and the minute. The almost universal praise lavished on the *Song* has undoubtedly been justified. It has not always been well considered, however. In the first place it is questionable how far many of its encomiasts really understand it. Before I had read Mr. Stead's introduction to *Jubilate Agno* a knowledge of some of Kipling's stories had convinced me that Smart was expressing in the *Song* the *arcana* of Freemasonry; and since I am not of that fraternity I suspect not only myself of being insufficiently equipped to comprehend it but others also, and particularly those who say that it presents no difficulty to the patient reader. Secondly, enthusiasm for the *Song* has damaged Smart's reputation as a poet by fostering what Mr. Edmund Blunden calls the myth that the writer was a sot who by accident wrote one consummate poem, and so distracting attention from his other verse. Particularly this is true in the matter of Smart's versification. The *Song* is a product of his later years, when (as happened with Milton) his rhythms had become more strongly marked, perhaps more grand, but certainly less fluid. This stiffening characterizes almost everything he published after 1763, and because of the interest which has been focused on these later poems his skill in handling the long stanza in the early pindaric odes, and the flexibility of his rhythms in octosyllabic and heroic couplets have been largely ignored. This is a pity, for there are few of Smart's early pieces, however trivial their subject, where the delicacy of ear, which is one of the essential qualities of a true poet, is not evident. The more I read him, the more I seem to hear an anticipation of the rhythms of the late A. E. Housman, and although there is probably no direct connexion, I think that the similarity may lie in the fact that they are both poets who had

fully absorbed the movement of the Latin hendeca-
syllabic line.

However this may be, that Smart was more than
ordinarily interested in the technique of versification
is clear from the introduction to his verse translation
of Horace,[1] and from the wide range of verse forms
that he used. It is also evident from the *Jubilate Agno*,
where, as Mr. Stead has pointed out, at least some of
the apparent incoherence may be explained as experi-
ment in new forms of verse in preparation for his
rendering of the Psalms. One case of this may perhaps
be instanced—a line which has been frequently cited as
evidence of Smart's madness:

*Let Ross house of Ross rejoice in the the great flabber
    dabber flat clapping fish with hands.*

Mr. Stead thinks there is a reference here to the floods
clapping their hands and another commentator has
suggested that 'Ross' may be the name of a fisherman
Smart had met in his travels. I would not venture to
disagree with either of them, but it has always seemed
to me that in this line Smart was trying to re-create
the visual and aural experience of watching a fisher-
man (or a fishmonger, for that matter) emptying a
catch of fish. In this case, of course, the 'hands' would
be human ones, and the syntactical disorder imposed
by the need to create a special sound effect.

Of *Jubilate Agno* as a whole there is no room to
speak. The publication of the poem in 1939 not only
enriched English poetry with some exquisite lines and
passages, but added considerably to our means of
assessing Smart's poetry. Once more, and with even
greater insistence, we are brought up against the
problem of personality—the personality of a man who
does not recognize that his misfortunes may in some

[1] See 'Critical Comments'.

degree be due to his own failings. The temptation to take sides, so evident in the passages cited in the critical appendix, is stronger than ever. Nevertheless, it is to be resisted. Enough harm has already been done by turning the *Song to David* into a miraculous *tour de force*. The balance will not be righted by portraying Smart as a persecuted mystic. To quote one of the more level-headed of the earlier commentators, 'Smart wrote enough to fill two volumes, and much of what he wrote is very good'. How good it remains for the reader of the following pages to discover.

Hatfield Broad Oak
  July 1947

ACKNOWLEDGEMENTS

ACKNOWLEDGEMENTS are tendered to the following:
Mr. W. F. Stead and Messrs. Jonathan Cape for permission to reprint the text of *Jubilate Agno*; the
Authorities of the British Museum for supplying
photostats of the *Psalms*, the *Parables* and *Jubilate
Agno*, and for much help from the staff of the Reading
Room; the Librarian of the Bodleian Library and the
Printer to the University of Oxford for permitting and
supplying respectively photostats of *Hymns for
Children*; the Librarian and Fellows of Pembroke
College for permission to collate the text of *A Song to
David*, for supplying a privately printed copy of the
'Tercentenary Ode', and for other kindness. To the
President and Council of the Bibliographical Society
for permission to reproduce the portrait of Smart; to
Mr. Stanley Horrocks, Borough Librarian of Reading,
and to the Editor of the *Reading Mercury* for much
help in connexion with this portrait and other matters.
To Mr. Middleton Murry, Professor Cyril Falls, Dr.
H. K. McKenzie, Miss Edith Sitwell, Messrs. Smith
Elder (for the extract from Browning's *Parleyings with
Certain People*), for permission to print extracts from
critical writings on Smart. The sources used in the Introduction and Notes have been acknowledged *ad loc*.
I would wish to mention in particular the work of the
late Professor E. G. Ainsworth and Dr. C. E. Noyes,
whose critical biography, *Christopher Smart*, so admirably documented, has helped me again and again; and
of Mr. W. F. Stead, whose Introduction and Notes to
Jubilate Agno have afforded continual enlightenment.
I regret that both Mr. Edmund Blunden's edition of
the *Hymns for Children* and Mr. Ruthven Todd's
Selections appeared too late for me to make use of

ACKNOWLEDGEMENTS

them. To those who have helped me with criticism and advice, my debt is too large for detailed acknowledgement. I must, however, express my thanks to Professor James R. Sutherland for much valued help and encouragement; to Mr. Norman Davis of Oriel College for obtaining for me the text of one poem; to Mr. Edmund Blunden for courteously setting me right about a doubtful attribution; to Mr. Geoffrey Grigson, whose wide knowledge of Smart has helped in so many ways; to Mr. William Palmer for reading the proofs of *Jubilate Agno*; and to my .wife, for whose patient assistance and encouragement the dedication of these volumes is an inconsiderable return.

SELECT BIBLIOGRAPHY

COLLECTIONS AND PERIODICALS

THE following is a list of collected editions up to 1791, and of some of the periodicals for which Smart wrote. The abbreviations in parenthesis are those used in the text to indicate the source of the poem. Where only a date is given in the text this shows that the poem was published by itself.

COLLECTIONS

Carmen Alexandri Pope, &c. (2nd edn.) 1746	(*CAP* 1746)
Poems on Several Occasions, 1752	(*PSO* 1752)
Poems, by Mr. Smart, (?) 1763	(*P* 1763)
Ode to the Right Honourable the Earl of Northumberland, 1764	(*Nd* 1764)
A Translation of the Psalms, &c., Hymns and Spiritual Songs for the Fasts and Festivals, &c., 1765	
The Parables of our Lord, 1768	
Hymns for the Amusement of Children, 1770	
The Poems of the Late Christopher Smart, 1791	(*R* 1791)

Collections of Smart's poems following closely *R* 1791 were made by Anderson, *British Poets*, vol. xi (1794), and Chalmers, *English Poets*, vol. xvi (1810). In 1924 Mr. Edmund Blunden published a selection containing *A Song to David*, some of the *Hymns* and a few other poems. *A Song to David* was first published separately in 1763 and was reprinted at the end of the *Psalms* in 1765. It has since been reprinted many times—in 1827, 1895, 1898, 1901, &c. The more important recent editions are Mr. Blunden's (1924), the Clarendon Press facsimile of the first edition

(1926), and that of Messrs. Shepard and Wood in *English Prose and Poetry* (1934).

PERIODICALS

The Student, or Oxford and Cambridge Monthly Miscellany	(*St* 1750, &c.)
The Midwife, or Old Woman's Magazine	(*Md* 1750, &c.)
The Gentleman's Magazine	(*GM* 1754, &c.)
The Universal Visiter and Monthly Memorialist	(*UV* 1756)

BIBLIOGRAPHIES

G. J. Gray, *A Bibliography of the Writings of Christopher Smart*, in *Transactions of the Bibliographical Society*, vol. vi, 1902. *Cambridge Bibliography of English Literature*, s.v. 'Smart' (a somewhat inadequate list of biographical and critical writings).

BIOGRAPHIES

There are three important accounts of Smart's life —Christopher Hunter's 'Memoir' prefixed to the collected edition of 1791, which contains many facts not obtainable in other contemporary writings; K. A. McKenzie's *Christopher Smart, sa Vie et ses Œuvres* (Paris, 1924); and Ainsworth and Noyes, *Christopher Smart* (*University of Missouri Studies*, no. 4, 1943), which is up to date and admirably documented. Other shorter 'lives', based mainly on Hunter, are by Anderson (*British Poets*, vol. xi), Chalmers (*English Poets*, vol. xvi), Seccombe (*Dictionary of National Biography*). Incidental biographical references are to be found, among other places, in Boswell, *Life of Samuel Johnson*, and *Correspondence*; Mrs. Piozzi, *Piozziana*;

Mme D'Arblay, *Diary*; Mrs. Le Noir, *Poems*, 1825 (Introduction); Napier, *Johnsoniana*; Gray, *Correspondence*.

Detailed studies of parts of Smart's life are numerous; the following are some of the most useful:

(On Smart's residence in Cambridge) Edmund Gosse, Correspondence in *Athenaeum*, nos. 3095 and 3110 (Feb., June 1887); C. D. Abbott, 'Christopher Smart's Madness', *Publications of the Modern Language Association*, xlv (1930).

(On Newbery) C. Welsh, *A Bookseller of the Last Century*.

(On Smart's residence in London) R. B. Botting, 'Christopher Smart in London', *Research Studies of the State College of Washington* (March 1939).

(On the *Universal Visiter* contract) R. B. Botting, 'Johnson, Smart and the *Universal Visiter*', *Modern Philology*, xxxvi; C. Jones, 'Christopher Smart, Richard Rolt and the *Universal Visiter*', *The Library*, xviii; S. Piggott, Correspondence in *The Times Literary Supplement*, June 13th, 1929.

(On Smart's madness) C. D. Abbott, *op. cit.*; W. F. Stead, Introduction, Notes, Appendices to *Rejoice in the Lamb*.

CRITICISM

Gentleman's Magazine, xxi (1751), xxiv (1754), *Monthly Review*, 1763–8, *Critical Review*, xv, xvi, xxviii, xxix.

Anderson, *op. cit.*; Chalmers, *op. cit.*; E. Gosse, *Gossip in a Library*; T. Seccombe, *Age of Johnson*; O. Elton, *English Literature from 1737 to 1880*; A. E. Housman, *The Name and Nature of Poetry*; E. Blunden, *A Song to David* (Introduction); R. E. Brittain, 'Christopher Smart and Dr. Delaney', *The Times Literary Supplement*, March 7th, 1936 'Christopher Smart's "Hymns for the Amusement of Children" ', *Papers of the Bibliographical Society of America*, xxxv; R. D. Havens, 'The Structure of Smart's *Song to David*', *Review of English Studies*, xiv (1938).

For detailed discussion of Smart's poetry as a whole, see McKenzie, *op. cit.*, and Ainsworth and Noyes, *op. cit.*, from which passages are quoted in the selection of critical comment.

CRITICAL COMMENTS

CRITICAL COMMENTS

CHRISTOPHER SMART

FOR my talent is to give an impression upon words by
punching, that when the reader casts his eye upon 'em,
he takes up the image from the mould wch I have
made.   *Jubilate Agno*

Besides the *Curiosa Felicitas*, so much of *Horace* by
himself, there is another poetical excellence, which
tho' possessed in a degree by every great genius, is
exceeding in our Lyric to surpass; I mean the beauty,
force, and vehemence of *Impression*: which leads me
to a rare and entertaining subject, not any where (I
think) insisted on by others.

Impression, then, is a talent or gift of almighty God,
by which a Genius is empowered to throw an emphasis
on a word or a sentence in such wise, that it cannot
escape any reader of sheer good sense, and true critical
sagacity. This power will sometimes keep it up thro'
the medium of a prose translation; especially in scrip-
ture, for in justice to truth and everlasting preemin-
ence, we must confess this virtue to be far more
powerful and abundant in the sacred writings.

The Works of Horace, 1767

THE CRITICAL REVIEW

Without venturing to criticize on the propriety of a
Protestant's offering up either hymns or prayers to the
dead, we must be of opinion, that great rapture and
devotion is discernable in this extatic song (*A Song to
David*). It is a fine piece of ruins, and must at once
please and affect a sensible mind.   1763

JAMES BOSWELL

I have sent you Smart's *Song to David*, which is a very curious composition, being a strange mixture of *dun obscure* and glowing genius at times ... His *Genius and Imagination* [sic] is very pretty. The other pieces have shivers of genius here and there, but are often ludicrously low.   *Correspondence* 1763

THE MONTHLY REVIEW

From the sufferings of this ingenious Gentleman, we could not but expect the performance before us [*A Song to David*] to be greatly irregular; but we shall certainly characterize it more justly if we call it irregularly great. There is a grandeur, a majesty of thought, not without a happiness of expression in the following stanzas (10, 17, 18, 21, 40). There is something remarkably great, and altogether original in the last-quoted stanza.

We meet with some passages, however, in this performance which are almost, if not altogether, unintelligible. Few Readers probably will see the Author's reason for distinguishing his seven pillars or monuments of the six days' creation, by the seven Greek letters he hath selected ... Our Poet's allusions also, in this little piece, relate frequently to subjects too little known, and far fetched. Thus, 'For adoration beasts embark', &c. We remember to have somewhere read of a certain quadruped which puts to sea on a piece of timber, in order to prey on fish. But we have no account of such embarkation in any natural Historian of credit ...

It would be cruel, however, to insist on the slight defects and singularities of this piece, for many reasons; and more especially if it be true,[1] as we are

---

[1] It was not true. of course. This is a typical example of the kind of criticism Smart had to put up with.

informed, that it was written when the Author was denied the use of pen, ink, and paper, and was obliged to indent his lines with the end of a key, upon the wainscot.   1763

This Ode [*to Northumberland*] is conceived in easy numbers, as every lyric performance ought to be: but there is in the later productions of Mr. Smart, a *tour* of expression, which we many times are at a loss to understand; and it often seems to us, that his words, as well as his sentiments, are rather too much under the influence of imagination. For this Ode, however, he merits the thanks of every true Protestant, for he fights with a truly British spirit against the Whore of Babylon. The last stanza is really very pretty . . .
                                                           1764

This version of the parables is, with great propriety, dedicated to Master Bonnell George Thornton, a child of three years old.   1768

We are inclined to believe that, after Gay, Smart is the most agreeable metrical fabulist in our language; his versification is less polished, and his analogues in general are perhaps less correct, than those of Gay or Moore: but in originality, in wit and in humour, the preference seems due to Smart.

The introductory lines of almost all these fables are singularly ingenious and happy; and in the course of each, the second line of most couplets presents us with an independent new idea. The best and most serious of these playful compositions is doubtless . . . *Care and Generosity* . . .   1792 [1]

[1] This is from a long and not unsympathetic review of Hunter's edition of the *Poems* (1791).

GOLDSMITH

[Mrs. Le Noir] recalls with pleasure ... his [Gold-smith's] skipping across the large, old-fashioned oaken wainscoted parlour, to snatch up a book that laid on the window-seat; it was a quarto edition of her Father's Poems. Opening it at the poem of the Mowers he read aloud—

Strong Labour got up with his pipe in his mouth
And stoutly strode over the dale—[1]

adding, 'There is not a man now living who could write such a line.'

(From the introduction to Mrs. Le Noir's
Poems, 1825)

LEIGH HUNT

This ... reminds me ... of poor Kit Smart, in whom a good deal of real genius seems to have wasted itself away in complexional weakness.   1846

ROBERT BROWNING

A Song where flute-breath silvers trumpet-clang,
And stations you for once on either hand
With Milton and with Keats, empowered to claim
Affinity on just one point ...
                              Such success
Befell Smart only out of throngs between
Milton and Keats that donned the singing-dress—
Smart, solely of such songmen, pierced the screen

[1] So printed by Hunter, but *not* in the quarto of 1752: see p. 102 of the present edition.

'Twixt thing and word, lit language straight from
    soul,—
Left no fine film-flake on the naked coal
Live from the censer ...
... here a poet was who always could—
Never before did—never after would—
Achieve the feat ...

Parleyings with Certain People, 1887

A. C. WARD

Gilfillan begins his life of Christopher Smart with
this remark: 'We hear of "Single-Speech Hamilton";
we have now to say something of "Single-Poem
Smart" '. That single poem was the *Song to David*.
Those who know anything of Smart will not accept
this summing-up. It may be his best piece, but Smart
wrote enough to fill two volumes, and much that he
wrote is very good ... He has a fine command of the
English language, wit, ingenuity, and an ear for
rhythm; but a good deal of sameness runs through all
his writings; the chill of Protestantism, if we may so
call it, seems to affect nearly every poet under the first
three Georges ...

Walford's *Antiquarian*, vol. viii (1885)

CYRIL FALLS

A more miserable and, but for one bright flower
budded in madness, a more worthless and barren life
than his, were hard to conceive. Even of his madness
we have no picture of a fine spirit wasting away in
melancholy, like that of his greater and like-circum-
stanced contemporary William Collins. When Dr.

Johnson, good, kindly soul, went to visit him in Bedlam, he returned to tell Boswell that he was growing fat. Boswell suggested that it might be for lack of exercise; but Johnson denied this, declaring that now he dug in the garden, whereas before, though he might walk as far as the ale-house, he was carried back. He added that he saw no reason for his confinement, since his maladies were not hurtful to society. He enumerated two: 'He insisted on people praying with him; and I'd as lief pray with Kit Smart as anyone else. Another charge was that he did not love clean linen; and I have no passion for it.' Johnson was probably right, but it is hard to see how confinement injured Smart, whilst it is at least to that confinement that we owe his one marvellous poem, *A Song to David* ... saving the incomparable Song ... Smart is a typical minor poet of an uninteresting age.

Let us beware ... of making claims too extravagant for poor Kit Smart. Only let us remember that, if we dub him a man of one poem, that poem is a long-sustained effort, and that it must set him in a category above, say, Wolfe, whose reputation rests upon eight stanzas.   *The Critic's Armoury*, 1924

EDITH SITWELL

But the whole poem [*A Song to David*] is bathed in the everlasting light of Heaven; the flowers are brighter than they are in our earthly meadows; there is no room in the heaven of this madman's mind for cruelty or injustice, or for anything but love. That Heaven was undimmed by the cruelties and by the darkness of Bedlam, unbroken by starvation, warm in the midst of that deathly cold. This madman of genius, this poet of genius, for all the barriers of his madness, continued to walk in the cool of the evening with his God.

The Pleasures of Poetry (First Series), 1930

1

W. F. STEAD

Not far from Coleridge in imagination and learning, he was even more ruinously weak in will. Coleridge searched himself, found out his faults, and in a measure resolved them; Smart did none of these things, probably because of a deficiency in analytical and constructive thought, two powers of the mind in which Coleridge excelled. Coleridge was always exploring the noumenal world with a view to discovering the unifying relations which sustain the whole; Smart saw things only in flashes. His mental processes were nearer those of Blake, with whom a good deal of this document [*Jubilate Agno*] shows a kindred spirit. Cowper and Smart compared as two victims of religious mania, exhibit contrasted self-portraits, the one all black, the other all white, since Cowper, whose life was nearly blameless, became convinced that he was damned, while Smart, who had wandered so far astray, never doubted his inheritance in New Canaan. Because he did not know himself, he hardly suspected his own faults, and went astray with a child's innocent conscience.

Rejoice in the Lamb (Introduction), 1939

K. A. McKENZIE

Nourri de pensée religieuse, saisi par une vive conscience du divin en toutes choses, l'esprit de Smart ne voyait pas de disconvenance dans les rapprochements entre l'humain et le divin qui nous semblent un peu surprenants. Ainsi il nous parle de 'the choir of Christ and Wren' (Hymne 13) . . .

De même, la pensée religieuse intervient dans une ode séculière, celle à l'Amiral Pocock, qui commence ainsi:

When Christ, the seaman, was aboard,
  Swift as an arrow to the White,
While Ocean his rude rapture roar'd,
  The Vessel gain'd the Haven with delight:
We therefore first to him the song renew,
Then sing of Pocock's praise, and make the point in
  view.

Analogue, mais plus raisonnée et moins surprenante, était sa méthode de traduire les *Psaumes*, en y remplaçant les éléments païens par des éléments chrétiens, et en les modifiant pour le culte de l'église d'Angleterre. La méthode d'ailleurs n'était pas nouvelle. Isaac Watts s'était plaint que tous les traducteurs précédents n'eussent fait que changer la langue du psalmiste, en laissant à sa pensée son caractère hébreu; Watts, lui, se proposa 'de modifier le livre des *Psaumes* pour le culte chrétien: et pour cela il faut ôter de David et d'Asaph, etc., toutes les caractéristiques sauf celles de Psalmiste et de Saint, et les faire parler toujours selon le Sens commun et le langage d'un Chrétien'. Ainsi, il exprime la pensée hébraïque en termes chrétiens: là où David 'parle de sacrifier des Boucs ou des Bœufs, je préfère parler du Sacrifice du Christ, l'Agneau de Dieu'. La méthode de Smart était analogue. Sa traduction est 'entreprise dans l'Esprit du Christianisme'. C'est-à-dire, 'toutes les expressions qui semblent contraires au Christ, sont omises, et des matières tirées de l'évangile mises à leur place; et comme elle (la traduction) vise surtout à l'office divin, le lecteur y trouvera des allusions diverses aux rites et aux cérémonies de l'église d'Angleterre, par lesquelles on veut rendre l'ouvrage en général plus utile et acceptable aux fidèles'. En effet, nous trouvons que Smart a fait ses modifications très librement, 'L'Eternel rachète l'âme des ses serviteurs' (Ps. xxxiv, 23), devient chez Smart,

The Lord his meritorious cross
Shall ransom all our souls.

'Tes flèches sont aiguës; les peuples tomberont sous
toi; elles entreront dans le cœur des ennemis du roi'
(Ps. xlv, 6), devient

> *Sharp is the voice of thy reproof*
> *When sin thy spirit grieves,*
> *Ev'n underneath the sacred roof*
> *Amidst the trading thieves.*

C'est là une adaptation étonnante, qui ne mérite
guère le nom de 'traduction'.

Christopher Smart, sa Vie et ses Œuvres, 1924

J. MIDDLETON MURRY

But the *Song to David* is not new: what will be new
to most people is the strange quality of Smart's *Hymns
and Spiritual Songs* ... These ... were printed
together with his versions of the Psalms and the
second edition of the *Song to David* in 1765. I imagine
from the internal evidence that Smart wrote the ver-
sions of the Psalms first, then being uplifted by the
splendour of the Psalmist's imagination and controlled
by his knowledge of the Psalmist's art, uttered the
Song to David, and finally, relaxed into a mood of
calm and simple serenity, composed the *Hymns and
Spiritual Songs.*

However this may be, there are marvellous things
in them, and these things are marvellous in a way
quite different from that of the *Song to David*. Con-
sider, for example, the last two verses of *The Nativity*.

> *Spinks and ouzels sing sublimely,*
> *'We too have a Saviour born';*

> *Whiter blossoms burst untimely*
> *On the blest Mosaic Thorn.*

> *God all-bounteous, all creative,*
> *Whom no ills from good dissuade,*
> *Is incarnate*, and a native
> Of the very world he made.

There is a simple miracle in that last line and a half: and one need not be a professing Christian to feel that it is the miracle of the Nativity itself. Or take lines from *St. Philip and St. James*:

> *And the lily smiles supremely*
> *Mentioned by the Lord on earth. . . .*

This is the true, the strange Christian *naïveté*: the sense of the knowledge that all living creatures are brothers of men, children of God, and can only be understood in virtue of the one love which unites them all. By this spirit the primaeval innocence of Eden (of which Rubens had a Pisgah-sight in his great picture) is restored, and for the moment that we share it we are no longer fallen away from our first perfection. It is the great Christian *naïveté* of St. Francis. It was to be manifested again, half a century later, in the poetry of John Clare, for the fitful yet unmistakable gleam plays over all Clare's work.

> *The very darkness smiles to wear*
> *The stars that show us God is there.*

It is a perception, a knowledge, a mode of understanding, which Christ himself brought into the world. 'Solomon in all his glory was not arrayed like one of these.' 'Are not two sparrows sold for a farthing?' Before Christ no one of whom memory remains to us had spoken words like these: before Him, this sense of communion in life between all living creatures did not exist. There is no record of it in the words of the wise before Him: the beautiful descriptions of nature in the ancient poets—and in spite of the common report, there *are* beautiful descriptions of nature in the ancient poets—are of another kind. They have not this immediacy of contact: the blood bond of brothers is not there. And, to speak truth, it is not in many poets of the Christian era: it is not, I believe, in Shakespeare, or in Dante, or in Milton, or even in Wordsworth. Wordsworth is too deliberate; there is a grave and deep philosophy in his attitude. But this *naïveté* is spontaneous, like the kiss one may sometimes surprise between two little children who believe themselves unwatched. I have seen such a kiss between two tiny staggerers in the Luxembourg Gardens. It is innocent, it is rapturous, and it is wise.

Discoveries, 1924

E. G. AINSWORTH AND C. E. NOYES

All this [a citation from *Parleyings with Certain People*] is very interesting, both as verse and as philosophy. That it does not tell the truth about the *Song to David* does not make it any the less worth reading. Yet, as recent writers point out, the mighty *Song* was a message altogether Smart's own. True, he wrote nothing so good before and nothing so good after, but by definition one does not surpass one's masterpiece. The *Song to David* was not a thing foreign to Smart. It is of a piece with his other religious verse—finer, stronger, sweeter, but of the same substance. There was no flame-transfigured moment when the god spoke through the tranced subject. The poetic imagination that brought forth the *Song to David* was alive in Pembroke, Grub Street, and Bedlam. It was a part of Smart's intellect and a part of his madness. *Christopher Smart,* 1943

ODES
AND ADDRESSES

Secular Ode on the Jubilee at Pembroke College, Cambridge, in 1743

I

GOD of science, light divine,
O'er all the world of learning shine;
    Shine fav'ring from th'etherial way:
But here with tenfold influence dwell,
Here all thy various rays compell
    To dignify this joyful day.
Nor thou, *Melpomene*, thy aid refuse,
Nor leave behind the comic muse;
    Mirthful mild, and gravely gay,
    Hither from your thrones away.
And thou, jolly *Bacchus*, shalt haste to come down,
While the full-flowing cup with fresh flow'rets we
    crown;
    But boast not here thy madding influence,
        For close beside thee *Pallas'* self shall stand,
        And hold thy temerarious hand,
    Forbidding rage to triumph over sense.
    And ye, illustrious-sacred shades,
Who whilom in these muse-resounding glades,
    High in rapture wont to stray,
Or trim the learned lamp, till dawn of day,
    Ye blessed sons of happier fates,
        Deign to look down from heav'n and see
        How lasting sweet the memory,
    Which to eternal fame fair virtue consecrates.
See, still fresh bloom your names thro' every age,
Still greatly live along the speaking page.

II

BUT chiefly thou, *Dan Spencer*, peerless bard,
    Sith in these pleasaunt groves you 'gan devise,

3

Of Red-cross knight, and virtue's high reward,
    And here first plann'd thy works of vast emprize,
Descend! nor thy inferior sons despise,
    Chaunting her praises on this festal day,
Who taught us, where the road to honour lies,
    Her steps still marking out the arduous way:
Blest is the theme I ween, and blessed be the lay.

III

BEHOLD, in virtue, and in beauty's pride,
Behold, at once, a widow and a bride!
        See all the nuptial revels at a stand,
        And *Hymen's* torch in *Libitina's* hand,
O what a scene! . . . .
        But, yonder, from on high, descend
    Religion, orphan-virtue's firmest friend,
        And laurell'd learning, mistress of the muse,
    Who, o'er the arts, sits on an eminence,
    By genius erected, and by sense,
        And with unbounded prospect all things
            views.
    With gentle hands they raise her drooping head,
And bid her trust in heav'n, nor wail the happy dead.
    All that is great and good she now pursues;
    She meditates a mansion for the muse,
        Nor will she lose a day;
    To you religion, wisdom and to you,
    She gives that prime, which pleasure calls her due,
        And folly wastes in wantonness away.
    She, by no specious flow'rs beguil'd,
    That deck *imagination's wild,*
        And witless youth decoy,
    Chose learning's *cultivated* glades,
    And virtue's *ever-blooming* shades,
        That give alone true joy.

4

IV

To *Granta* now, where gentle *Camus* laves,
The reedy shore, and rolls his silver waves,
  She flies, and executes, with bounteous hand,
  The work her mighty soul had plann'd,
And unborn minds she forms, and future souls
 she saves,
And to ensure that work to endless fame,
Left what can never die, her own illustrious name.
  Let others, with enthusiasm fill'd,
  Nunneries and convents build;
Where, decay'd with fasts and years,
  Melancholy loves to dwell,
  Moaping in her midnight cell,
And counts her beads, and mumbles o'er th'unmean-
 ing pray'rs.
  Religious joy, and sober pleasure,
  Virtuous ease, and learned leisure,
  Society and books, that give
  Th'important lesson how to live:
  These are gifts, are gifts divine,
  For, fair Pembroke, these were thine.

           UV 1756

To the King

STROPHE

As some vast vista, whose extent
Scarce bounded by the firmament
  From whence it's sweep begun;
Above, beneath, in every place,
Mark'd with some grand distinguish'd grace,
  Ends with the golden sun:

Thus GEORGE, thy reign, to the impartial view
    In all it's parts, in every light appears.
For ever happy, as for ever new,
        Rise the bright days, and roll the glorious
        years.
Yet—still—the voice, that bids the nations breathe
To hear fair justice, and the sword to sheathe,
'Tis this, th' exertion of thy godlike soul,
'Tis this confirms, compleats, and nobly crowns the
whole.

ANTISTROPHE

    Oh! born the nations to compose,
    How doubly sweet the olive blows
        O'er the triumphant palm!
    After the blast, how bland the breeze!
    How aimiably superb the seas,
        When hush'd into a calm!
Say by what miracle, what pow'rful charm,
    Plan'd and accomplish'd was th' august
    design?
Was it thy WILLIAM's formidable arm?
    Just and effectual, like the wrath Divine?
    Was it thy fleet that smoak'd the depth along
Swift as the eagle, as the lion strong?—
No—'twas that Wisdom bad the warfare cease,
Whose ways are pleasantness, and all whose paths
are PEACE.

EPODON

    Of Camus oft the solitary strand
        Poetically pensive will I haunt:
    And, as I view th' innumerable sand,
        Think on thy bounties; and with trans-
        port chaunt
    That now no more Bellona's brazen car
    Affrights Urania in her blisful seat;

6

Nor Stratagem, the subtlest snake of war,
    Plots to entangle evry Pilgrim's feet:
That now no lures our vagrant steps mis-
    lead;
    Except the harmless syrens of the mead,
Deftly secrete, in hawthorne ambuscade,
Charm the romantic rovers of the upland glade.
    Gratulatio Regis Academiae, 1748

A Solemn Dirge, Sacred to the Memory of His Royal Highness Frederic Prince of Wales

To His Royal Highness Prince George, The following little Poem,
On the much lamented death of his Father, is humbly inscribed
by the Author.

CHORUS

HENCE Clamour-loving Joy be gone,—
Come sober, serious Muse, come on,
And mournfully majestic flow,
In the dread Pomp of Regal Woe.

FIRST, MR. LOWE

Her Patron and her Father banish'd,
    Every Orphan Muse shall mourn,
Honour's fled, and Glory's vanish'd,
    To the death-devoted Urn.

SECOND, MISS BURCHELL

Sing some sad, some plaintive Ditty,
    Steept in Tears that endless flow;
Melancholy Notes of Pity,
    Notes that mean a World of Woe.

ODES AND ADDRESSES

THIRD, MR. LOWE

Charity no more shall charm us,
  But shall make a Virgin's Vow,
And Thou who fondly dreamt to warm us
  Hope, ah! where's thy Anchor now?

FOURTH, MISS BURCHELL

You his Offspring cease to languish,
  Claim not Sorrow for *your* Due;
We demand our Share of Anguish
  We were all his Children too.

FIFTH, MR. LOWE

Music's dumb, and Painting sighing,
  Drops her Pencil from her Hands.
Sculpture with her Sisters dying
  See! herself a Statue stands.

SIXTH, MISS BURCHELL

You, his Consort, think on Heaven,
  Blest, tho' immature he fled,
To him deathless Joys are given,
  Weep not for the happy dead.

SEVENTH, MR. LOWE

Weep for us—We Tears must borrow
  To express our Misery,
Private Grief to public Sorrow,
  Is a Riv'let to the Sea.

EIGHTH, MISS BURCHELL

Father! Master! Husband! Brother!
  Every blessed tender Name!
Ye must dye—till such another,
  Call you back to Life and Fame.

8

NINTH, MR. LOWE

Such another?—we possess him,
  To revive his Father's Fame,
Honour, Glory, Wisdom, bless him,
  Not another, but the same.

TENTH, MISS BURCHELL

Yes, he is the Kingdom's Glory,
  The Advice his Grandsire gave,
Shall secure his Fame in Story,
  'Twas, 'Be honest and be brave.'

CHORUS

George is *Albion's* Consolation,
  The King's Life's the common Weal:
Every Grief that wounds the Nation
  Long may he survive to heal!

1751

Ode to Lord Barnard

On his accession to that title.

Sis licet felix ubicunque mavis,
Et memor nostri.
Hor.

MELPOMENE, who charm'st the skies,
  Queen of the lyre and lute,
Say, shall my noble patron rise,
  And thou, sweet Muse, be mute?
Shall Fame, to celebrate his praise,
Her loudest, loftiest accents raise,
  And all her silver trumps employ,
And thou restrain thy tuneful hand,
And thou an idle list'ner stand
  Amidst the general joy?

Forbid it, all ye powers above
    That human hearts can try,
Forbid it gratitude and love,
    And every tender tye:
Was it not he, whose pious cares
Upheld me in my earliest years,
    And chear'd me from his ample store,
Who animated my designs,
In Roman and Athenian mines,
    To search for learning's ore?

The royal hand, my lord, shall raise
    To nobler heights thy name,
Who praises thee, shall meet with praise
    Ennobled in thy fame.
A disposition form'd to please,
With dignity endear'd by ease,
    And grandeur in good nature lost,
Have more of genuine desert,
Have more the merit of the heart,
    Than arts and arms can boast.

Can I forget fair Raby's towers,
    How awful and how great!
Can I forget such blissful bowers,
    Such splendour in retreat!
Where me, ev'n me, an infant bard,
Cleveland and Hope indulgent heard.
    (Then, Fame, I felt thy first alarms)
Ah, much lov'd pair!—tho' one is fled,
Still one compensates for the dead,
    In merit and in charms.

O more than compensation, sure!
    O blessings on thy life!
Long may the three-fold bliss endure,
    In daughters, sons, and wife!

Hope, copyist of her mother's mind,
Is loveliest, liveliest of her kind,
    Her soul with every virtue teems,
By none in wit or worth outdone,
With eyes, that shining on the sun,
    Defy his brightest beams.

Hark! Charity's cherubic voice
    Calls to her numerous poor,
And bids their languid hearts rejoice,
    And points to Raby's door;
With open heart and open hands,
There, Hospitality—she stands,
    A nymph, whom men and gods admire,
Daughter of heavenly Goodness she,
Her sister's Generosity,
    And Honour is her sire.

What though, my lord, betwixt us lie
    Full many an envious league,
Such vast extent of sea and sky,
    As even the eye fatigue;
Though interposing Ocean raves,
And heaves his Heaven-assaulting waves,
    While on the shores the billows beat,
Yet still my grateful Muse is free,
To tune her warmest strains to thee,
    And lay them at thy feet.

Goodness is ever kindly prone
    To feign what fate denies,
And others want of worth t'atone,
    Finds in herself supplies:
Thus dignity itself restrains,
By condescension's silken reins,

While you the lowly Muse upraise;
When such the theme, so mean the bard,
Not to reject is to reward,
   To pardon is to praise.

R 1791

To the Right Honourable Earl of Darlington

On his being appointed Paymaster of His Majesty's Forces.

> The royal hand, my lord, shall raise
> To nobler heights thy name;
> Who praises thee shall meet with praise,
> Ennobled in thy fame.
> *Smart's Ode.*

WHAT the prophetic Muse foretold is true,
And royal justice gives to worth its due;
The Roman spirit now breathes forth again,
And Virtue's temple leads to Honour's fane;
But not alone to thee this grant extends,
Nor in thy rise great Brunswick's goodness ends:
Whoe'er has known thy hospitable dome,
Where each glad guest still finds himself at home:
Whoe'er has seen the numerous poor that wait
To bless thy bounty at the expanded gate;
Whoe'er has seen thee general joy impart,
And smile away chagrin from every heart,
All these are happy—pleasure reigns confest,
And thy prosperity makes thousands blest.

UV 1756

Ode to Admiral Sir George Pocock

1

WHEN Christ, the seaman, was aboard,
  Swift as an arrow to the *White*,
While Ocean his rude rapture roar'd,
  The vessel gain'd the Haven with delight:
We therefore first to him the song renew,
Then sing of Pocock's praise, and make the point in
    view.

2

The Muse must humble e're she rise,
  And kneel to kiss her Master's feet,
Thence at one spring she mounts the skies
  And in New Salem vindicates her seat;
Seeks to the temple of th' Angelic choir,
And hoists the English Flag upon the topmost spire.

3

O Blessed of the Lord of Hosts,
  In either India most renown'd,
The Echo of the Eastern coasts,
  And all th'Atlantic shore thy name resound.—
The victor's clemency, the seaman's art,
The cool delib'rate head, the warm undaunted heart.

4

My pray'r was with thee, when thou sail'd
  With prophecies of sure success;
My thanks to Heav'n that thou prevail'd
  Shall last as long as I can breathe or bless;
And built upon thy deeds my song shall tow'r,
And swell, as it ascends, in spirit and in pow'r.

13

5

There is no thunder half so loud,
  As God's applauses in the height,
For those, that have his name avow'd,
  Ev'n *Christian* patriots valorous and great;
Who for the general welfare stand or fall,
And have no sense of self, and know no dread at all.

6

Amongst the numbers lately fir'd
  To act upon th' heroic plan,
Grace has no worthier chief inspir'd,
  Than that sublime, insuperable man,
Who could th'outnumb'ring French so oft defeat,
And from th'HAVANNAH stor'd his brave victorious
  fleet.

7

And yet how silent his return
  With scarce a welcome to his place—
Stupidity and unconcern,
  Were settled in each voice and on each face.
As private as myself he walk'd along,
Unfavour'd by a friend, unfollow'd by the throng.

8

Thy triumph, therefore, is not here,
  Thy glories for a while postpon'd,
The hero shines not in his sphere,
  But where the Author of all worth is own'd.—
Where *Patience* still persists to praise and pray
For all the Lord bestows, and all he *takes away*.

9

Nor HOWARD, FROBISHER, or DRAKE,
　Or VERNON's fam'd *Herculean* deed;
Not all the miracles of BLAKE,
　Can the great Chart of thine exploits exceed.—
Then rest upon thyself and dwell secure,
And cultivate the arts, and feed th' *increasing* poor.

10

O Name accustom'd and inur'd
　To fame and hardship round the globe,
For which fair Honour has insur'd
　The warrior's truncheon, and the consul's robe;
Who still, the more is *done* and *understood,*
Art easy of access, art affable and good.

11

O Name acknowledged and rever'd
　Where Isis plays her pleasant stream,
When'er thy tale is read or heard,
　The good shall bless thee and the wise esteem;
And they, whose offspring lately felt thy care,
Shall IN TEN THOUSAND CHURCHES make their daily
　　pray'r.

12

'Connubial bliss and homefelt joy,
　And ev'ry social praise be thine;
Plant thou the oak, the poor employ;
　Or plans of vast benevolence design;
And speed, when Christ his servant shall release,
From triumph over death to everlasting peace.'

P 1763

15

Ode to General Draper

... Utcunque ferant ea facta *minores*
Vincat amor patriae, laudumque immensa cupido.
Virg.

NOBLE in Nature, great in arms,

The Muses patron and thyself a bard,
Who sternly rushing from domestic charms

And for thy country tow'ring upon guard,
As born against the foes of human kind,
Preced'st the march alone, and leav'st all rank behind.
A little leisure for a thankful heart,

It's own peculiar workings to attend,
A little leisure to survey the Chart,

Of all thy labours bearing to their end;
To hail thee at the head of all renown,
To plan thy private peace, and weave thy laurel
    crown.

The Fame of Draper is a pile

Of God's erecting in th'embattled field;
An English fabrick in the Roman stile,

To which all meaner elevations yield;
What ho! ye brave lieutenants of the van,
Within a thousand furlongs not a single man.
My Muse is somewhat stronger than she was,

In spite of long calamity and time,
Arouse, Arouse ye! is there not a cause?

Arouse ye lively spirits of my prime!
Breathe, breathe upon the lyre thy parting breath,
There is no thought of him but triumphs after death.

Ye boys of Eton take your theme,

That heroes from heroic fathers come;
Ye sons of learned Granta draw the scheme

Of Archimedes, on the warrior's drum:
No more let champions scorn the man of parts,

16

For DRAPER comes like MARLBRO' from the school of
    arts.
O early train'd and practised in desert,
    The son of emulation from the womb,
In antient arms and eloquence expert;
    And student of the themes of Greece and Rome,
Thou chose ACHILLES from th' *Homeric* throng,
Who sinks upon thy deeds, tho' rais'd upon thy song.

A CHRISTIAN HERO is a name
    To bards of classic eminence unknown,
A heroe, that prefers a higher claim
    To God's applause, his country's and his own;
Than those, who, tho' the mirrour of their days,
Nor knew the Prince of Worth, nor principle of praise.
Advance, advance a little higher still—
    Th' Ideas of an Englishman advance!
Advance above his meaner strength or skill;
    Who solely grasps his pen or shakes his lance.
Thy talent ever flows to learning's hoard,
And bore to leisure fruit 'midst peril and the sword.

O ENGLISH aspect name and soul,
    All English to our joyful ears and eyes!
Thy chariot cleanly risk'd upon the goal
    Has brought thee winner of the Martial Prize;
And interval on interval succeeds,
Before thy second comes to signify his deeds.
A note above the Epic trumpet's reach
    Beyond the compass of the various lyre,
The song of all thy deeds, which sires shall teach
    Their children active prowess to inspire.—
Thou art a Master—whose exploits shall warm,
The valiant yet to come, and future heroes form.

It is an honest book, that writes
    Thy name as worthy honourable lot,

17

For fair and faithful thy detail recites,
    The merits of thy brethren on the spot;
From gallant MONSON foremost of th'array,
To him that came the last, yet help'd to win the day.
What tho' no sense of gratitude be shown
    As heretofore, to chiefs of meaner rank;
No mason hew thy figure from a stone,
    Or painter daub thee staring on a plank;
No groupe of Aldermen proclaim thee free,
And in the Tayler's College give thee thy degree?

What tho' no bonfires be display'd,
    Nor windows light up the nocturnal scene;
What tho' the merry ringer is not paid,
    Nor rockets shoot upon the STILL SERENE;
Tho' no matross upon the rampart runs,
To send out thy report from loud redoubling guns?
What tho' thy precious health does not go round,
    Where'er the gourmandizing sinner dines;
Thy name be kept in secrecy profound,
    O'er female converse and loquacious wines;
What tho' th' astonish'd rustic does not fawn,
On DRAPER made of wax, or on the bellows drawn?

No coin the medalists devise,
    With thankful captives crowding the *Reverse*;
Or *Plutus* leading *Merit* to the prize,
    Or ALBION wailing More's untimely hearse;
What tho' no bawling ballad-singers rend
The skies with joy for thee, or dirges for thy friend?
Not monumental marble or the life
    Upon the rival canvas aptly feign'd,
Nor City-Speaker, licensed by his wife,
    To skrew up panegyric bridg'd and strain'd;
Not glass adorn'd with mottos and with boughs,
Nor fires that light the mob to roar and to carouse.

18

Not the round peal or guns salute,
   Pronouncing still that DRAPER is the toast;
Not youth and blooming beauty, bearing fruit
   To Justice, as they make A MAN their boast;
Not all the prose and verse of all the Grub-street news.
Not any thing they have denied to Thee,
   Is half so great as that which thou possess;
The patriot's hand, the honest parson's knee,
   And the GREAT BRITISH MONARCH's love express;
And If I may presume upon my mite,
This rough unbidden verse, that aims to do thee right.

Stupendous, surely, is thy chance,
   If such a man as thou shou'd be despis'd ;
Advance—thy fav'rite word—advance, advance
   To take thy rank with worthies in the skies;
The Captain of ten thousand in the sphere,
Where *Michael* draws the sword or throws the glitt'-
   ring spear.
Thyself and seed for which there is no doom,
   Race rising upon race in goodly pride;
Shall ever flourish root, and branch, and bloom,
   Shall flourish tow'ring high and spreading wide;
To carry God's applauses in their heart,
To shew an ENGLISH face, and act an ENGLISH part.
                        P 1763

Ode to the Earl of Northumberland

On his being appointed Lord Lieutenant of Ireland, presented on
the birth-day of Lord Warkworth.

WHATE'ER distinguish'd patriots rise,
The times and manners to revise,
   And drooping merit raise,
The song of triumph still pursues
Their footsteps, and the moral muse
   Dwells sweetly on their praise.

It is a task of true delight,
The ways of goodness to recite,
  And all her works refin'd;
Tho' modest greatness under rate
Its lustre; 'tis as fix'd as fate,
  Says truth with music join'd.

All hail to this auspicious morn,
When we, for gallant Warkworth born,
  Our gratulations pay:
Tho' virtue all the live-long year,
Refuse her eulogy to hear,
  She must attend to-day.

All hail to that transcendant fair,
That crown'd thy wishes with an heir,
  And bless'd her native land:
Still shoots thy undegenerate line,
Like oak from oak, and pine from pine,
  As goodly and as grand.

O how illustrious and divine
Were all the heroes of thy line,
  'Gainst Rome's ambitious cheat!
Born all these base insidious arts,
Which work the most in weakest hearts,
  To dare and to defeat!

Live then in triumph o'er deceit,
That with new honours we may greet
  The house of ARMS and ARTS,
'Till blest experience shall evince
How fairly you present that prince,
  Who's sovereign of our hearts.

In pity to our sister isle
With sighs we lend thee for a while;
   20

O be thou soon restor'd,
Tho' Stanhope, Hallifax were there,
We never had a man to spare
Our love could less afford.

Nd 1764

To the Honourable Mrs. Draper

NOBLE, lovely, and judicious,
Making worth thy aim and prize,
Hear the verse the muse officious
Now presents thee to revise.

Thine is exquisite discernment,
Zealous for thy country's cause
Thou hast heap'd the best preferment
On the prince of all applause.

Thus I greet thee at a distance,
Checking love by learning awe;
Grandeur gives the muse assistance,
And the lighter thoughts withdraw.

All ideas are untainted
When we think on heav'nly things;
Cherubs without sex are painted,
Form'd alone of heads and wings.

When of Cherubs we conjecture,
'Tis because we dwell on thee;
Looks and life thou art a lecture
On th' angelical degree.

Take the laurel for thy frontlet,
On thy breast the myrtles place,
For young DRAPER wears the gauntlet
Of all chivalry and grace.

Nd 1764

On being asked by Colonel Hall to make
Verses upon Kingsley at Minden

I

THIS task of me why does thou crave?
Thyself ingenious, learn'd, and brave,
   And equal to th' immortal theme!
The scenes that you beheld display,
And draw the picture of the day
   With which thy great ideas teem.

But if like me you are at fault,
Nor can your utmost thought exalt,
   But needs must do the subject wrong;
Then let us both at once confess
Our meanness, and the man address
   Who soars above our song.

II

'O heart-allow'd, by conscience prais'd,
As the vast envy thou hast rais'd,
   Such is the terror of thine arm:
The Muses and the Arts have join'd
The grudging silence of mankind,
   And our weak hands thy deeds disarm.

'Say leader of the glorious few,
What can impoverish'd fancy do
   On paper, canvas, or on stone?
Thy work so great, thy name so bright,
That God himself, with all his might
   Must give th'applause alone.'

Nd 1764

Female Dignity

Inscribed and Applied to Lady Hussey Delaval.

I

WHATE'ER the sense, whate'er the face,
  Whate'er the beauties all combin'd;
'Tis DIGNITY, that gives the grace,
  And forms the Fair, as first design'd.
Thro' life we have a sterling rule
  To make the noblest points our aim;
And DIGNITY commands the school
  Of all that excellence, we claim.

II

O never yet the gift of chance,
  Or bought by wealth, or forced by pow'r;
For Thee, the champion grasps his lance,
  For Thee, the flights of Fancy tow'r.
Thine is the great and perfect praise
  Of fathers kind, and lovers true;
Stern censure smiles thy worth to blaze,
  And owns the myrtle wreath thy due.

III

'Tis DIGNITY, supports the song
  By sense to choicest sounds allied;
The Muses do the Graces wrong,
  Unless her influence preside.
O Fountain of all female worth,
  That play'd so sweet and so sublime;
To feed the flow of decent mirth,
  The PRIDE of Place, the LIFE of TIME.

IV

Hail Condescension, heav'nly mild,
  By which no Majesty is lost;
Thee Faith and Truth their Queen have styl'd,
  And still with awful love accost.
On Thee, ten thousand blessings wait,
  In bright succession without pause;
If, CHARMER, thou hast found thy mate,
  His name is HONOUR and Applause.

PSO 1764

EPIGRAMS
AND EPITAPHS

On a Malignant Dull Poet

WHEN the viper its venom has spit, it is said,
That its fat heals the wound which its poison has
    made;
Thus it fares with the blockhead who ventures to write;
His dulness an antidote proves to his spite.

Privileges of the University of Cambridge

Inscriptions on an Æolian Harp

On one End.

PARTEM aliquam, O venti, divûm referatis ad aures!

On one Side.

Salve, quæ fingis proprio modulamine carmen,
    Salve, Memnoniam vox imitata lyram!
Dulcè O divinùmque sonas sine pollicis ictu,
    Dives naturæ simplicis, artis inops!
Talia, quæ incultæ dant mellea labra puellæ,
    Talia sunt faciles quæ modulantur aves.

On the other Side.

Hail, heav'nly harp, where Memnon's skill is shown,
That charm'st the ear with music all thine own!
Which, though untouch'd, can'st rapt'rous strains
    impart,
O rich of genuine nature, free from art!
Such the wild warblings of the sylvan throng,
So simply sweet the untaught virgin's song.

On the other End.

CHRISTOPHORUS SMART HENRICO BELL ARMIGERO.

St 1750

Epigram extempore on a Cold Poet

FRIGIDIO's muse, from ardour free,
    Whene'er he tunes his lyre,
Gives him a *leaden policy*
    T'insure his works from fire.

St 1750

On Seeing the Picture of Miss R——
G——N

Drawn by Mr. Varelst, of Threadneedle-street.

SHALL candid PRIOR, in immortal lays,
Thy ancestor with generous ardour praise;
Who, with his pencil's animating pow'r,
In liveliest dies immortaliz'd a flow'r?
And shall no just, impartial bard be found,
Thy more exalted merits to resound!
Who giv'st to beauty a perpetual bloom,
And lively grace, which age shall not consume;
Who mak'st the speaking eyes with meaning roll,
And paint'st at once the body, and the soul.

St 1751

On the Merit of Brevity

IF you think that my Works are too puft up with
    Levity,
Yet at least approbation is due to my Brevity,
The Praises of which shou'd be now more egregious,
As our Bards at this Time are confoundedly tedious.

Md 1752

28

The Physician and the Monkey

A LADY sent lately for one Doctor *Drug*,
To come in an Instant, and clyster poor Pug—
As the Fair one commanded he came at the Word,
And did the Grand-Office in Tie-Wig and Sword.
   The Affair being ended, so sweet and so nice!
He held out his Hand with, 'You know, Ma'm, my
     price.'
'Your Price!' says the Lady—'Why, Sir, he's a Brother,
And Doctors must never take Fees of each other.'
                            Md 1751

The Miser and the Mouse

An Epigram from the Greek

To a Mouse says a Miser, 'My dear Mr. Mouse,
Pray what may you please for to want in my House?'
Says the Mouse, 'Mr. Miser, pray keep yourself quiet,
You are safe in your Person, your Purse, and your
    Diet:
A Lodging I want, which ev'n you may afford,
But none wou'd come here to beg, borrow, or board.'
                            Md 1751

On a Woman who was Singing Ballads for Money to Bury Her Husband

FOR her Husband deceas'd, *Sally* chants the sweet
    Lay,
   Why, Faith, this is singular Sorrow;
But (I doubt) since she *sings* for a dead Man To-day,
   She'll *cry* for a live one To-morrow.

                       Md 1751

Apollo and Daphne

WHEN Phœbus was am'rous, and long'd to be rude,
Miss Daphne cry'd pish! and ran swift to the Wood,
And rather than do such a naughty Affair,
She became a fine Laurel to deck the God's Hair.
The Nymph was (no Doubt) of a cold Constitution,
For sure to turn Tree was a strange Resolution;
But in this she resembled a true modern Spouse,
For she fled from his Arms to distinguish his Brows.

Md 1751

An Epigram of Sir Thomas More,
imitated

ONCE on a time I fair *Dorinda* kiss'd,
Whose *Nose* was too distinguish'd to be miss'd;
'My dear,' says I, 'I fain would kiss you closer,
But tho' your lips say *Aye*—your Nose says, No,
    Sir.'—
The Maid was equally to Fun inclin'd,
And plac'd her lovely Lily-Hand BEHIND;
'Here, Swain,' she cry'd, 'may'st thou securely kiss,
Where there's no Nose to interrupt thy bliss.'

Md 1751

Epigram from Martial, Lib. viii, Ep. 69

Imitated by Mrs. Midnight.

No Praise the grutching *Rosalinda* yields
To Bards, till they are in th' *Elysian Fields*,
She says that every Modern is a Dunce,
Forgetting Homer was a Modern once.
Die—die, she cries—and then I'll deign a Smile,
Your Servant, Ma'm,—but 'tis not worth my while.

Md 1752

30

On a Lady throwing Snow-balls at her Lover

From the Latin of Petronius Ascanius.

WHEN, wanton fair, the snowy orb you throw,
I feel a fire before unknown in snow,
E'en coldest snow I find has pow'r to warm
My breast, when flung by *Julia's* lovely arm.
T' elude love's powerful arts I strive in vain,
If ice and snow can latent fires contain.
These frolicks leave; the force of beauty prove;
With equal passion cool my ardent love.

GM 1754

Επικτητος

Imitated from the Greek.

BY birth a servant, and in body maim'd;
By want a beggar;—worth, to beg asham'd:
Hardships like these to certain bliss commend;
For hence I boast immortal God my friend.

Nd 1764

Epigramma Sannazarii

Translated.

WHEN in the Adriatic Neptune saw
Fair Venice stand, and give all ocean law;
Now Jove (he cried) the tow'rs of Mars compare,
And Rome's eternal bulwarks, if you dare:
If Tiber beats the main declare the odds,
Whose the mean craft of man, and which the plan of
Gods.

Nd 1764

31

After Dining with Mr. Murray

Imitated from Catullus.

O THOU, of British orators the chief
That *were*, or *are* in *being*, or belief;
All eminence and goodness as thou art,
Accept the gratitude of Poet Smart,—
The meanest of the tuneful train as far,
As thou transcend'st the brightest at the bar.

Nd 1764

Epigram from Martial, Book 1, Ep. 26

WHEN Brutus' fall wing'd fame to Porcia brought,
Those arms her friends conceal'd, her passion sought.
She soon perceiv'd their poor officious wiles,
Approves their zeal, but at their folly smiles.
What Cato taught, heaven sure cannot deny,
Bereav'd of all, we still have pow'r to die.
Then down her throat the burning coal conveyed,
'Go now, ye fools, and hide your swords,' she said.

1791

On the Death of Master [Newbery]

After a lingering illness.

HENCEFORTH be every tender Tear supprest,
Or let us weep for Joy, that he is blest;
From Grief to Bliss, from Earth to Heav'n remov'd,
His Mem'ry honour'd, as his Life belov'd.
That heart o'er which no evil e'er had pow'r;
That disposition Sickness could not sour!

That Sense so oft to riper years deny'd
That patience hero's might have own'd with pride!
His painful Race undauntedly he ran,
And on the eleventh Winter died a MAN.

Md 1751

The Famous General Epitaph

From Demosthenes.

THESE for their country's cause were sheath'd in arms
    And all base imputations dare despise;
And nobly struck with glory's dreadful charms
    Made death their aim, eternity their prize.
For never could their mighty spirits yield,
    To see themselves and country-men in chains;
And Earth's kind bosom hides them in the field
    Of battle, so the Will Supreme ordains;
To conquer chance and errour's not reveal'd,
    For mortals sure mortality remains.

PSO 1764

On the Sudden Death of a Clergyman

IF, like th' Orphean lyre, my song could charm,
    And light to life the ashes in the urn,
Fate of his iron dart I would disarm,
    Sudden as thy disease should'st thou return,
Recall'd with mandates of despotic sounds,
And arbitrary grief, that will not hear of bounds.
    But, ah! such wishes, artless Muse, forbear;
        'Tis impotence of frantic love,
    Th' enthusiastic flight of wild despair,
        To hope the Thracian's magic power to prove.
    Alas! thy slender vein,
    Nor mighty is to move, nor forgetive to feign,
    Impatient of a rein,

33

Thou canst not in due bounds the struggling measures
      keep,
—But thou alas! canst weep—
Thou canst—and o'er the melancholy bier
Canst lend the sad solemnity a tear.
Hail! to that wretched corse, untenanted and cold,
And hail the peaceful shade loos'd from its irksome
      hold.
   Now let me say thou'rt free,
     For sure thou paid'st an heavy tax for life,
   While combating for thee,
Nature and mortality
   Maintain'd a daily strife.
High on a slender thread thy vital lamp was plac'd
   Upon the mountain's bleakest brow,
To give a noble light superior was it rais'd,
But more expos'd by eminence it blaz'd;
     For not a whistling wind that blew,
     Nor the drop descending dew,
     Nor a bat that idly flew,
   But half extinguish'd its fair flame—but now
See—hear the storms tempestuous sweep—
Precipitate it falls—it falls—falls lifeless in the deep.
Cease, cease, ye weeping youth,
Sincerity's soft sighs, and all the tears of truth.
   And you, his kindred throng, forbear
   Marble memorials to prepare,
And sculptur'd in your breasts his busto wear.
    'Twas thus when Israel's legislator dy'd,
    No fragile mortal honours were supply'd,
     But even a grave denied.
Better than what the pencil's dawb can give,
Better than all that Phidias ever wrought,
Is this—that what he taught shall live,
   And what he liv'd for ever shall be taught.
                     St 1751

Epitaph on Henrietta, Late Dutchess
of Cleveland

BORN in those days, when Charity revived
And from the Champion of the Church derived,
We claim a portion in the HOUSE of GRACE
For her, whose relicts shall adorn the place;
For her, who cherish'd with a mother's care,
And fill'd the Orphan's mouth with praise and pray'r.
Form'd for these deeds she bore her fruit *above*,
And left no issue of connubial love.
Yet was the noble matron well sustain'd,
And true politeness serv'd, where prudence reign'd.
She check'd all thoughts wherein the temper lurks,
By keeping Fancy busied on her works.—
A taste for hist'ry with a gen'rous aim,
And strict attention to her country's fame.—
A skill in picture, genius in design,
'Twas nature copy'd nature line for line.
Such were her merits when her faith was tried,
And to attain diviner things she died.—
Amen,—The paths of life so justly trod,
Bespeak the welcome due, thro' CHRIST, from GOD.

PSO 1764

Epitaph on Henry Fielding, Esq.

THE Master of the GREEK and ROMAN page,
The lively scorner of a venal age,
Who made the publick laugh, at publick vice,
Or drew from sparkling eyes the pearls of price;
Student of nature, reader of mankind,
In whom the patron, and the bard were join'd;
As free to give the plaudit, as assert,
And faithful in the practice of desert.

35

Hence pow'r consign'd the laws to his command,
And put the scales of Justice in his hand;
To stand protector of the Orphan race,
And find the female penitent a place.
From toils like these, too much for age to bear,
From pain, from sickness, and a world of care;
From children, and a widow in her bloom,
From shores remote, and from a foreign tomb,
Call'd by the WORD of Life, thou shalt appear,
To *please* and *profit* in a higher sphere,
Where endless hope, unperishable gain,
Are what the scriptures *teach* and *entertain*.

PSO 1764

Sacred to the Memory of the Rev'd James Sheeles, A.B., &c.

O YOUNG, yet apt and able in the word,
And at the morning-call to CHRIST preferr'd!
Our hope was longer time, and more commands,
So great the harvest, and so scarce the hands!
See how the likeliest are not lent to last,
And love officious calculates too fast.
—If God had left thy lot to human praise,
A father's pray'r had multiplied thy days.
But since to grieve is now the talk injoin'd,
We've learnt full well to weep and be resign'd;
Nay more, adore and bless the great decree,
And, in the spirit, still commune with Thee.
Let God's good will, at our expence be done,
As CHRIST demands a brother and a son.

PSO 1764

Epitaph on the Late Duke of Argyle

To Death's grim shades let meaner spirits fly,
Here rests JOHN CAMPBELL who shall never die.

Nd 1764

Epitaph on the Rev. Mr. Reynolds

At St. Peter's in the Isle of Thanet.

WAS rhetoric on the lips of sorrow hung,
Or cou'd affliction lend the heart a tongue,
Then should my soul, in noble anguish free,
Do glorious justice to herself and thee.
But ah! when loaded with a weight of woe,
Ev'n nature, blessed nature is our foe.
When we should praise, we sympathetic groan,
For sad mortality is all our own.
Yet but a word: as lowly as he lies,
He spurns all empires and asserts the skies.
Blush, power! he had no interest here below;
Blush, malice! that he dy'd without a foe;
The universal friend, so form'd to engage,
Was far too precious for this world and age.
Years were deny'd, for (such his worth and truth)
Kind Heaven has call'd him to eternal youth.

R 1791

FABLES

Fashion and Night

Quam multa prava atque injusta fiunt moribus?
Terent.

FASHION, a motley Nymph of Yore,
The *Cyprian* Queen to *Proteus* bore:
Various herself, in various Climes,
She moulds the Manners of the Times;
And turns in every Age and Nation,
The chequer'd Wheel of Variegation;
True Female, that ne'er knew her Will,
Still changing, tho' immortal still.
One Day as the inconstant Maid
Was careless on her Sofa laid,
Sick of the Sun, and tir'd with Light,
She thus invok'd the gloomy Night:
'Come—these malignant Rays destroy,
Thou skreen of Shame, and Rise of Joy.
Come from thy Western Ambuscade,
Queen of the Rout and Masquerade;
Nymph, without thee no Cards advance,
Without thee halts the loitering Dance
Till you approach, all, all's Restraint,
Nor is it safe to game or paint;
The Belles and Beaux thy Influence ask,
Put on the Universal Mask;
Let us invert, in thy Disguise,
That odious Nature, we despise.'
She ceas'd—the sable mantled Dame
With slow Approach, and awful, came;
And frowning with sarcastic Sneer,
Reproach'd the Female Rioteer:
'That Nature you abuse, my Fair,
Was I created to repair,
And contract with a friendly Shade,

The Pictures Heaven's rich Pencil made;
And with my Sleep—alluring Dose,
To give laborious Art Repose;
To make both Noise and Action cease,
The Queen of Secrecy and Peace.
But thou a Rebel, vile, and vain,
Usurp'st my lawful old Domain;
My Sceptre thou affect'st to sway,
And all the various Hours are Day;
With Clamours of unreal Joy,
My Sister Silence you destroy;
The blazing Lamp's unnatural Light
My Eye balls weary and affright;
But if I am allow'd one Shade,
Which no intrusive Eyes invade,
There all the atrocious Imps of Hell,
Theft, Murder, and Pollution dwell;
Think then how much, thou Toy of chance,
Thy Praise is likely Worth t' inhance;
Blind Thing that run'st without a Guide,
Thou Whirlpool in a rushing Tide,
No more my Fame with Praise pollute,
But damn me into some Repute.'

Md 1752

Where's the Poker?

THE Poker lost, poor *Susan* storm'd,
And all the Rites of Rage perform'd;
As scolding, crying, swearing, sweating,
Abusing, figitting, and fretting.
'Nothing but Villainy, and Thieving;
Good Heavens! what a World we live in?
If I don't find it in the Morning,
I'll surely give my Master Warning,
He'd better far shut up his Doors,

42

Than keep such good-for-nothing Whores;
For wheresoe'er their Trade they drive,
We *vartous* Bodies cannot thrive.'
Well may poor *Susan* grunt and groan;
Misfortunes never come alone,
But tread each other's Heels in Throngs,
For the next Day she lost the Tongs:
The Salt-box, Cullender, and Grate,
Soon shar'd the same untimely fate.
In vain she Vails and Wages spent
On new ones—for the new ones went.
There'd been, (she swore) some Dev'l or Witch in,
To rob or plunder all the Kitchin.
One Night she to her Chamber crept
(Where for a Month she had not slept,
Her Master being, to her seeming
A better playfellow than dreaming)
Curse on the Author of these Wrongs,
In her own Bed she found the Tongs,
(Hang *Thomas* for an idle Joker!)
And there, good lack! she found the Poker;
With Salt-box, Pepper-box, and Kettle,
With all the culinary Mettle.—
Be warn'd, ye fair, by *Susan's* crosses,
Keep chaste, and guard yourselves from Losses;
For if young Girls delight in Kissing,
No wonder, that the Poker's missing.

Md 1752

The Tea Pot and Scrubbing Brush

A TAWDRY *Tea-pot, A-la-mode,*
Where Art her utmost Skill bestow'd,
Was much esteem'd for being old,
And on its Sides with Red and Gold

43

Strange Beasts were drawn, in Taste *Chinese*,
And frightful Fish, and hump-back Trees.
High in an elegant Beaufet,
This pompous Utensil was set,
And near it, on a Marble Slab,
Forsaken by some careless Drab,
A veteran *Scrubbing-brush* was plac'd,
And the rich Furniture disgrac'd.
The *Tea-pot* soon began to flout,
And thus its Venom *spouted* out:
'Who from the Scullery or Yard,
Brought in this low, this vile Black-guard,
And laid in insolent Position,
Among us People of Condition?
Back to the Helper in the Stable,
Scour the Close-stool, or Wash-house Table;
Or cleanse some horsing block, or Plank,
Nor dare approach us Folk of Rank.
Turn—brother Coffee-pot, your Spout,
Observe the nasty stinking lout,
Who seems to scorn my Indignation,
Nor pays due Homage to my Fashion;
Take, sister Sugar-dish, a View,
And cousin, Cream-pot, pray do you.'
'Pox on you all,' replies old *Scrub*,
'Of Coxcombs ye confederate Club.
Full of Impertinence, and Prate,
Ye hate all Things that are sedate.
None but such ignorant Infernals,
Judge, by Appearance, and Externals:
Train'd up in Toil and useful Knowledge,
I'm Fellow of the Kitchen College,
And with the Mop, my old Associate,
The Family Affairs negociate.—
Am Foe to Filth, and Things obscene,
Dirty by making others clean.—
Not shining, yet I cause to shine,

44

My Roughness makes my Neighbours fine;
You're fair without, but foul within,
With Shame impregnated, and Sin;
To *you* each impious Scandal's owing,
You set each Gossip's Clack a-going.—
How Parson *Tythe* in secret sins,
And how Miss *Dainty* brought forth Twins:
How dear delicious *Polly Bloom*,
Owes all her Sweetness to Perfume;
Though grave at Church, at Cards can bet,
At once a Prude and a Coquette.—
'Twas better for each *British* Virgin,
When on roast Beef, strong Beer, and Sturgeon,
Joyous to Breakfast they sat round,
Nor was asham'd to eat a Pound.
These were the Manners, these the Ways,
In good Queen *Bess's* golden Days;
Each Damsel ow'd her Bloom and Glee,
To wholesome Elbow-grease, and me.
But now they center all their Joys
In empty Rattle traps and Noise.
Thus where the Fates send *you*, they send
Flagitious Times, which ne'er will mend,
'Till some Philosopher can find,
A *scrubbing-brush* to scour the Mind.'

Md 1752

Care and Generosity

OLD Care, with Industry and Art,
At length so well had play'd his part;
He heap'd up such an ample store,
That Av'rice could not sigh for more:
Ten thousand flocks his shepherd told,
His coffers overflow'd with gold;

45

The land all round him was his own.
With corn his crowded granaries groan.
In short, so vast his charge and gain,
That to possess them was a pain:
With happiness oppress'd he lies,
And much too prudent to be wise.
Near him there liv'd a beauteous maid,
With all the charms of youth array'd;
Good, amiable, sincere and free,
Her name was Generosity.
'Twas hers the largess to bestow
On rich and poor, on friend and foe.
Her doors to all were open'd wide,
The pilgrim there might safe abide:
For th' hungry and the thirsty crew,
The bread she broke, the drink she drew;
There Sickness laid her aching head,
And there Distress cou'd find a bed.—
Each hour with an all-bounteous hand,
Diffus'd she blessings round the land:
Her gifts and glory lasted long,
And numerous was th' accepting throng.
At length pale Penury seiz'd the dame,
And Fortune fled, and Ruin came,
She found her riches at an end,
And that she had not made one friend.—
All curs'd her for not giving more,
Nor thought on what she'd done before;
She wept, she rav'd, she tore her hair,
When lo! to comfort her came Care.—
And cry'd, 'My dear, if you will join
Your hand in nuptial bonds with mine;
All will be well—you shall have store,
And I be plagu'd with Wealth no more.
Tho' I restrain your bounteous heart,
You still shall act the generous part.'—
The Bridal came—great was the feast,

And good the pudding and the priest;
The bride in nine moons brought him forth
A little maid of matchless worth:
Her face was mix'd of care and glee,
They christen'd her Œconomy;
And styled her fair Discretion's Queen,
The mistress of the golden mean.
Now Generosity confin'd,
Is perfect easy in her mind;
Still loves to give, yet knows to spare,
Nor wishes to be free from Care.

PSO 1752

The Bag-wig and the Tobacco-Pipe

A BAG-WIG of a jauntee air,
Trick'd up with all a barber's care,
Loaded with powder and perfume,
Hung in a spendthrift's dressing-room:
Close by its side, by chance convey'd,
A black Tobacco-pipe was laid;
And with its vapours far and near,
Outstunk the essence of Monsieur;
At which its rage, the thing of hair,
Thus, bristling up, began declare.

'Bak'd dirt! that with intrusion rude
Break's in upon my solitude,
And whose offensive breath defiles
The air for forty thousand miles—
Avaunt—pollution's in thy touch—
O barb'rous English! horrid Dutch!
I cannot bear it—Here, Sue, Nan,
Go call the maid to call the man,
And bid him come without delay,
To take this odious pipe away.

47

Hideous! sure some one smoak'd thee, Friend,
Reversely, at his t'other end.
Oh! what mix'd odours! what a throng
Of salt and sour, of stale and strong!
A most unnatural combination,
Enough to mar all perspiration—
Monstrous! again—'twou'd vex a saint:
Susan, the drops—or else I faint!'
The pipe (for 'twas a pipe of soul)
Raising himself upon his bole,
In smoke, like oracle of old,
Did thus his sentiments unfold.
'Why, what's the matter, Goodman Swagger,
Thou flaunting French, fantastic bragger?
Whose whole fine speech is (with a pox)
Ridiculous and heterodox.
'Twas better for the English nation
Before such scoundrels came in fashion,
When none sought hair in realms unknown,
But every blockhead bore his own.
Know, puppy, I'm an English pipe,
Deem'd worthy of each Briton's gripe,
Who, with my cloud-compelling aid,
Help our plantations and our trade,
And am, when sober and when mellow,
An upright, downright, honest fellow.
Tho' fools, like you, may think me rough,
And scorn me, 'cause I am in buff,
Yet your contempt I glad receive,
'Tis all the fame that you can give:
None finery or fopp'ry prize,
But they who've something to disguise;
For simple nature hates abuse,
And plainness is the dress of Use.'

PSO 1752

The Brocaded Gown and Linen Rag

FROM a fine lady to her maid,
A gown descended of brocade.
French!—Yes, from *Paris*—that's enough,
That wou'd give dignity to stuff.
By accident or by design,
Or from some cause, I can't divine;
A linen rag (sad source of wrangling!)
On a contiguous peg was dangling
Vilely besmear'd—for late it's master,
It serv'd in quality of plaister.
The gown, contemptuous beholder,
Gave a *French* shrug from either shoulder,
And rustling with emotion furious,
Bespoke the rag in terms injurious.
'Unfit for tinder, lint, or *fodder*,
Thou thing of filth, and (what is odder)
Discarded from thy owner's issue,
Dar'st thou proceed 'gainst gold tissue?
Instant away—or in this place,
Begar me give you *coup de grace*.'
  To this reply'd the honest rag,
Who lik'd a jest, and was a wag;
'Tho' thy glib tongue without a halt run,
Thou shabby, second-hand, subaltern,
At once so ancient and so easy,
At once so gorgeous and so greasy;
I value not your gasconading,
Nor all thy *a-la-mode* parading;
But to abstain from words imperious,
And to be sober, grave, and serious,
(Tho', says friend *Horace*, 'tis no treason,
At once to giggle, and to reason.)
When me you lesson, friend, you dream,
For know I am not what I seem.
Soon by the mill's refining motion,

49

The sweetest daughter of the ocean,
Fair *Medway*, shall with snowy hue,
My virgin purity renew,
And give me re-inform'd existence,
A good retention and subsistence.
Then shall the sons of genius join
To make my second life divine.
O *Murray*, let me then dispense,
Some portion of thy eloquence;
For *Greek* and *Roman* rhetoric shine,
United and improved in thine.
The spirit-stirring sage alarms,
And *Ciceronian* sweetness charms.
Th' *Athenian Akinside* may deign,
To stamp me deathless with his pen,
While flows approv'd by all the nine
Th' immortal soul of every line.
Collins, perhaps, his aid may lend,
Melpomene's selected friend.
Perhaps our great Augustan *Gray*
May grace me with a *Doric* lay;
With sweet, with manly words of woe,
That nervously pathetic flow.
What, *Mason*, may I owe to you?
Learning's first pride, and Nature's too;
On thee she cast her sweetest smile,
And gave thee Art's correcting file;
That file, which with assiduous pain,
The viper *Envy* bites in vain.—
Such glories my mean lot betide,
Hear, tawdry fool, and check thy pride.—
Thou, after scouring, dying, turning,
(If haply thou escape a burning)
From gown to petticoat descending,
And in a beggar's mantle ending,
Shalt in a dunghill or a sty,
'Midst filth and vermin rot and dye.'

GM 1754

The Duellists

WHAT's honour, did your lordship say?
My lord, I humbly crave a day.—
'Tis difficult, and in my mind,
Like substance, cannot be defin'd.
It deals in numerous externals,
And is a legion of infernals;
Sometimes in riot and in play,
'Tis breaking of the Sabbath day:
When 'tis consider'd as a passion,
I deem it lust and fornication.
We pay our debts in honour's cause,
Lost in the breaking of the laws:
'Tis for some selfish impious end,
To murder the sincerest friend;
But wou'd you alter all the clan,
Turn out an honourable man.
Why take a pistol from the shelf,
And fight a duel with yourself.—
'Twas on a time, the Lord knows when,
In Ely, or in Lincoln fen,
A frog and mouse had long disputes,
Held in the language of the brutes,
Who of a certain pool and pasture,
Shou'd be the sovereign and master.
'Sir,' says the frog, and damn'd his blood,
'I hold that my pretension's good;
Nor can a brute of reason doubt it,
For all that you can squeak about it.'
The mouse, averse to be o'erpower'd,
Gave him the lie, and call'd him coward;
Too hard for any frog's digestion,
To have his froghood call'd in question!
A bargain instantly was made,
No mouse of honour could evade,

51

On the next morn, as soon as light,
With desperate bullrushes to fight;
The morning came—and man to man,
The grand monomachy began;
Need I recount how each bravado,
Shone in montant and in passado;
To what a height their ire they carry'd,
How oft they thrusted and they parry'd;
But as these champions kept dispensing,
Finesses in the art of fencing,
A furious vulture took upon her,
Quick to decide this point of honour,
And, lawyer like, to make an end on't,
Devour'd both plaintiff and defendant.
Thus, often in our British nation,
(I speak by way of application)
A lie direct to some hot youth.
The giving which perhaps was truth,
The treading on a scoundrel's toe,
Or dealing impudence a blow,
Disputes in politics and law,
About a feather and a straw;
A thousand trifles not worth naming,
In whoring, jockeying, and gaming,
Shall cause a challenge's inditing,
And set two loggerheads a fighting,
Meanwhile the father of despair,
The prince of vanity and air,
His querry, like an hawk discovering,
O'er their devoted heads hangs hovering,
Secure to get in his tuition,
These volunteers for black perdition.

R 1791

The Snake, the Goose, and Nightingale

Humbly addressed to the hissers and cat-callers attending
both Houses.

WHEN rul'd by truth and nature's ways,
When just to blame, yet fix'd to praise,
As votary of the Delphic god,
I reverence the critic's rod;
But when inflam'd with spite alone,
I hold all critics but as one;
For though they class themselves with art,
And each man takes a different part;
Yet whatso'er they praise and blame;
They in their motives are the same,
    Forth as she waddled in the brake,
A grey goose stumbled on a snake,
And took th' occasion to abuse her,
And of rank plagiarism accuse her.
"Twas I,' quoth she, 'in every vale,
First hiss'd the noisy nightingale;
And boldly cavill'd at each note,
That twitter'd in the woodlark's throat:
I, who sublime and more than mortal,
Must stoop to enter at the portal,
Have ever been the first to show
My hate to every thing that's low;
While thou, mean mimic of my manner,
(Without inlisting to my banner)
Dar'st in thy grov'ling situation,
To counterfeit my sibilation.'
    The snake enrag'd, reply'd, 'Know, madam,
I date my charter down from Adam;
Nor can I, since I bear the bell,
E'er imitate where I excell.
Had any other creature dar'd
Once to aver, what you've averr'd,

53

I might have been more fierce and fervent,
But you're a goose,—and so your servant.'
'Truce with your folly and your pride,'
The warbling Philomela cry'd;
'Since no more animals we find
In nature of the hissing kind,
You should be friends with one another,
Nay, kind as brother is to brother.
For know, thou pattern of abuse,
Thou snake art but a crawling goose;
And thou dull dabbler in each lake,
Art nothing but a feather'd snake.'

R 1791

Mrs. Abigail and the Dumb Waiter

WITH frowning brow, and aspect low'ring,
As Abigail one day was scow'ring,
From chair to chair she past along,
Without soliloquy or song;
Content, in humdrum mood, t'adjust
Her matters to disperse the dust.—
Thus plodded on the sullen fair,
'Till a dumb-waiter claim'd her care;
She then in rage, with shrill salute,
Bespoke the inoffensive mute:—
'Thou stupid tool of vapourish asses,
With thy brown shelves for pots and glasses;
Thou foreign whirligig, for whom
Us honest folks must quit the room;
And, like young misses at a christ'ning,
Are forc'd to be content with list'ning;
Though thou'rt a fav'rite of my master's,
I'll set thee gadding on thy castors.'
This said—with many a rough attack,

She scrubb'd him 'till she made him crack;
Insulted stronger still and stronger,
The poor dumb thing could hold no longer.—
'Thou drab, born mops and brooms to dandle,
Thou haberdasher of small scandal,
Factor of family abuse,
Retailer of domestic news;
My lord, as soon as I appear,
Confines thee in thy proper sphere;
Or else, at ev'ry place of call,
The chandler's shop, or cobler's stall,
Or ale-house, where (for petty tales,
Gin, beer, and ale are constant vails)
Each word at table that was spoke,
Wou'd soon become the public joke,
And cheerful innocent converse,
To scandal warp'd—or something worse.—
Whene'er my master I attend,
Freely his mind he can unbend;—
But when such praters fill my place,
Then nothing should be said—but grace.'

GM 1755

The Country Squire and the Mandrake

THE Sun had rais'd above the mead
His glorious horizontal head;
Sad *Philomela* left her thorn;
The lively linnets hymn'd the morn,
And nature, like a waking bride,
Her blushes spread on every side;
The cock (as usual) crow'd up *Tray*,
Who nightly with his master lay;
The faithful spaniel gave the word,
TRELOOBY at the signal stirr'd,

And with his gun, from wood to wood,
The man of prey his course pursu'd;
The dew and herbage all around,
Like pearls and emeralds on the ground,
The uncultur'd flowers that rudely rise,
Where smiling freedom art defies,
The lark, in transport, tow'ring high,
The crimson curtains of the sky,
Affected not *Trelooby's* mind—
For what is beauty to the blind?
Th' amorous voice of *Sylvan* love,
Form'd charming concerts in the grove;
Sweet *Zephyr* sigh'd on *Flora's* breast,
And fann'd the blackbird in her nest;
Whisp'ring he leapt from leaf to leaf;
But what is musick to the deaf?

At length while poring on the ground,
With monumental look profound,
A curious vegetable caught
His—something similar to thought:
Wond'ring, he ponder'd, stooping low
(*Trelooby* always lov'd a show)
And on the *Mandrake's* vernal station,
Star'd with prodigions observation.
Th' affronted *Mandrake* with a frown.
Address'd in rage the wealthy clown.

'Proud member of the rambling race,
That vegetate from place to place,
Pursue the leveret at large,
Nor near thy blunderbuss discharge.
Disdainful tho' thou look'st on me,
What art thou, or what can'st thou be?
Nature, that markt thee as a fool,
Gave no materials for the school?
In what consists thy work and fame?
The preservation of the. game.—
For what? thou avaritious elf,

But to destroy it all thy-self;
To lead a life of drink and feast,
T' oppress the poor, and cheat the priest,
Or triumph in a virgin lost,
Is all the manhood thou canst boast.—
Pretty! in nature's various plan,
To see a weed that's like a man,
But 'tis a grievous thing indeed,
To see a man so like a weed.'

GM 1755

The Wholesale Critic and the Hop Merchant

HAIL to each ancient sacred shade
Of those, who gave the Muses aid,
Skill'd verse mysterious to unfold,
And set each brilliant thought in gold.
Hail Aristotle's honour'd shrine,
And, great Longinus, hail to thine;
Ye too, whose judgments ne'er could fail,
Hail Horace, and Quintilian hail;
And, dread of every Goth and Hun,
Hail Pope, and peerless Addison.

Alas! by different steps and ways
Our modern critics aim at praise,
And rashly in the learned arts,
They judge by prejudice and parts;
For crampt by a contracted soul,
How shou'd they comprehend the whole?

I know of many a deep-learn'd brother,
Who weighs one science by another,
And makes 'mongst bards poetic schism,
Because he understands the prism;
Thinks in acuteness he surpasses,

From knowledge of the optic-glasses.
There are some critics in the nation,
Profoundly vers'd in gravitation;
Who like the bulky and the great,
And judge by quantity and weight.
Some who're extremely skill'd in building,
Judge by proportion, form, and gilding,
And praise with a sagacious look
The architecture of a book.

    Soon as the hops arriv'd from Kent,
Forth to the quay the merchant went,
Went critically to explore
The merit of the hops on shore.
Close to a bag he took his standing,
And at a venture thrust his hand in;
Then, with the face of a physician,
Their colour scann'd and their condition;
He trusts his touch, his smell, his eyes,
The goods at once approves and buys.

    Catchup, so dextrous, droll, and dry,
It happen'd Catchup there was by,
Who like Iago, arch on all,
Is nothing, if not critical.
He with a sneer and with a shrug,
With eye of hawk, and face of pug,
Cry'd; 'Fellow, I admire thy fun,
Thou most judiciously hast done,
Who from one handful buyst ten ton.
Does it not enter in thy crown,
Some may be mouldy, some be brown;
The vacancies with leaves supplied,
And some half pick'd and some half dry'd?'
The merchant, who Tom Catchup knew,
(A merchant and a scholar too)
Said, 'What I've done is not absurd,
I know my chap and take his word.—
On thee, thou caviller at large,

I here retort thy random charge,
Who, in an hypercritic rage,
Judgest ten volumes by a page;
Whose wond'rous comprehensive view
Grasps more than Solomon e'er knew;
With every thing you claim alliance,
Art, trade, profession, calling, science;
You mete out all things by one rule,
And are an universal fool.
Though swoln with vanity and pride,
You're but one driv'ller multiplied,
A prig—that proves himself by starts,
As many dolts—as there are arts.'

R 1791

The English Bull Dog, Dutch Mastiff, and Quail

ARE we not all of race divine,
Alike of an immortal line?
Shall man to man afford derision,
But for some casual division;
To malice, and to mischief prone,
From climate, canton, or from zone,
Are all to idle discord bent,
These Kentish men—those men of Kent;
And parties and distinction make,
For parties and distinction's sake.
Souls sprung from an etherial flame,
However clad, are still the same;
Nor should we judge the heart or head,
By air we breathe, or earth we tread.
Dame Nature, who, all meritorious,
In a true Englishman is glorious;
Is lively, honest, brave and bonny,

59

In Monsieur, Taffy, Teague, and Sawney.
Give prejudices to the wind,
And let's be patriots of mankind.
Bigots, avaunt, sense can't endure ye,
But fabulists should try to cure ye.
    A snub-nos'd dog to fat inclin'd
Of the true hogan mogan kind,
The favourite of an English dame,
Mynheer Van Trumpo was his name:
One morning as he chanc'd to range,
Met honest Towzer on the 'Change;
'And whom have we got here, I beg,'
Quoth he,—and lifted up his leg;
'An English dog can't take an airing,
But foreign scoundrels must be staring.
I'd have your French dogs and your Spanish,
And all your Dutch and all your Danish,
By which our species is confounded,
Be hang'd, be poison'd, or be drowned;
No mercy on the race suspected,
Greyhounds from Italy excepted:
By them my dames ne'er prove big-bellied,
For they, poor toads, are Farrinellied.
Well, of all dogs it stands confess'd,
Your English bull dogs are the best;
I say it, and will set my hand to't,
Cambden records it, and I'll stand to't.
'Tis true we have too much urbanity,
Somewhat o'ercharg'd with soft humanity;
The best things must find food for railing,
And every creature has its failing.'
    'And who are you?' reply'd Van Trump,
(Curling his tail upon his rump)
'Vaunting the regions of distraction,
The land of party and of faction.
In all fair Europe, who but we,
For national economy;

For wealth and peace, that have more charms,
Than learned arts, or noisy arms?
You envy us our dancing bogs,
With all the music of the frogs;
Join'd to the Tretchscutz's bonny loon,
Who on the cymbal grinds the tune.
For poets, and the Muses nine,
Beyond comparison we shine:
Oh! how we warble in our gizzards,
With X X's, H H's and with Z Z's.
For fighting—now you think I'm joking;
We love it better far than smoking.
Ask but our troops, from man to boy,
Who all surviv'd at Fontenoy.
'Tis true, as friends, and as allies,
We're ever ready to devise;
Our loves, or any kind assistance,
That may be granted at a distance;
But if you go to brag, good bye t'ye,
Nor dare to brave the High and Mighty.'
    'Wrong are you both,' rejoins a quail,
Confin'd within its wiry jail:
'Frequent from realm to realm I've rang'd
And with the seasons, climates chang'd.
Mankind is not so void of grace,
But good I've found in every place:
I've seen sincerity in France,
Amongst the Germans complaisance;
In foggy Holland wit may reign,
I've known humility in Spain;
Free'd was I by a turban'd Turk,
Whose life was one entire good work;
And in this land, fair freedom's boast,
Behold my liberty is lost.
Despis'd Hibernia have I seen,
Dejected like a widow'd queen;
Her robe with dignity long worn,

And cap of liberty were torn;
Her broken fife, and harp unstrung,
On the uncultur'd ground were flung;
Down lay her spear, defil'd with rust,
And book of learning in the dust;
Her loyalty still blameless found,
And hospitality renown'd:
No more the voice of fame engross'd,
In discontent and clamour lost.—
Ah! dire corruption, art thou spread,
Where never viper rear'd it's head?
And didst thy baleful influence sow,
Where hemlock nor the nightshade grow.
Hapless, disconsolate, and brave,
Hibernia! who'll Hibernia save?
Who shall assist thee in thy woe,
Who ward from thee the fatal blow?
'Tis done, the glorious work is done,
All thanks to Heaven and Hartington.'

R 1791

The Citizen and the Red Lion of Brentford

I LOVE my friend—but love my ease,
And claim a right myself to please;
To company however prone,
At times all men wou'd be alone.
Free from each interruption rude,
Or what is meant by solitude.
My villa lies within the bills,
So—like a theatre it fills:
To me my kind acquaintance stray,
And Sunday proves no sabbath day;
Yet many a friend and near relation,

Make up a glorious congregation;
They crowd by dozens and by dozens,
And bring me all their country cousins.
Though cringing landlords on the road,
Who find for man and horse abode;
Though gilded grapes to sign-post chain'd,
Invite them to be entertain'd,
And straddling cross his kilderkin,
Though jolly Bacchus calls them in;
Nay—though my landlady wou'd trust 'em,
Pilgarlic's sure of all the custom;
And his whole house is like a fair,
Unless he only treats with air.
What? shall each pert half witted wit,
That calls me Jack, or calls me Kit,
Prey on my time, or on my table?
No—but let's hasten to the fable.

The eve advanc'd, the Sun declin'd,
Ball to the booby-hutch was join'd,
A wealthy cockney drove away,
To celebrate Saint Saturday;
Wife, daughter, pug, all crouded in,
To meet at country house their kin.
Thro' Brentford, to fair Twickenham's bow'rs,
The ungreas'd grumbling axle scow'rs,
To pass in rural sweets a day,
But there's a lion in the way:
This lion a most furious elf,
Hung up to represent himself,
Redden'd with rage, and shook his mane,
And roar'd, and roar'd, and roar'd again.
Wond'rous, tho' painted on a board,
He roar'd, and roar'd, and roar'd, and roar'd.
'Fool!' (says the majesty of beasts)
'At whose expense a legion feasts,
Foe to yourself, you those pursue,
Who're eating up your cakes and you;

63

Walk in, walk in, (so prudence votes)
And give poor Ball a feed of oats,
Look to yourself, and as for ma'm,
Coax her to take a little dram;
Let Miss and Pug with cakes be fed,
Then, honest man, go back to bed;
You're better, and you're cheaper there,
Where are no hangers on to fear.
Go buy friend Newbery's new Pantheon,
And con the tale of poor Acteon,
Horn'd by Diana, and o'erpower'd,
And by the dogs he fed devour'd.
What he receiv'd from charity,
Lewdness perhaps may give to thee;
And tho' your spouse my lecture scorns,
Beware his fate, beware his horns.'

　　'Sir,' says the Cit, (who made a stand,
And strok'd his forehead with his hand)
'By your grim gravity and grace,
You greatly wou'd become the mace.
This kind advice I gladly take,—
Draw'r, bring the dram, and bring a cake,
With good brown beer that's brisk and humming.'
'A coming, sir! a coming, coming!'
The Cit then took a hearty draught,
And shook his jolly sides and laugh'd.
Then to the king of beasts he bow'd,
And thus his gratitude avow'd.—
'Sir, for your sapient oration,
I owe the greatest obligation.
You stand expos'd to sun, and show'r,
I know Jack Ellis of the Tow'r;
By him you soon may gain renown,
He'll show your highness to the town;
Or, if you chuse your station here,
To call forth Britons to their beer,
As painter of distinguish'd note,

64

He'll send his man to clean your coat.'
The lion thank'd him for his proffer,
And if a vacancy shou'd offer,
Declar'd he had too just a notion,
To be averse to such promotion.
The citizen drove off with joy,
'For London—Ball—for London—hoy.'
Content to bed he went his way,
And is no bankrupt to this day.

R 1791

Madam and the Magpie

YE thunders roll, ye oceans roar,
And wake the rough resounding shore;
Ye guns in smoke and flames engage,
And shake the ramparts with your rage;
Boreas distend your chops and blow;
Ring, ring, ye bonny bells of Bow;
Ye drums and rattles, rend the ears,
Like twenty thousand Southwark fairs;
Bellow, ye bulls, and bawl, ye bats,
Encore, encore, ye amorous cats;
In vain, poor things, ye squeak and squall,
Soft Sylvia shall out-tongue you all:
But here she comes—there's no relief,
She comes, and blessed are the deaf.
'A magpie! why, you're mad, my dear,
To bring a chattering magpie here.
A prating play thing, fit for boys—
You know I can't endure a noise.—
You brought this precious present sure,
My headache and my cough to cure.
Pray hand him in and let him stain
Each curtain, and each counterpane;

65

Yes, he shall roost upon my toilet,
Or on my pillow—he can't spoil it:
He'll only make me catch my death.—
O Heavens! for a little breath!—
Thank God, I never knew resentment,
But am all patience and contentment,
Or else, you paltry knave, I shou'd
(As any other woman wou'd)
Wring off his neck, and down your gullet
Cram it, by way of chick or pullet.—
Well, I must lock up all my rings,
My jewels, and my curious things:
My Chinese toys must go to pot;
My dear, my pinchbecks—and what not?
For all your magpies are, like lawyers,
At once thieves, brawlers, and destroyers.—
You for a wife have search'd the globe,
You've got a very female Job,
Pattern of love, and peace, and unity,
Or how cou'd you expect impunity?
O Lord! this nasty thing will bite,
And scratch and clapper, claw and fight.
O monstrous wretch, thus to devise,
To tear out your poor Sylvia's eyes.
You're a fine Popish plot pursuing,
By presents to affect my ruin;
And thus for good are ill retorting
To ME, who brought you such a fortune;
To ME, you low-liv'd clown, to ME,
Who came of such a family;
ME, who from age to age possess'd
A lion rampant on my crest;
ME, who have fill'd your empty coffers.
ME, who'd so many better offers;
And is my merit thus regarded,
Cuckold, my virtue thus rewarded.
O 'tis past sufferance—Mary—Mary,

I faint—the citron, or the clary.'
    The poor man, who had bought the creature,
Out of pure conjugal good-nature,
Stood at this violent attack,
Like statues made by Roubilliac,
Though form'd beyond all skill antique,
They can't their marble silence break;
They only breathe, and think, and start,
Astonish'd at their maker's art.
Quoth Mag, 'Fair Grizzle, I must grant,
Your spouse a magpye cannot want:
For troth (to give the Dev'l his due)
He keeps a rookery in you.
Don't fear I'll tarry long, sweet lady,
Where there is din enough already,
We never should agree together,
Although we're so much of a feather;
You're fond of peace, no man can doubt it,
Who make such wond'rous noise about it;
And your tongue of immortal mould
Proclaims in thunder you're no scold.
Yes, yes, you're sovereign of the tongue,
And like the king can do no wrong;
Justly your spouse restrains his voice,
Nor vainly answers words with noise;
This storm, which no soul can endure,
Requires a very different cure;
For such sour verjuice dispositions,
Your crabsticks are the best physicians.'

                                    R 1791

A Story of a Cock and a Bull

YES—we excell in arts and arms,
In learning's lore and beauty's charms.
The seas wide empire we engross,
All nations hail the British cross;
The land of liberty we tread,
And woe to his devoted head,
Who dares the contrary advance,
One Englishman's worth ten of France.
These these, are truths, what man won't write for,
Won't swear, won't bully, or won't fight for;
Yet (tho' perhaps I speak thro' vanity)
Wou'd we'd a little more humanity;
Too far, I fear, I've drove the jest,
So leave to cock and bull the rest.

    A bull, who'd listen'd to the vows
Of above fifteen hundred cows;
And serv'd his master fresh and fresh,
With hecatombs of special flesh,
Like to an hermit or a dervise,
(Grown old and feeble in the service)
Now left the meadow's green parade,
And sought a solitary shade.
The cows proclaim'd in mournful lowing,
The bull's deficiency in wooing,
And to their disappointed master,
All told the terrible disaster.

    'Is this the case' (quoth Hodge) 'O rare!
But hold, to morrow is the fair.
Thou to thy doom, old boy, art fated,
To morrow—and thou shalt be baited.'
The deed was done—curse on the wrong!
Bloody description, hold thy tongue.—
Victorious yet the bull return'd,
And with stern silence inly mourn'd.

    A vet'ran, brave, majestic cock,

68

Who serv'd for hour glass, guard, and clock,
Who crow'd the mansion's first relief,
Alike from goblin and from thief;
Whose youth escap'd the Christmas skillet,
Whose vigour brav'd the Shrovetide billet,
Had just return'd in wounds and pain,
Triumphant from the barbarous main.—
By riv'let's brink, with trees o'ergrown,
He heard his fellow sufferer's moan;
And greatly scorning wounds and smart,
Gave him three cheers with all his heart.

'Rise, neighbour, from that pensive attitude,
Brave witness of vile man's ingratitude;
And let us both with spur and horn,
The cruel reasoning monster scorn.—
Methinks at every dawn of day,
When first I chant my blithsome lay,
Methinks I hear from out the sky,
All will be better by and by;
When bloody, base, degenerate man,
Who deviates from his Maker's plan;
Who Nature and her works abuses,
And thus his fellow servants uses,
Shall greatly, and yet justly want,
The mercy he refus'd to grant;
And (while his heart his conscience purges)
Shall wish to be the brute he scourges.'

R 1791

The Blockhead and Beehive

THE fragrance of the new-mown hay
Paid incense to the god of day;
Who issuing from his eastern gate,
Resplendent rode in all his state:

Rous'd by the light from soft repose,
Big with the Muse, a bard arose,
And the fresh garden's still retreat
He measured with poetic feet.
The cooling, high, o'er-arching shade,
By the embracing branches made,
The smooth shorn sod, whose verdant gloss,
Was check'd with intermingled moss,
Cowslips, like topazes that shine,
Close by the silver serpentine,
Rude rustics which assert the bow'rs,
Amidst the educated flow'rs.
The lime tree and sweet-scented bay,
(The sole reward of many a lay)
And all the poets of the wing,
Who sweetly without salary sing,
Attract at once his observation,
Peopling thy wilds, Imagination!
'Sweet Nature, who this turf bedews,
Sweet Nature, who's the thrush's Muse!
How she each anxious thought beguiles,
And meets me with ten thousand smiles!
O infinite benignity!
She smiles, but not alone on me;
On hill, on dale, on lake, on lawn,
Like Celia when her picture's drawn;
Assuming countless charms and airs,
'Till Hayman's matchless art despairs,
Pausing like me he dreads to fall
From the divine original.'
    More had he said—but in there came
A lout—Squire Booby was his name.—
The bard, who at a distant view
The busy prattling blockhead knew,
    Retir'd into a secret nook,
And thence his observations took.
Vex'd he cou'd find no man to tease,

70

The squire 'gan chattering to the bees,
And pertly with officious mien,
He thus address'd their humming queen:
'Madam, be not in any terrours;
I only come t'amend your errours;
My friendship briefly to display,
And put you in a better way.
Cease, madam, (if I may advise)
To carry honey on your thighs,
Employ ('tis better, I aver)
Old Grub, the fairies' coach-maker;
For he who has sufficient art
To make a coach, may make a cart.
To these you'll yoke some sixteen bees,
Who will dispatch your work with ease;
And come and go, and go and come,
To bring your honey harvest home.—
Ma'am, architecture you're not skill'd in,
I don't approve your way of building;
In this there's nothing like design,
Pray learn the use of Gunter's line.
I'll serve your highness at a pinch,
I am a scholar every inch,
And know each author I lay fist on,
From Archimedes down to Whiston.—
Though honey making be your trade,
In chemistry you want some aid.—
Pleas'd with your work, altho' you sing,
You're not quite right—'tis not the thing.
Myself wou'd gladly be an actor,
To help the honey manufacture.—
I hear for war you are preparing,
Which I should like to have a share in:
Yet though the enemy be landing,
'Tis wrong to keep an army standing.—
If you'll ensure me from the laws,
I'll write a pamphlet in your cause.—

I vow, I am concern'd to see
Your want of state-economy.
Of nothing living I pronounce ill,
But I don't like your privy-council.
There is, I know, a certain bee,
(Wou'd he was from the ministry)
Which certain bee, if rightly known,
Wou'd prove no better than a drone;
There are (but I shall name no names,
I never love to kindle flames)
A pack of rogues with crimes grown callous,
Who greatly wou'd adorn the gallows;
That with the wasps, for paltry gold,
A secret correspondence hold,
Yet you'll be great—your subjects free,
If the whole thing be left to me.—'

Thus, like the waters of the ocean,
His tongue had run in ceaseless motion,
Had not the queen ta'en up in wrath,
This thing of folly and of froth.

'Impertinent and witless meddler,
Thou smattering, empty, noisy pedler!
By vanity, thou bladder blown,
To be the football of the town.
O happy England, land of freedom,
Replete with statesmen, if she need 'em,
Where war is wag'd by Sue or Nell,
And Jobson is a Machiavel!—
Tell Hardwick that his judgment fails,
Show Justice how to hold her scales.—
To fire the soul at once, and please,
Teach Murray and Demosthenes;
Say Vane is not by goodness grac'd,
And wants humanity and taste.—
Tho' Pelham with Mæcenas vies,
Tell Fame she's false, and Truth she lies;
And then return, thou verbal Hector,

And give the bees another lecture.'
  This said, the portal she unbarr'd,
Calling the bees upon their guard,
And set at once about his ears
Ten thousand of her grenadiers.—
Some on his lips and palate hung,
And the offending member stung.
'Just' (says the bard from out the grot)
'Just, though severe, is your sad lot,
Who think, and talk, and live in vain,
Of sweet society the bane.
Business misplac'd is a mere jest,
And active idleness at best.'

R 1791

The Herald and Husband-Man

—— Nobilitas sola est atque unica virtus.
Juvenal.

I with friend Juvenal agree,
Virtue's the true nobility;
Has of herself sufficient charms,
Altho' without a coat of arms.
Honestus does not know the rules,
Concerning Or and Fez, and Gules,
Yet sets the wond'ring eye to gaze on,
Such deeds no herald e'er could blazon.
Tawdry achievements out of place,
Do but augment a fool's disgrace;
A coward is a double jest,
Who has a lion for his crest;
And things are come to such a pass,
Two horses may support an ass;
And on a gamester or buffoon,
A moral motto's a lampoon.

An honest rustic having done
His master's work 'twixt sun and sun,
Retir'd to dress a little spot,
Adjoining to his homely cot,
Where pleas'd, in miniature, he found
His landlord's culinary ground,
Some herbs that feed, and some that heal,
The winter's medicine or meal.
The sage, which in his garden seen,
No man need ever die I ween;
The marjoram comely to behold,
With thyme, and ruddiest marygold,
And mint and pennyroyal sweet,
To deck the cottage windows meet,
And baum, that yields a finer juice
Than all that China can produce;
With carrots red, and turnips white,
And leeks, Cadwallader's delight;
And all the savory crop that vie
To please the palate and the eye.
Thus, as intent, he did survey
His plot, a Herald came that way,
A man of great escutcheon'd knowledge,
And member of the motley college.
Heedless the peasant pass'd he by,
Indulging this soliloquy;
'Ye gods! what an enormous space,
'Twixt man and man does Nature place;
While some by deeds of honour rise,
To such a height, as far out-vies
The visible diurnal sphere;
While others, like this rustic here,
Grope in the groveling ground content,
Without or lineage or descent,
Hail, Heraldry! mysterious art,
Bright patroness of all desert,
Mankind would on a level lie,

And undistinguish'd live and die;
Depriv'd of thy illustrious aid,
Such! so momentous is our trade.'
   'Sir,' says the clown, 'why sure you joke,'
(And kept on digging as he spoke)
'And prate not to extort conviction,
But merrily by way of fiction.
Say, do your manuscripts attest,
What was old father Adam's crest;
Did he a nobler coat receive
In right of marrying Mrs. Eve;
Or had supporters when he kiss'd her,
On dexter side, and side sinister;
Or was his motto, prithee speak,
English, French, Latin, Welch, or Greek;
Or was he not, without a lye,
Just such a nobleman as I?
Virtue, which great defects can stifle,
May beam distinction on a trifle;
And honour, with her native charms,
May beautify a coat of arms;
Realities somewhat will thrive,
E'en by appearance kept alive;
But by themselves, Gules, Or, and Fez,
Are cyphers neither more or less:
Keep both thy head and hands from crimes,
Be honest in the worst of times:
Health's on my countenance impress'd,
And sweet content's my daily guest,
My fame alone I build on this,
And Garter King at Arms may kiss.'—

                            R 1791

The Pig

In every age, and each profession,
Men err the most by prepossession,
But when the thing is clearly shown,
And fairly stated, fully known,
We soon applaud what we deride,
And penitence succeeds to pride.---
A certain baron on a day,
Having a mind to show away,
Invited all the wits and wags,
Foot, Massey, Shutter, Yates and Skeggs,
And built a large commodious stage,
For the choice spirits of the age;
But above all, among the rest,
There came a genius who profess'd
To have a curious trick in store,
Which never was perform'd before.
Thro' all the town this soon got air,
And the whole house was like a fair;
But soon his entry as he made,
Without a prompter, or parade,
'Twas all expectance, all suspense,
And silence gagg'd the audience.
He hid his head behind his wig,
And with such truth took off a pig,
All swore 'twas serious, and no joke,
For doubtless underneath his cloak,
He had conceal'd some grunting elf,
Or, was a real hog himself.
A search was made, no pig was found—
With thund'ring claps the seats resound,
And pit, and box, and galleries roar,
With—O rare! bravo! and encore.
Old Roger Grouse, a country clown,
Who yet knew something of the town,

THE PIG

Beheld the mimic and his whim,
And on the morrow challeng'd him,
Declaring to each beau and bunter,
That he'd out-grunt th' egregious grunter.
The morrow came—the crowd was greater—
But prejudice and rank ill-nature
Usurp'd the minds of men and wenches,
Who came to hiss, and break the benches.
The mimic took his usual station,
And squeak'd with general approbation.
'Again, encore! encore!' they cry—
'Twas quite the thing—'twas very high:
Old Grouse conceal'd, amidst the racket,
A real pig beneath his jacket—
Then forth he came—and with his nail
He pinch'd the urchin by the tail.
The tortur'd pig from out his throat,
Produc'd the genuine nat'ral note.
All bellow'd out—'twas very sad!
Sure never stuff was half so bad!
'That like a pig!'—each cry'd in scoff,
'Pshaw! Nonsense! blockhead! Off! Off! Off!'
The mimic was extoll'd; and Grouse
Was hiss'd, and catcall'd from the house.—
'Soft ye, a word before I go,'
Quoth honest Hodge—and stooping low
Produc'd the pig, and thus aloud
Bespoke the stupid partial croud:
'Behold, and learn from this poor creature,
How much you critics know of Nature.'

R 1791

Reason and Imagination

A fable; [address'd to Mr. Kenrick].

[AMIDST the ample field of things
The doubtful Muse suspends her wings;
While Thoughts, Imagination's host,
Keep hov'ring over Reason's post
Maintain'd, O *Truth*, upon thy base,
Whose voice, and whose Angelic face,
Are what the prudent love and hear,
And by no other star they steer.

In vain fair *Fancy* decks her bow'rs,
And tempts with fruit and tempts with flow'rs;
Her wiles in ev'ry mode express'd,
Or leudly strip'd, or proudly dress'd;
Try all the little arts she can,
Firm stands the Attribute of Man;
And solid, weighty, deep, and sound,
Asserts its right and keeps its ground.

'Twas in the famous *Sabine* grove
Where Wit so oft with Judgment strove,
Where Wisdom grac'd th' Horatian lyre,
Like weight of metal, play'd by fire;
Where Elegance and sense conferr'd,
Just at the coming of the Word,
Who chose his reasons to convey
A plain and a familiar way,
Then would you taste the immortal tale,
First bless the banquet, and regale.]

Imagination, in the flight
Of young desire and gay delight,
Began to think upon a mate;
As weary of a single state;

For sick of change, as left at will,
And cloy'd with entertainment still,
She thought it better to be grave,
To settle, to take up, and save.
She therefore to her chamber sped,
And thus at first attir'd her head.
Upon her hair, with brilliants graced,
Her tow'r of beamy gold she plac'd;
Her ears with pendant jewels glow'd
Of various water, curious mode,
As nature sports the wintry ice,
In many a whimsical device.
Her eye-brows arch'd, upon the stream
Of rays, beyond the piercing beam;
Her cheeks in matchless colour high,
She veil'd to fix the gazer's eye;
Her paps, as white as Fancy draws,
She cover'd with a crimson gauze;
And on her wings she threw perfume
From buds of everlasting bloom.
Her zone, ungirded from her vest,
She wore across her swelling breast;
On which, in gems, this verse was wrought,
'I make and shift the scenes of thought.'
In her right hand a wand she held,
Which Magick's utmost pow'r excell'd;
And in her left retain'd a Chart,
With figures far surpassing art,
Of other natures, suns and moons,
Of other moves to higher tunes.
The Sylphs and Sylphids, fleet as light,
The Fairies of the gamesome night,
The Muses, Graces, all attend
Her service, to her journey's end:
And Fortune, sometimes at her hand,
Is now the fav'rite of her band,

Dispatch'd before the news to bear,
And all th' adventure to prepare.

    Beneath an holm-tree's friendly shade,
Was Reason's little cottage made;
Before, a river deep and still;
Behind, a rocky soaring hill.
Himself, adorn'd in seemly plight,
Was reading to the Eastern light;
And ever, as he meekly knelt,
Upon the Book of Wisdom dwelt.
The Spirit of the shifting wheel,
Thus first essay'd his pulse to feel.—
'The Nymph supreme o'er works of wit,
O'er labour'd plan, and lucky bit,
Is coming to your homely cot,
To call you to a nobler lot;
I, *Fortune*, promise wealth and pow'r,
By way of matrimonial dow'r:
Preferment crowns the golden day,
When fair Occasion leads the way.'
Thus spake the frail, capricious dame,
When she that sent the message came.—

    'From first Invention's highest sphere,
I, Queen of Imag'ry, appear;
And throw myself at Reason's feet,
Upon a weighty point to treat.
You dwell alone, and are too grave;
You make yourself too much a slave;
Your shrewd deductions run a length,
'Till all your Spirits waste their strength:
Your fav'rite logic is full close;
Your morals are too much a dose;
You ply your studies 'till you risk
Your senses—you should be more brisk—
The Doctors soon will find a flaw,
And lock you up in chains and straw.

But, if you are inclin'd to take
The gen'rous offer which I make,
I'll lead you from this hole and ditch,
To gay Conception's top-most pitch;
To those bright plains, where crowd in swarms
The spirits of fantastic forms;
To planets populous with elves;
To natures still above themselves,
By soaring to the wond'rous height
Of notions, which they still create;
I'll bring you to the pearly cars,
By dragons drawn, above the stars;
To colours of Arabian glow;
And to the heart-dilating show
Of paintings, which surmount the life:
At once your tut'ress, and your wife.'—
——'Soft, soft,' (says Reason) 'lovely friend;
Tho' to a parley I attend,
I cannot take thee for a mate;
I'm lost, if e'er I change my state.
But whensoe'er your raptures rise,
I'll try to come with my supplies;
To muster up my sober aid,
What time your lively pow'rs invade;
To act conjointly in the war
On dullness, whom we both abhor;
And ev'ry sally that you make,
I must be there, for conduct's sake;
Thy correspondent, thine ally;
Or any thing, but bind and tye—
But, ere this treaty be agreed,
Give me thy wand and winged steed:
Take thou this compass and this rule,
That wit may cease to play the fool;
And that thy vot'ries who are born
For Praise, may never sink to scorn.'

FABLES

[O Kenrick, happy in the view
Of *Reason*, and of *Fancy* too;
Whose friendship of a few days growth,
Is ripe and greater than them both;
Thou reconcil'st with Euclid's scheme,
The tow'ring flight, the golden dream,
With thoughts at once restrain'd and free,
I dedicate this tale to THEE.
But now, a vet'ran for the prize,
I claim a license to advise.
Let not a fondness for the sage,
Decoy thee from a brighter page,
THE BOOK OF SEMPITERNAL BLISS,
The lore where nothing is amiss,
The truth to full perfection brought,
Beyond the sage's deepest thought;
Beyond the poet's highest flight;
Then let Invention reason right,
And free from prejudice and hate,
And false retirement's vain debate,
Since GOD's the WORD, that *Christians* read,
Be love their everlasting deed.]

P 1763

82

MISCELLANEOUS
POEMS

The Pretty Bar-Keeper of the Mitre

Written at College, 1741.

'RELAX, sweet girl, your wearied mind,
  And to hear the poet talk,
Gentlest creature of your kind,
  Lay aside your spunge and chalk;
Cease, cease the bar-bell, nor refuse
To hear the jingle of the Muse.

'Hear your numerous votries prayers,
  Come, O come and bring with thee
Giddy whimsies, wanton airs
  And all love's soft artillery;
Smiles and throbs, and frowns, and tears,
With all the little hopes and fears.'

She heard—she came—and e'er she spoke,
  Not unravish'd you might see
Her wanton eyes that wink'd the joke,
  E'er her tongue could set it free.
While her forc'd blush her cheeks inflam'd,
And seem'd to say she was asham'd.

No handkerchief her bosom hid,
  No tippet from our sight debars
Her heaving breasts with moles o'erspread,
  Markt, little hemispheres, with stars;
While on them all our eyes we move,
Our eyes that meant immoderate love.

In every gesture, every air,
  Th' imperfect lisp, the languid eye,
In every motion of the fair
  We awkward imitators vie,

85

And, forming our own from her face,
Strive to look pretty, as we gaze.

If e'er she sneer'd, the mimic crowd
    Sneer'd too, and all their pipes laid down;
If she but stoop'd, we lowly bow'd,
    And sullen if she 'gan to frown
In solemn silence sat profound—
But did she laugh?—the laugh went round.

Her snuff-box if the nymph pull'd out,
    Each JOHNIAN in responsive airs
Fed with the tickling dust his snout,
    With all the politesse of bears.
Dropt she her fan beneath her hoop,
Ev'n stake-stuck CLARIANS *strove* to stoop.

The sons of culinary KAYS
    Smoking from the eternal treat,
Lost in ecstatic transport gaze,
    As though the fair was good to eat;
Ev'n gloomiest KING's-MEN, pleas'd awhile,
'Grin horribly a ghastly smile.'

But hark, she cries, 'My mamma calls,'
    And strait she's vanish'd from our sight;
'Twas then we saw the empty bowls,
    'Twas then we first perceiv'd it night;
While all, sad synod, silent moan,
Both that she went—and went alone.

                                                    St 1750

86

To Lyce

AT length Mother Gunter the Gods hear my prayer,
They have heard me at length, Mother Gunter,
You're grown an old Woman yet romp drink and
    swear,
And attest the tricks of Pounter.

You invoke with a voice that tremblingly squeaks
Brisk Cupid tho sure of denial;
He Shuns you and basks in the blossomly cheeks
Of Miss Gubbins who plays on the Viol.

He flies from the trunk that is sapless and bare
To the pliant young Branches he comes up;
Age has hail'd on thy face, and has snow'd on thy
    hair,
And thy green Teeth have eat all thy Gums up.

Nor thy Sack, nor thy Necklace, thy watch, nor thy
    Ring,
Have restored thee to youth, or retarded
Those years which Old Time and his friend Vincent
    Wing
In the Almanack long have recorded.

O where is that beauty, that bloom and that grace,
Those lips that would breath Inspiration,
That steal me away from myself, and gave place,
To no Creature save Joan in the nation.

But poor Joan is dead, and has left you her years
As a Legacy which gracious Heaven
Has join'd to your own, which a Century clears,
And is just Mad'm the age of a Raven.

87

There remains a memento to each jolly soul,
Who of Venus's Club's a staunch member,
That Love hot as fire must be burnt to a coal,
As the Broomstick concludes in an Ember.

MS. in Pembroke Hall Library, c. 1750-1

On Taking a Batchelor's Degree

Exegi monumentum ære perennius, &c.
Hor., Od., iii, 30.

'Tis done:—I tow'r to that degree,
    And catch such heav'nly fire,
That HORACE ne'er could rant like me,
    Nor is *King's* chapel higher.—
My name in sure recording page
    Shall time itself o'erpow'r,
If no rude mice with envious rage
    The buttery books devour.
A title too with added grace,
    My name shall now attend,
Till to the church with silent pace
    A nymph and priest ascend.
Ev'n in the schools I now rejoice,
    Where late I shook with fear,
Nor heed the *Moderator's* voice
    Loud thundering in my ear.
Then with *Æolian* flute I blow
    A soft *Italian* lay,
Or where *Cam's* scanty waters flow,
    Releas'd from lectures, stray.
Meanwhile, friend BANKS, my merits claim
    Their just reward from you,
For HORACE bids us challenge fame,
    When once that fame's our due,

Invest me with a graduate's gown,
   Midst shouts of all beholders,
My head with ample square-cap crown,
   And deck with hood my shoulders.

St 1750

On an Eagle

Confin'd in a college court.

IMPERIAL bird, who wont to soar
   High o'er the rolling cloud,
Where *Hyperborean* mountains hoar
   Their heads in Ether shroud;—
Thou servant of almighty Jove,
Who, free and swift as thought, could'st rove
   To the bleak north's extremest goal;—
Thou, who magnanimous could'st bear
The sovereign thund'rer's arms in air,
   And shake thy native pole!

Oh cruel fate! what barbarous hand,
   What more than *Gothic* ire,
At some fierce tyrant's dread command,
   To check thy daring fire,
Has plac'd thee in this servile cell,
Where Discipline and Dulness dwell,
   Where Genius ne'er was seen to roam;
Where ev'ry selfish soul's at rest,
Nor ever quits the carnal breast,
   But lurks and sneaks at home!

Tho' dim'd thine eye, and clipt thy wing,
   So grov'ling! once so great!
The grief-inspired Muse shall sing
   In tend'rest lays thy fate.

What time by thee scholastic Pride
Takes his precise, pedantic stride,
   Nor on thy mis'ry casts a care,
The stream of love ne'er from his heart
Flows out, to act fair pity's part;
   But stinks, and stagnates there.

Yet useful still, hold to the throng—
   Hold the reflecting glass,—
That not untutor'd at thy wrong
   The passenger may pass:
Thou type of wit and sense confin'd,
Cramp'd by the oppressors of the mind,
   Who study downward on the ground;
Type of the fall of *Greece* and *Rome*;
While more than mathematic gloom,
   Envelopes all around!

St 1750

Prologue to '*A Trip to Cambridge*', *or* '*The Grateful Fair*'

In ancient days, as jovial Horace sings,
When laurell'd bards were lawgivers and kings,
Bold was the comic muse without restraint,
To name the vicious and the vice to paint;
Th' enliven'd picture from the canvas flew,
And the strong likeness crowded in the view.
Our author practises more general rules,
He is no niggard of his knaves and fools:
Both small and great, both pert and dull his muse
Displays, that everyone may pick and chuse.
The rules dramatic though he scarcely knows,
Of time and place, and all the piteous prose
The pedant Frenchmen snuffle though their nose.

Fools who personate what Homer should have done,
Like tattling watches they correct the sun.
Critics, like posts, undoubtedly may show
The way to Pindus, but they cannot go.
Whene'er immortal Shakespeare's works are read,
He wins the heart before he strikes the head.
Swift to the soul the piercing image flies,
Swifter than *Harriot's* wit, or *Harriot's* eyes;
Swifter than some romantic traveller's thought;
Swifter than British fire when *William* fought.
Fancy precedes, and conquers all the mind;
Deliberating judgment slowly comes behind;
Comes to the field with blunderbus and gun,
Like heavy *Falstaff*, when the work is done.
Fights when the battle's o'er with wondrous pain,
By Shrewsbury's clock, and nobly slays the slain.
The critic's censures are beneath our care,
We strive to please the generous and the fair;
To their decision we submit our claim,
We write not, speak not, breathe not, but for them.

R 1791

Princess Perriwinkle's Soliloquy

(*Enter the* Princess Perriwinkle *sola, attended by four-
teen maids of great honour.*)

SURE such a wretch as I was never born,
By all the world deserted and forlorn;
This bitter-sweet, this honey-gall to prove,
And all the oil and vinegar of love.
Pride, Love, and Reason will not let me rest,
But make a devilish bustle in my breast.
To wed with Fizgig, Pride, Pride, Pride denies,
Put on a Spanish padlock, Reason cries;
But tender gentle Love with every wish complies.

91

Pride, Love and Reason fight till they are cloy'd,
And each by each in mutual wounds destroy'd.
Thus when a Barber and a Collier fight,
The Barber beats the luckless Collier—white.
The dusty Collier heaves his pond'rous sack,
And, big with vengeance, beats the Barber—black.
In comes the Brickdust man, with grime o'erspread,
And beats the Collier and the Barber—red.
Black, red and white in various clouds are toss'd,
And in the dust they raise, the combatants are lost.

R 1791

An *Occasional Prologue Occasion'd by [the] two Occasional Prologues*

To be spoken either by Mr. *Garrick* or Mr. *Barry*, or both, assisted
in the delivery thereof by Mrs. *Midnight*, being the first time of her
appearing on any Stage.

KIND hearted Friends—behold these Sobs and Sighing!
I'd ask your Pardon—but—I can't for crying.
'Twas vile in me your Honours to offend,
And if you'll make me better—why—I'll mend.
'Twas wholly to my Brother-Bluster owing;
He was the Man *did do* this sad *Misdoing*;
He was the Man whose proud indignant Spirit,
Hating a Rival, strove to hide my Merit.
Ah Brother! Brother! think on *Johnny Gay*,
Think on the Moral giv'n us in his Play;
And let's like *Peachum,* and his Brother *Lockit,*
Our' own Affronts—with others Money, pocket.

Enter Mrs. Midnight *in haste.*

Great is the Noise, and clam'rous is the Clash,
When two such *weighty Wights* together dash!
Wit's Mirth oft takes its Rise from *Folly's* Ire,
As *Flint* strikes *Steel*, and Quarrels into *Fire*.

92

I, even I, old woman as I am,
Have just Pretence your Poetry to damn;
To fix the Standard between wrong and right,
And call you both a couple of—Good night.

*They bow to Mrs. Midnight, and then retire; after
which, the old Lady sings the following Simile.*

While *Garrick* smart, and blust'ring *Barry* jar,
Like Rough and Smooth, or Oil and Vinegar,
I, like an hard-boil'd Egg come in between,
And mix their Matters, as I intervene;
I form (for Rhyme's sake add, with JUST INTENTION)
Betwixt the fighting Fluids a Convention;
Which being thus conjoin'd, please ev'ry Palate,
And make a pretty Figure in a Sallad.

N.B. *If any Reader has any Objection to the above as
a* PROLOGUE, *let him signify such his Dislike in the Daily
Advertiser, and it shall be call'd an* INTERLUDE.

Md 1751

On seeing the incomparable Mons. TIMBERTOE *dance at Mrs.* MIDNIGHT'S *Oratory*

BEHOLD great TIMBERTOE—illustrious Name!
Exalts the Dance, and capers into Fame.
Tho' his Left Leg a Victim fell to Fate,
His right officiates for its absent Mate;
And with a Wooden Supplement engages,
All Tastes, all Ranks, all Sexes, and all Ages.
Each Fair is dubious, which should win her Heart,
The Limb of Nature, or the Stump of Art;
And smiles to see this active Artist do,
More with one Foot than others can with two.

General Advertiser, May 22, 1752

An Occasional Prologue and Epilogue
to Othello

As it was acted at the Theatre-Royal in Drury-Lane, on Thursday
the 7th of March, 1751, by persons of distinction, for their
diversion.

WHILE mercenary Actors tread the Stage,
And hireling Scribblers lash or lull the Age,
Our's be the Task t' instruct, and entertain,
Without one Thought of Glory or of Gain.
Virtue's her own—from no external Cause—
She gives, and she demands the Self-applause:
Home to her Breast she brings the heart-felt Bays,
Heedless alike of Profit, and of Praise.
This now perhaps is wrong—yet this we know,
'Twas Sense and Truth a Century ago:
When *Britain*, with transcendant Glory crown'd,
For high Achievements, as for Wit renown'd,
Cull'd from each growing Grace the purest part,
And cropt the Flowers from every blooming Art,
Our noblest Youth would then embrace the task
Of comic Humour, or the mystic masque.
'Twas theirs t' incourage worth, and give to Bards
What now is spent in *Boxing* and in *Cards*:
Good Sense their Pleasure—Virtue still their Guide,
And *English* Magnanimity—their Pride.
Methinks I see with Fancy's magic Eye,
The Shade of *Shakespear*, in yon azure Sky.
On yon High Cloud behold the Bard advance,
Grasping all Nature with a single Glance:
In various Attitudes around him Stand
The Passions, waiting for his dread Command.
First kneeling Love before his Feet appears,
And musically sighing melts in Tears.
Near him fell Jealousy with Fury burns,
And into Storms the amorous Breathings turns

94

Then Hope with Heavenward looks, and Joy draws
    near,
While palsied Terrour trembles in the Rear.
   Such *Shakespear's* train of Horror and Delight,
And such we hope to introduce to-night.
But if, tho' just in Thought, we fail in Fact,
And good Intention ripens not to act,
Weigh our Design, your Censure still defer,
When Truth's in View 'tis glorious e'en to err.

1751

Epilogue Spoken by Desdemona

TRUE Woman to the last—my *peroration*
I come to speak in spight of Suffocation;
To show the present and the Age to come,
We may be choak'd, but never can be dumb.
Well now methinks I see you all run out,
And haste away to lady *Bragwell's* Rout;
Each modish sentiment to hear and weigh,
Of those who nothing think, and all things say.
Prudella first in Parody begins,
(For Nonsense and Buffoonery are Twins)
'Can Beaux the Court for Theatres exchange?
I swear by Heaven 'tis strange, 'tis passing strange;
And very whimsical, and mighty dull,
And pitiful, and wond'rous pitiful:
I wish I had not heard it'—blessed Dame!
Whene'er she speaks her Audience wish the same.
Next *Neddy Nicely*—'Fye, O fye, good lack,
A nasty man to make his Face all black.'
Then lady *Stiffneck* shows her pious Rage,
And wonders we shou'd act—upon a Stage.
'Why Ma'me,' says *Coquetilla*, 'a Disgrace?
Merit in any Form may shew her Face:

95

In this dull Age the Male Things ought to play,
To teach them what to do, and what to say.'
In short, they all with diff'rent Cavils cram us,
And only are unanimous to *damn us*:
But still there are a fair judicious few,
Who judge unbias'd, and with Candour view;
Who value Honesty, though clad in Buff,
And Wit, though dress'd in an old *English* ruff.
Behold them here—I beaming Sense descry,
Shot from the living Lustre of each Eye.
Such meaning Smiles each blooming Face adorn,
As deck the Pleasure-painted Brow of Morn;
And shew the Person of each matchless Fair,
Though rich to Rapture, and above compare,
Is, ev'n with all the Skill of Heavn design'd,
But an imperfect Image of their Mind;
While Chastity unblemish'd and unbrib'd
Adds a majestic Mien that scorns to be describ'd:
Such (we will vaunt), and only such as these,
'Tis our Ambition, and our Fame to please.

1751

Epilogue to 'The Apprentice'

(*Enters reading a Play Bill.*)

A VERY pretty bill—as I'm alive!
The part of—nobody—by Mrs. Clive!
A paltry scribbling fool—to leave me out—
He'll say, perhaps—he thought I cou'd not *spout*.
Malice and envy to the last degree!
And why?—I wrote a farce as well as he,
And fairly ventur'd it—without the aid
Of prologue dress'd in black, and face in masquerade;
Oh! Pit—have pity—see how I'm dismay'd!
Poor soul! this canting stuff will never do.

Unless like Bayes he bring his hangman too.
But granting that from these same obsequies,
Some pickings to our bard in black arise;
Should your applause to joy convert his fear,
As *Pallas* turns to feast—*Lardella's* bier;
Yet 'twould have been a better scheme by half
T' have thrown his weeds aside, and learnt with me to
    laugh.
I cou'd have shown him, had he been inclin'd,
A spouting junto of the female kind.
There dwells a milliner in yonder row,
Well dress'd, full voic'd, and nobly built for show,
Who, when in rage she scolds at *Sue* and *Sarah*,
Damn'd, damn'd dissembler!—thinks she's more than
    Zara.
She has a daughter too that deals in lace,
And sings—*O ponder well*—and *Chevy Chase*,
And fain wou'd fill the fair *Ophelia's* place.
And in her cock'd up hat, and gown of camblet,
Presumes on something—*touching the lord Hamlet*.
A cousin too she has with squinting eyes,
With waddling gait, and voice like *London Cries*;
Who for the stage too short by half a story,
Acts *Lady Townly*—thus—in all her glory.
And while she's traversing her scanty room,
Cries—'Lord! my lord, what can I do at home!'
In short, we've girls enough for all the fellows,
The ranting, whining, starting, and the jealous,
The *Hotspurs*, *Romeos*, *Hamlets*, and *Othellos*.
Oh! little do these silly people know,
What dreadful trials—actors undergo.
Myself—who most in harmony delight,
Am scolding here from morning until night.
Then take advice from me, ye giddy things,
Ye royal milliners, ye apron'd kings;
Young men beware, and shun our slippery ways,
Study arithmetic, and shun our plays;

And you, ye girls, let not our tinsel train
Enchant your eyes, and turn your madd'ning brain;
Be timely wise, for oh! be sure of this;
A shop, with virtue, is the height of bliss.

R 1791

Epilogue

Spoken by Mr. Shuter, at Covent-Garden, after the Play of the
Conscious Lovers, acted for the benefit of the Middlesex Hospital
for lying-in women, 1755, in the character of a man-midwife.

(Enters with a child.)

WHOE'ER begot thee, has no cause to blush:
Thou'rt a brave chopping boy, *(child cries)* nay, hush!
      hush! hush!
A workman, faith! a man of rare discretion,
A friend to Britain, and to our profession:
With face so chubby, and with looks so glad,
O rare roast beef of England—here's a lad!

(Shows him to the Company.)

(Child makes a noise again.)

Nay if you once begin to puke and cough,
Go to the nurse. Within!—here take him off.
Well, Heav'n be prais'd, it is a peopling age,
Thanks to the bar, the pulpit, and the stage;
But not to th' army—that's not worth a farthing,
The captains go too much to Covent Garden,
Spoil many a girl,—but seldom make a mother,
They foil us one way—but we have them t'other.

(Shakes a box of pills.)

The nation prospers by such joyous souls,
Hence smokes my table, hence my chariot rolls.
Tho' some snug jobs, from surgery may spring,
Man-midwifry, man-midwifry's the thing!
Lean shou'd I be, e'en as my own anatomy,

98

By mere cathartics and by plain phlebotomy.
Well, besides gain, besides the pow'r to please,
Besides the music of such birds as these,

(Shakes a purse.)

It is a joy refin'd, unmix'd and pure,
To hear the praises of the grateful poor.
This day comes honest Taffy to my house,
'Cot pless her, her has sav'd her poy and spouse;
Her sav'd her Gwinnifrid, or death had swallow'd
    her,
Tho' creat crand creat crand crand child of Cad-
    wallader.'
Cries Patrick Touzl'em, 'I am bound to pray,
You've sav'd my Sue in your same physick way,
And further shall I thank you yesterday.'
Then Sawney came and thank'd me for my love,
(I very readily excus'd *his glove*)
He bless'd the mon, e'en by St. Andrew's cross,
'Who cur'd his bonny bearn and blithsome lass.'
  But merriment and mimicry apart,
Thanks to each bounteous hand and gen'rous heart
Of those, who tenderly take pity's part;
Who in good-natur'd acts can sweetly grieve,
Swift to lament, but swifter to relieve.
Thanks to the lovely fair ones, types of heaven,
Who raise and beautify the bounty given;
But chief to him in whom distress confides,
Who o'er this noble plan so gloriously presides.

1791

A Morning Piece

Or an hymn for the hay-makers.

Quin etiam Gallum noctem explaudentibus alis
Auroram clara consuetum voce vocare.
Lucret.

BRISK Chanticleer his matins had begun,
   And broke the silence of the night.
 And thrice he call'd aloud the tardy sun,
    And thrice he hail'd the dawn's ambiguous light;
Back to their graves the fear-begotten phantoms
        run.

  Strong Labour got up.—With his pipe in his
         mouth,
      He stoutly strode over the dale,
  He lent new perfumes to the breath of the south,
     On his back hung his wallet and flail.
Behind him came Health from her cottage of thatch,
Where never physician had lifted the latch.

First of the village COLIN was awake,
And thus he sung reclining on his rake.
        Now the rural graces three
        Dance beneath yon maple tree;
        First the vestal Virtue, known
        By her adamantine zone;
        Next to her in rosy pride,
        Sweet Society the bride;
        Last Honesty, full seemly drest
        In her cleanly home-spun vest.
The abbey bells in wak'ning rounds
      The warning peal have giv'n;
And pious Gratitude resounds
      Her morning hymn to heav'n.

All nature wakes—the birds unlock their throats,
And mock the shepherd's rustic notes.

100

A NOON-PIECE

All alive o'er the lawn,
      Full glad of the dawn,
         The little lambkins play,
Sylvia and Sol arise,—and all is day—
         Come, my mates, let us work,
         And all hands to the fork,
While the Sun shines, our hay-cocks to make,
         So fine is the day,
         And so fragrant the hay,
That the meadow's as blith as the wake.

         Our voices let's raise
         In Phœbus's praise,
Inspir'd by so glorious a theme,
         Our musical words
         Shall be join'd by the birds,
And we'll dance to the tune of the stream.

St 1750

A Noon-Piece

Or, The Mowers at Dinner.

Jam pastor umbras cum grege languido,
Rivumque fessus quærit, & horridi
    Dumeta Silvani, caretque
        Ripa vagis taciturna ventis.

Hor.

THE Sun is now too radiant to behold,
And vehement he sheds his liquid rays of gold:
   No cloud appears thro' all the wide expanse;
         And short, but yet distinct, and clear,
         To the wanton whistling air
The mimic shadows dance.

         Fat Mirth, and Gallantry the gay,
         And romping Ecstasy 'gin play.

101

Now myriads of young Cupids rise,
And open all their joy-bright eyes,
Filling with infant prate the grove,
And lisp in sweetly-fault'ring love.
In the middle of the ring,
Mad with May, and wild of wing,
Fire-ey'd Wantonness shall sing.

By the rivulet on the rushes,
Beneath a canopy of bushes
Where the ever-faithful *Tray*,
Guards the dumplings and the whey,
Collin Clout and *Yorkshire* Will
From the leathern flasket swill.

Their scythes upon the adverse bank
   Glitter 'mongst th' entangled trees,
Where the hazles form a rank,
   And court'sy to the courting breeze.

Ah! HARRIOT! sovereign mistress of my heart,
   Could I thee to these meads decoy,
New grace to each fair object thou'dst impart,
   And heighten ev'ry scene to perfect joy.

On a bank of fragrant thyme,
Beneath yon stately, shadowy pine,
We'll with the well-disguised hook
Cheat the tenants of the brook;
Or where coy Daphne's thickest shade
Drives amorous Phœbus from the glade,
There read Sidney's high-wrought stories
Of ladies charms, and heroes glories;
Thence fir'd, the sweet narration act,
And kiss the fiction into fact.

Or satiate with Nature's random scenes,
Let's to the gardens regulated greens,

Where Taste and Elegance command
Art to lend her dædal hand,
Where Flora's flock, by nature wild,
To discipline are reconcil'd,
And laws and order cultivate,
Quite civiliz'd into a state.

From the Sun and from the show'r,
Haste we to yon boxen bow'r,
Secluded from the teizing pry
Of Argus curiosity:
There, while Phœbus' golden mean,
The gay meridian is seen,
E'er decays the lamp of light,
And length'ning shades stretch out to night—
Seize, seize the hint—each hour improve
(This is morality in love)
Lend, lend thine hand—O let me view
Thy parting breasts, sweet avenue!
Then,—then thy lips, the coral cell
Where all th' ambrosial kisses dwell!
Thus we'll each sultry noon employ
In day-dreams of ecstatic joy.

St 1750

A Night-Piece

Or, Modern Philosophy.

Dicetur meritâ nox quoque nœniâ.
Hor.

'TWAS when bright Cynthia with her silver car,
Soft stealing from Endymion's bed,
Had call'd forth ev'ry glit'ring star,
And up th' ascent of heav'n her brilliant host had led.

Night with all her negroe train,
Took possession of the plain;

103

In an hearse she rode reclin'd,
Drawn by screech-owls slow and blind:
Close to her, with printless feet,
Crept Stillness in a winding sheet.
Next to her deaf Silence was seen,
Treading on tip-toes over the green;
Softly, lightly, gently she trips,
Still holding her fingers seal'd to her lips.
    Then came sleep serene and bland,
    Bearing a death watch in his hand;
    In fluid air around him swims
    A tribe grotesque of mimic dreams.

    You could not see a sight,
       You could not hear a sound,
    But what confess'd the night,
       And horrour deepen'd round.

    Beneath a plantain's melancholy shade,
    SOPHRON the wise was laid:
And to the answ'ring wood these sounds convey'd:
       While others toil within the town,
       And to fortune smile or frown,
       Fond of trifles, fond of toys,
       And married to that woman, Noise;
       Sacred Wisdom be my care,
       And fairest Virtue, Wisdom's heir.

His speculations thus the sage begun,
   When, lo! the neighbouring bell
In solemn sound struck one:—
   He starts—and recollects---he was engag'd to Nell.
Then up he sprang nimble and light,
   And rapp'd at fair Elenor's door;
He laid aside Virtue that night,
   And next morn por'd in Plato for more.

St 1750

104

The Widow's Resolution

A Cantata.

RECITATIVE

SYLVIA, the most contented of her kind,
Remain'd in joyless widowhood resign'd:
In vain to gain her ev'ry shepherd strove,
Each passion ebb'd, but grief, which drowned love.

AIR

'Away,' she cry'd, 'ye swains, be mute,
Nor with your odious fruitless suit
    My loyal thoughts controul;
My grief on Resolution's rock
Is built, nor can Temptation shock
    The purpose of my soul.

'Though blithe Content with jocund air,
May ballance comfort against care,
    And make me life sustain;
Yet ev'ry joy has wing'd its flight,
Except that pensive dear delight
    That takes it's rise from pain.'

RECITATIVE

She said:—A youth approach'd of manly grace,
A son of MARS, and of th' Hibernian race:—
In flow'ry rhetoric he no time employ'd,
He came—he woo'd—he wedded and enjoy'd.

AIR

Dido thus of old protested,
    Ne'er to know a second flame,
But alas! she found she jested,
    When the stately *Trojan* came.

C.S.—I   105   L

Nature a disguise may borrow,
    Yet this maxim true will prove,
Spite of pride, and spite of sorrow,
    She that has an heart must love.

What on Earth is so enchanting
    As beauty weeping on her weeds!
Thro' flowing eyes, on bosom panting
    What a rapturous ray proceeds?

Since from death there's no returning,
    When th' old lover bids adieu,
All the pomp and farce of mourning
    Are but signals for a new.

St 1750

The Distressed Damsel

OF all my experience how vast the amount,
Since fifteen long winters I fairly can count!
Was ever a damsel so sadly betray'd,
To live to these years and yet still be a maid?

Ye heroes, triumphant by land and by sea,
Sworn vot'ries to love, yet unmindful of me;
You can storm a strong fort, or can form a blockade,
Yet ye stand by like dastards, and see me a maid.

Ye lawyers so just, who with slippery tongue,
Can do what you please, or with right, or with wrong,
Can it be or by law or by equity said,
That a buxom young girl ought to dye an old maid.

Ye learned physicians, whose excellent skill
Can save or demolish, can cure or can kill,

106

To a poor, forlorn damsel contribute your aid,
Who is sick—very sick—of remaining a maid.

You Fops, I invoke not to list to my song,
Who answer no end, and to no sex belong,
You echoes of echoes, and shadows of shade—
For if I had you—I might still be a maid.

St 1750

Chaucer's 'Recantation'

RECITATIVE

OLD Chaucer once to this re-echoing grove
Sung of the 'sweet bewitching tricks of love',
But soon he found, he sullied his renown,
And arm'd each charming bearer with a frown:
Then self-condemn'd anew his lyre he strung,
And in repentant strains his recantation sung.

AIR

I

Long since unto her native sky
Fled heav'n-descended constancy;
Now nought that's stable's to be had;
The world's grown mutable and mad;
Save women—they, we must confess
Are miracles of stedfastness,
And every witty pretty dame
Bears for her motto—still *the same*.

II

The flow'rs that in the vale are seen,
The white, the yellow, blue and green,

107

In brief complection idly gay,
Still set with every setting day;
Dispers'd by wind or chill'd by frost,
Their odours gone, their colours lost:
But what is true, tho' passing strange,
The women never—fade or change.

III

The wise man said that all was vain,
And folly's universal reign;
Wisdom its vot'ries oft enthrals,
Riches torment and pleasure palls;
And 'tis, good lack, a general rule,
That each man soon or late's a fool:
In women 'tis th'exception lies,
For they are wond'rous—wond'rous wise.

IV

This earthly ball with noise abounds,
And from its emptiness it sounds,
Fame's deaf'ning din, the hum of men,
The lawyers plea, and poets pen:
But women here no one suspects,
Silence distinguishes their sex:
For, poor dumb things, so meek's their mould,
You can scarce hear them—when they scold.

CHORUS

An hundred mouths, an hundred tongues,
An hundred pair of iron lungs,
Five heralds and five thousands criers,
With throats whose accent never tires;
Ten speaking trumpets of a size
Would deafness with their din surprize;
Your praise, sweet nymphs, shall sing and say;
And those that will believe it—may.

London Magazine, 1750

Sweet William

By a prattling stream, on a midsummer's eve,
Where the woodbine and jess'mine their boughs
    interweave,
'Fair Flora,' I cry'd, 'to my harbour repair,
For I must have a chaplet for sweet William's hair.'

She brought me the vi'let that grows on the hill,
The vale-dwelling lilly, and gilded jonquill:
But such languid odours how cou'd I approve,
Just warm from the lips of the lad that I love.

She brought me, his faith and his truth to display,
The undying myrtle, and ever-green bay:
But why these to me, who've his constancy known?
And Billy has lawrels enough of his own.

The next was the gift that I could not contemn,
For she brought me two roses that grew on a stem:
Of the dear nuptial tie they stood emblems confest,
So I kiss'd 'em, and press'd them quite close to my
    breast.

She brought me a sun-flow'r—This, fair one's your
    due,
For it once was a maiden, and love-sick like you:
Oh! give it me quick, to my shepherd I'll run,
As true to his flame, as this flow'r to her Sun.

St 1750

The Fair Recluse

YE antient patriarchs of the wood,
　　That veil around these awful glooms,
Who many a century have stood
　　In verdant age, which ever blooms!

Ye Gothic tow'rs by vapours dense.
　　Obscur'd into severer state!
In pastoral magnificence,
　　At once so simple and so great!

Why all your jealous shades on me,
　　Ye hoary elders do ye spread?
Fair innocence shou'd still be free,
　　Nought shou'd be chain'd, but what we dread.

Say, must these tears for ever flow,
　　Can I from patience learn content,
While solitude still nurses woe,
　　And leaves me leisure to lament?

My guardian see—who wards off peace,
　　Whose cruelty is his employ;
Who bids the tongue of transport cease,
　　And stops each avenue to joy.

Freedom of air alone is giv'n,
　　To aggravate, not sooth my grief,
To view th' immensely-distant heav'n,
　　My nearest prospect of relief.

St 1751

The Decision

MY Florio, wildest of his sex,
(Who sure the veriest saint wou'd vex)
    From beauty roves to beauty;
Yet, tho' abroad the wanton roam,
Whene'er he deigns to stay at home,
    He always minds his duty.

Something to every charming she,
In thoughtless prodigality,
    He's granting still and granting;
To Phyllis that, to Cloe this,
And every madam, every miss;
    Yet I find nothing wanting.

If haply I his will displease,
Tempestuous as th' autumnal seas
    He foams and ranges ever;
But when he ceases from his ire,
I cry, 'Such spirit, and such fire,
    Is surely wond'rous clever.'

I ne'er want reason to complain;
But sweet is pleasure after pain,
    And every joy grows greater.
Then trust me, damsels, whilst I tell,
I should not like him half so well,
    If I cou'd make him better.

St 1751

The Author Apologizes to a Lady for His being a Little Man

Natura nusquam magis, quam in minimis tota est.
Pliny.

Ολιγον τε φιλον τε.
Hom.

YES, contumelious fair, you scorn
The amorous dwarf that courts you to his arms,
      But ere you leave him quite forlorn,
   And to some youth gigantic yield your charms,
   Hear him—oh hear him, if you will not try,
And let your judgment check th' ambition of your eye.

      Say, is it carnage makes the man?
      Is to be monstrous really to be great?
      Say, is it wise or just to scan
   Your lover's worth by quantity or weight?
   Ask your mamma and nurse, if it be so;
Nurse and mamma I ween shall jointly answer, no.

      The less the body to the view,
      The soul (like springs in closer durance pent)
      Is all exertion, ever new,
   Unceasing, unextinguish'd, and unspent;
   Still pouring forth executive desire,
As bright, as brisk, and lasting, as the vestal fire.

      Does thy young bosom pant for fame:
      Woud'st thou be of posterity the toast?
      The poets shall ensure thy name,
   Who magnitude of *mind* not *body* boast.
   Laurels on bulky bards as rarely grow,
As on the sturdy oak the virtuous mistletoe.

      Look in the glass, survey that cheek—
      Where FLORA has with all her roses blush'd;
      The shape so tender,—look so meek—

The breasts made to be press'd, not to be
      crush'd—
Then turn to me,—turn with obliging eyes,
Nor longer nature's works, in miniature, despise.

Young AMMON did the world subdue,
Yet had not more external man than I;
    Ah! charmer, should I conquer you,
With him in fame, as well as size, I'll vie.
Then, scornful nymph, come forth to yonder g rove,
Where I defy, and challenge, all thy utmost love.

St 1751

The Talkative Fair

FROM Morn to Night, from Day to Day
At all Times and at every Place,
You scold, repeat, and sing, and say,
Nor are there Hopes you'll ever cease.

Forbear, my *Celia*, oh! forbear,
If your own Health, or ours you prize;
For all Mankind that hear you, swear
Your Tongue's more killing than your Eyes.

Your Tongue's a Traitor to your Face,
Your Fame's by your own Noise obscur'd;
All are distracted, while they gaze
But if they listen all are cur'd.

Your Silence would acquire more Praise,
Then all you say, or all I write;
One Look ten thousand Charms displays;
Then hush—and be an Angel quite.

Md 1751

113

The Silent Fair

FROM all her fair loquacious Kind,
So different is my *Rosalind*,
That not one Accent can I gain
To crown my Hopes, or sooth my Pain.

Ye Lovers, who can construe Sighs,
And are the Interpreters of Eyes,
To Language all her Looks translate,
And in her Gestures read my Fate.

And if in them you chance to find
Aught that is gentle, aught that's kind;
Adieu mean Hopes of being great,
And all the Littleness of State.

All Thoughts of Grandeur I'll despise,
Which from Dependance take their Rise;
To serve her shall be my Employ,
And Love's sweet Agony my Joy.

Md 1752

The Power of Innocence

To Miss C****.

THE blooming Damsel, whose Defence
Is adamantine Innocence,
Requires no Guardian to attend
Her Steps, for Modesty's her Friend
Tho' her fair Arms are weak to wield
The glitt'ring Spear, and massy Shield;
Yet safe from Force and Fraud combin'd,
She is an *Amazon* in Mind.

114

With this Artillery she goes,
Not only 'mongst the harmless Beaux;
But e'vn unhurt and undismay'd,
Views the long Sword and fierce Cockade,
Though all a Syren as she talks,
And all a Goddess as she walks,
Yet Decency each Motion guides,
And Wisdom o'er her Tongue presides.

Place her in *Russia's* showery Plains,
Where a perpetual Winter reigns;
The Elements may rave and range,
Yet her fix'd Mind will never change.
Place her, Ambition, in thy Towers,
'Mongst the more dangerous golden Show'rs,
E'vn there she'd spurn the venal Tribe,
And fold her Arms against the Bribe.

Leave her, defenceless and alone,
A pris'ner in the torrid Zone,
The Sunshine there might vainly vie
With the bright Lustre of her Eye;
But *Phœbus* self, with all his Fire,
Cou'd ne'er one unchaste Thought inspire;
But Virtue's Path she'd still pursue,
And still, my Fair, wou'd copy you.

Md 1751

To Mecaenas

THY noble Birth, *Mecaenas* springs
From an illustrious Race of Kings,
    That in *Etruria* reign'd;
Thy kind Protection is my Boast,

My all without Thee, had been lost,
My Patron and my Friend.

Some in Olympick Games delight,
Where Clouds of Dust obscure the Sight,
    And darken all the Skies;
Striving who first shall reach the Goal,
Their kindling wheels around to roll,
    And gain the glorious Prize.

The Palm obtain'd, so great the Odds,
It ranks the Victors with the Gods,
    That rule the World below:
Others by low Intrigues elate,
To shine a Minister of State,
    All less Pursuits forego.

Some lur'd with Hopes of ample Gain,
Their Garners fill with *Lybian* Grain,
    Awaiting Times of Dearth:
Some wedded to paternal Fields
Admire the Store that Labour yields,
    Employ'd to till the Earth.

Offer to these *Peruvian* Mines,
Or all the glittering Wealth that shines,
    On *India*'s distant Shore;
They would not tempt the stormy Main,
Where Winds unequal War maintain,
    And Waves incessant roar.

The Merchant views, with Fear aghast,
The Fury of the *Northern* Blast,
    When lofty Billows foam;
Praises the Country's calm Retreats,
Yet soon his shatter'd Bark refits,
    In trackless Paths to roam.

TO MECAENAS

Some cheer the Hours with racy Wine,
The Product of the Massick Vine,
    Reclin'd beneath a Shade;
Or near a mossy sacred Source,
Where Streams begin their silent Course,
    Their listless Limbs are laid.

Others are pleas'd when Monarchs jarr,
Admiring all the Pomp of War,
    And ev'ry warlike Air;
When Trumpets fainting Hearts inspire,
And Clarions kindle martial Fire,
    Detested by the Fair.

The Sportsman bent to chace the Hind,
To all Delights besides is blind,
    His Spouse intreats in vain;
Despising wint'ry Skies he bounds,
Attended by fagacious Hounds,
    O'er Hill, and Dale, and Plain.

Politer Arts, *Mecaenas*, share,
Thy calmer Hours and banish Care,
    Th' Employment of the Wise;
An Ivy Wreath thy Temples binds,
And Honour due t'exalted Minds,
    The Kindred of the Skies.

I love to sing the cooling Grove,
Where Nymphs and Fawns in Measures move;
    And if the Muses aid:
Euterpe shall the Flute inspire;
And *Polyhymnia* touch the Lyre,
    Deep in a sacred Shade.

Thus rais'd above the vulgar Throng,
To noble Themes I'll suit my Song,

And if you rank my Name;
Among the tuneful Lyrick Train,
My Works shall envious Time disdain;
Secure of deathless Fame.

Md 1751

A beautiful Passage in the Anti-Lucretius of the Cardinal De Polignac ...

Englished by Mary Midnight.

THE witless Hen, disturb'd by causeless Fright,
With droll Amusement oft diverts the Sight,
For if the Nurse, ev'n to herself unknown,
Mistakes the Duck's Production for her own,
Soon as the Eggshell's broke and just alive,
Forth to the Pond the little Dabblers drive,
And by their first Efforts they plainly prove,
That Swimming is the very Thing they love;
Then mindful of their Birthright high and low,
Thro' all their Manor of the Marsh they go.
Swift to their Aid th' imagined Parent flies,
With Beak, and Wing, and Foot, and Voice, and Eyes,
Gives every Hint, and each Remonstrance tries.
But when she sees her quaking Brats proceed,
High Time she thinks to rave and scold indeed.
About she works 'midst Rushes, Reeds and Sedge,
And blunders round, and round, and round the Edge,
Flutters each Feather while her Eyeballs roll,
And all th' Old Woman centers in her Soul:
For why? the sober Matron errs thro' Zeal,
Nor sees the safe Impunity they feel;
Takes Nature's Instinct merely for a Whim,
And thinks it very odd a Duck shou'd swim.

Md 1752

Idleness

GODDESS of ease, leave Lethe's brink,
    Obsequious to the Muse and me;
For once endure the pain to think,
    Oh! sweet insensibility!

Sister of peace and indolence,
    Bring, Muse, bring numbers soft and slow
Elaborately void of sense,
    And sweetly thoughtless let them flow.

Near some cowslip-painted mead,
    There let me doze out the dull hours,
And under me let Flora spread,
    A sofa of her softest flow'rs.

Where, Philomel, your notes you breathe
    Forth from behind the neighbouring pine,
And murmurs of the stream beneath
    Still flow in unison with thine.

For thee, O Idleness, the woes
    Of life we patiently endure,
Thou art the source whence labour flows,
    We shun thee but to make thee sure.

For who'd sustain war's toil and waste,
    Or who th' hoarse thund'ring of the sea,
But to be idle at the last,
    And find a pleasing end in thee.

PSO 1752

119

On Good Nature

HAIL cherub of the highest heav'n,
Of look divine, and temper ev'n,
    Celestial sweetness, exquisite of mien,
    Of ev'ry virtue, ev'ry praise the queen!

Soft gracefulness, and blooming youth,
Where, grafted on the stem of truth,
    That friendship reigns, no interest can divide,
    And great humility looks down on pride.

Oh! curse on Slander's vip'rous tongue,
That daily dares thy merit wrong;
    Ideots usurp thy title, and thy frame,
    Without or virtue, talent, taste, or name.

Is apathy, is heart of steel,
Nor ear to hear, nor sense to feel,
    Life idly inoffensive such a grace,
    That it shou'd steal thy name and take thy place?

No—thou art active—spirit all—
Swifter than lightning, at the call
    Of injur'd innocence, or griev'd desert,
    And large with liberality's thy heart.

Thy appetites in easy tides
(As reason's luminary guides)
    Soft flow—no wind can work them to a storm,
    Correctly quick, dispassionately warm.

Yet if a transport thou canst feel
'Tis only for thy neighbours weal:
    Great, generous acts thy ductile passions move,
    And smilingly thou weep'st with joy and love.

Mild is thy mind to cover shame,
Averse to envy, slow to blame,
    Bursting to praise, yet still sincere and free
    From flatt'ry's fawning tongue, and bending
      knee.

Extensive, as from west to east,
Thy love descends from man to beast,
    Nought is excluded, little, or infirm,
    Thou canst with greatness stoop to save a worm.

Come, goddess, come with all thy charms,
For Oh! I love thee, to my arms—
    All, all my actions guide, my fancy feed,
    So shall *existence* then be *life* indeed.

                           PSO 1752

Against Ill Nature

OFFSPRING of folly and of pride,
To all that's odious, all that's base allied;
   Nurs'd up by vice, by pravity misled,
By pedant affectation taught and bred:
   Away, thou hideous hell-born spright,
Go, with thy looks of dark design,
   Sullen, sour, and saturnine;
Fly to some gloomy shade, nor blot the goodly light.
   Thy planet was remote, when I was born;
'Twas Mercury that rul'd my natal morn,
   What time the Sun exerts his genial ray,
And ripens for enjoyment every growing day;
   When to exist is but to love and sing,
And sprightly Aries smiles upon the spring.

   There in yon lonesome heath,
Which Flora, or Sylvanus never knew,

Where never vegetable drank the dew,
Or beast, or fowl attempts to breathe;
  Where Nature's pencil has no colours laid;
But all is blank, and universal shade;
  Contrast to figure, motion, life and light,
There may'st thou vent thy spight,
  For ever cursing, and for ever curs'd,
Of all th' infernal crew the worst;
  The worst in genius, measure and degree;
For envy, hatred, malice, are but parts of thee.

Or would'st thou change the scene, and quit thy den,
  Behold the heav'n-deserted fen,
Where spleen, by vapours dense begot and bred,
  Hardness of heart, and heaviness of head,
Have rais'd their darksome walls, and plac'd their
      thorny bed;
  There may'st thou all thy bitterness unload,
There may'st thou croak in concert with the toad,
  With thee the hollow howling winds shall join,
Nor shall the bittern her base throat deny,
  The querulous frogs shall mix their dirge with thine,
Th' ear-piercing hern, the plover screaming high,
  Millions of humming gnats fit œstrum shall supply.

Away—away—behold an hideous band
  An herd of all thy minions are at hand,
Suspicion first with jealous caution stalks,
  And ever looks around her as she walks,
With bibulous ear imperfect sounds to catch,
  And prompt to listen at her neighbours latch.
  Next Scandal's meagre shade,
Foe to the virgins, and the poet's fame,
  A wither'd, time-deflower'd old maid,
That ne'er enjoy'd love's ever sacred flame.
  Hypocrisy succeeds with saint-like look,
  And elevates her hands and plods upon her book.

Next comes illiberal scrambling Avarice,
   Then Vanity, and Affectation nice—
See, she salutes her shadow with a bow
   As in short Gallic trips she minces by,
Starting antipathy is in her eye,
   And squeamishly she knits her scornful brow.
To thee, Ill-Nature, all the numerous group
   With lowly reverence stoop—
They wait thy call, and mourn thy long delay.
   Away—thou art infectious—haste away.

                        PSO 1752

The Judgment of Midas

A masque.

Auriculas Asini Mida Rex habet.
                 Juv.

PERSONS REPRESENTED

APOLLO.
PAN.
TIMOLUS, God of the Mountain.
MIDAS.
CALLIOPE.
MELPOMENE.
AGNO, ⎱
MELINOE, ⎰ two Wood-Nymphs.
SATYRS, &c.

Timolus, Melinoe, and Agno, two Wood-nymphs

TIMOLUS

AGNO, to day we wear our acorn crown,
The parsley wreath be thine; it is most meet
We grace the presence of these rival gods
With all the honours of our woodland weeds.

123

Thine was the task, Melinoe, to prepare
The turf-built theatre, the boxen bow'r,
And all the sylvan scenery.

MELINOE

That task,
Sire of these shades, is done. On yester eve,
Assisted by a thousand friendly fays
While fav'ring Dian held her glitt'ring lamp,
We ply'd our nightly toils, nor ply'd we long,
For Art was not the mistress of our revels,
'Twas gentle Nature, whom we jointly woo'd;
She heard, and yielded to the forms we taught her,
Yet still remain'd herself—— Simplicity,
Fair Nature's genuine daughter, was there too,
So soft, yet so magnificent of mien,
She shone all ornament without a gem.
The blithsome Flora, ever sweet and young,
Offer'd her various store: we cull'd a few
To robe, and recommend our darksome verdure,
But shunn'd to be luxuriant.—

TIMOLUS

It was well.
Agno, thy looks are pensive: what dejects
Thy pleasure-painted aspect? Sweetest nymph,
That ever trod the turf, or sought the shade,
Speak, nor conceal a thought.

AGNO

King of the woods,
I tremble for the royal arbiter.
'Tis hard to judge, whene'er the great contend,
Sure to displease the vanquish'd: when such pow'rs
Contest the laurel with such ardent strife,
'Tis not the sentence of fair equity,
But 'tis their pleasure that is right or wrong.

124

THE JUDGMENT OF MIDAS

TIMOLUS

'Tis well remark'd, and on experience founded.
I do remember that my sister Ida
(When as on her own shadowy mount we met,
To celebrate the birth-day of the Spring,
And th' orgies of the May) wou'd oft recount
The rage of the indignant goddesses,
When shepherd Paris to the Cyprian queen,
With hand obsequious gave the golden toy.
Heav'n's queen, the sister and the wife of Jove,
Rag'd like a feeble mortal; fall'n she seem'd,
Her deity in human passions lost:
Ev'n Wisdom's goddess, jealous of her form,
Deem'd her own attribute her second virtue.
Both vow'd and sought revenge.

AGNO

     If such the fate
Of him who judg'd aright, what must be his
Who shall mistake the cause? for much I doubt
The skill of Midas, since his fatal wish,
Which Bacchus heard, and curs'd him with the gift.
Yet grant him wise, to err is human still,
And mortal is the consequence.

MELINOE

     Most true.
Besides, I fear him partial; for with Pan
He tends the sheep-walks all the live-long day,
And on the braky lawn to the shrill pipe
In aukward gambols he affects to dance,
Or tumbles to the tabor—'tis not likely
That such an umpire shou'd be equitable,
Unless he guess at justice.

TIMOLUS

Soft—no more—
'Tis ours to wish for Pan, and fear from Phœbus,
Whose near approach I hear. Ye stately cedars,
Forth from your summits bow your awful heads,
And reverence the gods. Let my whole mountain
    tremble,
Not with a fearful, but religious awe,
And holiness of horror. You, ye winds,
That make soft, solemn music 'mongst the leaves,
Be all to stillness hush'd; and thou, their echo,
Listen, and hold thy peace; for see they come.

Scene *opens, and discovers* Apollo, *attended by* Clio *and*
    Melpomene, *on the right hand of* Midas, *and* Pan *on*
    the left, whom Timolus, *with* Agno *and* Melinoe, *join.*

MIDAS

Begin, celestial candidates for praise,
Begin the tuneful contest: I, mean while,
With heedful notice and attention meet,
Will weigh your merits, and decide your cause.

APOLLO

From Jove begin the rapturous song,
To him our earliest lays belong,
   We are his offspring all;
'Twas he, whose looks supremely bright,
Smil'd darksome chaos into light,
   And fram'd this glorious ball.

PAN

Sylvanus, in his shadowy grove,
The seat of rural peace and love,

Attends my Doric lays;
By th' altar on the myrtle mount,
Where plays the wood-nymph's favourite fount,
   I'll celebrate his praise.

CLIO

Parnassus, where's thy boasted height,
Where, Pegasus, thy fire and flight,
Where all your thoughts so bold and free,
Ye daughters of Mnemosyne?
If Pan o'er Phœbus can prevail,
And the great god of verse shou'd fail?

AGNO

From nature's works, and nature's laws,
We find delight, and seek applause;
The prattling streams and zephyrs bland,
And fragrant flow'rs by zephyrs fann'd,
The level lawns and buxom bow'rs,
Speak Nature and her works are ours.

MELPOMENE

What were all your fragrant bow'rs,
Splendid days, and happy hours,
Spring's verdant robe, fair Flora's blush,
And all the poets of the bush?
What the paintings of the grove,
Rural music, mirth and love?
Life and ev'ry joy wou'd pall,
If Phœbus shone not on them all.

MELINOE

We chant to Phœbus, king of day,
The morning and the evening lay,
But Pan, each satyr, nymph and fawn,
Adore as laureat of the lawn;

From peevish March to joyous June,
He keeps our restless souls in tune,
Without his oaten reed and song,
Phœbus, thy days wou'd seem too long.

APOLLO

Am I not he, who, prescious from on high,
Send a long look thro' all futurity?
Am I not he, to whom alone belong
The powers of Med'cine, Melody and Song?
Diffusely lib'ral, as divinely bright,
Eye of the universe and sire of light.

PAN

O'er cots and vales, and every shepherd swain,
In peaceable pre-eminence I reign;
With pipe on plain, and nymph in secret grove,
The day is music, and the night is love.
I, blest with these, nor envy nor desire
Thy gaudy chariot, or thy golden lyre.

CLIO

Soon as the dawn dispels the dark,
    Illustrious Phœbus 'gins t' appear,
Proclaimed by the herald lark,
    And ever-wakeful chanticleer,
The Persian pays his morning vow,
And all the turban'd easterns bow.

AGNO

Soon as the evening shades advance,
    And the gilt glow-worm glitters fair,
For rustic gambol, gibe and dance,
    Fawns, nymphs and dryads all prepare,
Pan shall his swains from toil relieve,
And rule the revels of the eve.

THE JUDGMENT OF MIDAS

MELPOMENE

In numbers as smooth as Callirhoe's stream,
Glide the silver ton'd verse when Apollo's the theme;
While on his own mount Cyparissus is seen,
And Daphne preserves her immutable green.
We'll hail Hyperion with transport so long,
Th' inventor, the patron, and subject of song.

MELINOE

While on the calm ocean the halcyon shall breed,
And Syrinx shall sigh with her musical reed,
While fairies, and satyres, and fawns shall approve
The music, the mirth, and the life of the grove,
So long shall our Pan be than thou more divine,
For he shall be rising when thou shalt decline.

MIDAS

No more—To Pan and to his beauteous nymphs
I do adjudge the prize, as is most due.

Enter two Satyres, *and crown* MIDAS *with a pair of ass's ears*.

APOLLO

Such rural honours all the gods decree,
To those who sing like Pan, and judge like thee.

[*Exeunt omnes.*
PSO 1752

129

Ode to a Virginia Nightingale

Which was cured of a fit in the bosom of a young lady, who
afterwards nursed the author in a dangerous illness.

SWEET bird! whose fate and mine agree,
    As far as proud humanity
        The parallel will own;
    O let our voice and hearts combine,
    O let us fellow warblers join,
        Our patroness to crown.

When heavy hung thy flagging wing,
When thou could'st neither move nor sing,
    Of spirits void and rest;
A lovely nymph her aid apply'd,
She gave the bliss to Heav'n allied,
    And cur'd thee on her breast.

Me too the kind indulgent maid,
With gen'rous care and timely aid,
    Restor'd to mirth and health;
Then join'd to her, O may I prove
By friendship, gratitude and love,
    The poverty of wealth.

GM 1754

Fanny, Blooming Fair

WHEN Fanny, blooming fair,
    First caught my ravish'd sight,
Pleas'd with her shape and air,
    I felt a strange delight:
Whilst eagerly I gaz'd,
    Admiring ev'ry part,
And ev'ry feature prais'd,
    She stole into my heart.

AD XANTHIAM PHOCEUM

In her bewitching eyes
   Ten thousand loves appear;
There Cupid basking lies,
   His shafts are hoarded there.
Her blooming cheeks are dy'd
   With colour all her own,
Excelling far the pride
   Of roses newly blown.

Her well turn'd limbs confess
   The lucky hand of Jove;
Her features all express
   The beauteous queen of love.
What flames my nerves invade
   When I behold the breast
Of that too charming maid
   Rise suing to be prest!

Venus round Fanny's waist
   Has her own cestus bound,
There guardian Cupids grace,
   And dance the circle round.
How happy may he be,
   Who shall her zone unloose!
That bliss to all but me,
   May Heav'n and she refuse.

R 1791

Ad Xanthiam Phoceum

In imitation of Horace.

COLLIN, oh! cease thy friend to blame,
Who entertains a servile flame.
Chide not—believe me, 'tis no more
Than great Achilles did before,

Who nobler, prouder far than he is,
Ador'd his chambermaid Briseis.

The thund'ring Ajax Venus lays
In love's inextricable maze.
His slave Tecmessa makes him yield,
Now mistress of the sevenfold shield.
Atrides with his captive play'd,
Who always shar'd the bed she made.

'Twas at the ten years siege, when all
The Trojans fell in Hector's fall,
When Helen rul'd the day and night,
And made them love and made them fight;
Each hero kiss'd his maid, and why,
Tho' I'm no hero, may not I?

Who knows? Polly perhaps may be
A piece of ruin'd royalty.
She has (I cannot doubt it) been
The daughter of some mighty queen;
But fate's irremeable doom
Has chang'd her sceptre for a broom.

Ah! cease to think it—how can she,
So generous, charming, fond, and free,
So lib'ral of her little store,
So heedless of amassing more,
Have one drop of plebeian blood
In all the circulating flood?

But you, by carping at my fire,
Do but betray your own desire—
Howe'er proceed—made tame by years,
You'll raise in me no jealous fears.
You've not one spark of love alive,
For, thanks to heav'n, you're forty-five.

PSO 1752

Song

WHERE shall Celia fly for shelter,
In what secret grove or cave?
Sighs and sonnets sent to melt her
From the young, the gay, the brave,
Tho' with prudish airs she starch her,
Still she longs, and still she burns;
CUPID shoots like HAYMAN's archer,
Wheresoe'er the damsel turns.

Virtue, wit, good sense, and beauty,
If discretion guide us not,
Sometimes are the ruffian's booty,
Sometimes are the booby's lot:
Now they're purchas'd by the trader,
Now commanded by the peer;
Now some subtle mean invader
Wins the heart, or gains the ear.

O discretion, thou'rt a jewel,
Or our grandmammas mistake;
Stinting flame by baiting fewel,
Always careful and awake!
Wou'd you keep your pearls from tramplers,
Weigh the license, weigh the banns:
Mark my song upon your samplers,
Wear it on your knots and fans.

Nd 1764

The Sweets of Evening

THE sweets of evening charm the mind,
Sick of the sultry day;
The body then no more confin'd,
But exercise with freedom join'd,
When Phœbus sheathes his ray.

133

While all-serene the summer Moon
    Sends glances thro' the trees,
And Philomel begins her tune,
Asteria too shall help her soon
    With voice of skilful ease.

A nosegay, every thing that grows,
    And music, every sound
To lull the Sun to his repose;
The skies are coloured like the rose
    With lively streaks around.

Of all the changes rung by time
    None half so sweet appear,
As those when thoughts themselves sublime,
And with superior natures chime
    In fancy's highest sphere.

Nd 1764

On a Bed of Guernsey Lilies

Written in September 1763.

I

YE beauties! O how great the sum
    Of sweetness that ye bring;
On what a charity ye come
    To bless the latter spring!
How kind the visit that ye pay,
Like strangers on a rainy day,
    When heartiness despair'd of guests:
No neighbour's praise your pride alarms,
No rival flow'r surveys your charms,
    Or heightens, or contests!

II

Lo, thro' her works gay nature grieves
How brief she is and frail,
As ever o'er the falling leaves
Autumnal winds prevail.
Yet still the philosophic mind
Consolatory food can find,
And hope her anchorage maintain:
We never are deserted quite;
'Tis by succession of delight
That love supports his reign.

Nd 1764

Ode on Saint Cecilia's Day

Hanc Vos, Pierides festis cantate calendis
Et testudineâ, Phoebe superbe, lyrâ
Hoc solemne sacrum multos celebretur in annos,
Dignior est vestro nulla puella choro.
Tibullus.

THE ARGUMENT

Stanza I, II. Invocation of Men and Angels to join in the praise of S. Cecilia. The Divine origin of Musick. Stanza III. Art of Musick, or it's miraculous power over the brute and inanimate Creation exemplified in Waller, and Stanza IV, V, in Arion. Stanza VI. The Nature of Musick, or it's power over the Passions. Instances of this in it's exciting pity. Stanza VII. In promoting Courage and Military Virtue. Stanza VIII. Excellency of Church Musick. Air to the memory of Mr. Purcell.—Praise of the Organ and it's Inventress Saint Cecilia.

I

FROM your lyre-enchanted tow'rs,
Ye musically mystic Pow'rs,

135

Ye, that inform the tuneful spheres,
Inaudible to mortal ears,
While each orb in Ether swims
Accordant to th' inspiring hymns;
 Hither Paradise remove
 Spirits of Harmony and Love!
Thou too, divine *Urania*, deign t' appear,
 And with thy sweetly-solemn lute
 To the grand argument the numbers suit;
  Such as sublime and clear,
  Replete with heavenly love,
 Charm th' enraptur'd souls above.
Disdainful of fantastic play,
 Mix on your ambrosial tongue
 Weight of sense with sound of song,
 And be angelically gay.

CHORUS
Disdainful, &c. &c.

II

And you, ye sons of Harmony below,
How little less than angels, when ye sing!
With emulation's kindling warmth shall glow,
 And from your mellow-modulating throats
 The tribute of your grateful notes
 In Union of Piety shall bring.
Shall Echo from her vocal cave
Repay each note, the Shepherd gave,
And shall not we our mistress praise
And give her back the borrow'd lays?
But farther still our praises we pursue;
 For ev'n *Cecilia*, mighty maid,
 Confess'd she had superior aid—
She did—and other rites to greater pow'rs are due.
 Higher swell the sound and higher:
 Let the winged numbers climb:

To the heav'n of heav'ns aspire,
　　Solemn, sacred, and sublime:
From heav'n music took it's rise,
Return it to it's native skies.

CHORUS

Higher swell the sound, &c. &c.

III

Musick's a celestial art;
　　Cease to wonder at it's pow'r,
Tho' lifeless rocks to motion start,
　Tho' trees dance lightly from the bow'r,
　Tho' rolling floods in sweet suspence
Are held, and listen into sense.
In *Penshurst's* plains when *Waller*, sick with love,
Has found some silent solitary grove,
Where the vague moon-beams pour a silver flood
Of trem'lous light athwart th' unshaven wood,
　　Within an hoary moss-grown cell,
He lays his careless limbs without reserve,
And strikes, impetuous strikes each quer'lous nerve
　　　Of his resounding shell.
　　In all the woods, in all the plains
　　Around a lively stillness reigns;
　　The deer approach the secret scene,
　　And weave their way thro' labyrinths green;
　　While *Philomela* learns the lay,
　　And answers from the neighbouring bay.
　　But *Medway*, melancholy mute,
　　　Gently on his urn reclines,
　　And all-attentive to the lute,
　　　In uncomplaining anguish pines:
　　The crystal waters weep away,
　　And bear the tidings to the sea:
　　　Neptune in the boisterous seas

C.S.—I. 　　　　137 　　　　　　N

Spreads the placid bed of peace,
    While each blast,
    Or breathes it's last,
Or just does sigh a symphony and cease.

Neptune, &c. &c.

IV

Behold *Arion*—on the stern he stands
    Pall'd in theatrical attire,
To the mute strings he moves th' enliv'ning hands,
    Great in distress, and wakes the golden lyre:
While in a tender Orthian strain
He thus accosts the Mistress of the main:
    By the bright beams of *Cynthia's* eyes
    Thro' which your waves attracted rise,
        And actuate the hoary deep;
    By the secret coral cell,
    Where love, and joy, and *Neptune* dwell
        And peaceful floods in silence sleep;
    By the sea-flow'rs, that immerge
    Their heads around the grotto's verge,
        Dependent from the stooping stem;
    By each roof-suspended drop,
    That lightly lingers on the top,
        And hesitates into a gem;
    By thy kindred wat'ry Gods,
    The lakes, the riv'lets, founts and floods,
    And all the pow'rs that live unseen
    Underneath the liquid green;
  Great *Amphitrite* (for thou can'st bind
  The storm, and regulate the wind)
Hence waft me, fair goddess, oh, waft me away,
Secure from the men and the monsters of prey!

CHORUS

Great Amphitrite, &c. &c.

V

He sung—The winds are charm'd to sleep,
Soft stillness steals along the deep,
  The *Tritons* and the *Nereids* sigh
  In soul-reflecting sympathy,
And all the audience of waters weep.
But *Amphitrite* her Dolphin sends—the same,
Which erst to *Neptune* brought the nobly perjur'd
    Dame—
 Pleas'd to obey, the beauteous monster flies,
  And on his scales as the gilt sun-beams play,
  Ten thousand variegated dies
   In copious streams of lustre rise,
Rise o'er the level main and signify his way—
  And now the joyous bard, in triumph bore,
Rides the voluminous wave, and makes the wish'd for
    shore.
   Come, ye festive, social throng
  Who sweep the lyre, or pour the song,
   Your noblest melody employ,
   Such as becomes the mouth of joy,
   Bring the sky-aspiring thought,
   With bright expression richly wrought,
And hail the Muse ascending on her throne,
The main at length subdued, and all the world her
    own.

CHORUS

Come, ye festive, &c. &c.

VI

But o'er th' affections too she claims the sway,
 Pierces the human heart, and steals the soul away,

139

And as attractive sounds move high or low,
Th' obedient ductile passions ebb and flow.
Has any nymph her faithful lover lost,
  And in the visions of the night,
  And all the day-dreams of the light,
In sorrow's tempest turbulently tost—
  From her cheeks the roses die,
The radiations vanish from her sun-bright eye,
    And her breast, the throne of love,
    Can hardly, hardly, hardly move,
      To send th' ambrosial sigh.
But let the skilful bard appear,
And pour the sounds medicinal in her ear;
  Sing some sad, some plaintive ditty,
    Steept in tears, that endless flow,
  Melancholy notes of pity,
    Notes that mean a world of woe;
She too shall sympathize, she too shall moan,
And pitying others' sorrows sigh away her own.

CHORUS

Sing some sad, some &c. &c.

VII

  Wake, wake the kettle-drum, prolong
  The swelling trumpet's silver song,
  And let the kindred accents pass
  Thro' the horn's meandring brass.
Arise—The patriot muse invites to war,
  And mounts *Bellona's* brazen car;
    While *Harmony*, terrific Maid!
    Appears in martial pomp array'd:
  The sword, the target, and the lance
She wields, and as she moves, exalts the Pyrrhic dance.
      Trembles the earth, resound the skies—
      Swift o'er the fleet, the camp she flies

With thunder in her voice and lightning in her eyes.
    The gallant warriours engage
    With inextinguishable rage,
      And hearts unchil'd with fear;
    Fame numbers all the chosen bands,
    Full in the front fair *Vict'ry* stands
      And *Triumph* crowns the rear.

CHORUS

The gallant warriors, &c. &c.

VIII

But hark the Temple's hollow'd roof resounds,
And *Purcell* lives along the solemn sounds—
    Mellifluous, yet manly too,
      He pours his strains along,
    As from the lyon Sampson slew,
      Comes sweetness from the strong.
    Not like the soft *Italian* swains,
      He trills the weak enervate strains,
        Where sense and musick are at strife;
    His vigorous notes with meaning teem,
      With fire, with force explain the theme,
      And sing the subject into life.
Attend—he sings *Cecilia*—matchless Dame!
 'Tis She—'tis She—fond to extend her fame,
On the loud chords the notes conspire to stay,
And sweetly swell into a long delay,
    And dwell delighted on her name.
    Blow on, ye sacred organs, blow,
    In tones magnificently slow;
    Such is the musick, such the lays,
    Which suit your fair Inventress' praise:
    While round religious silence reigns,
    And loitering winds expect the strains.
    Hail majestic mournful measure
    Source of many a pensive pleasure!

Best pledge of love to mortals giv'n,
As pattern of the rest of heav'n!
And thou chief honour of the veil,
Hail, harmonious Virgin, hail!
When *Death* shall blot out every name,
And *Time* shall break the trump of Fame,
Angels may listen to thy lute;
Thy pow'r shall last, thy bays shall bloom,
When tongues shall cease, and worlds consume,
And all the tuneful spheres be mute.

GRAND CHORUS.

When Death *shall blot out every name*, &c.
CAP 1746

The Hop-Garden

A georgic.—In two books.

Me quoque Parnassi per lubicra culmina raptat
Laudis amor: studium sequor insanabile vatis,
Ausus non operam, non formidare poetæ
Nomen, adoratum quondam, nunc pæne procaci
Monstratum digito.——

Van. Præd. Rust.

BOOK THE FIRST

THE land that answers best the farmer's care,
And silvers to maturity the Hop:
When to inhume the plants; to turn the glebe;
And wed the tendrils to th' aspiring poles:
Under what sign to pluck the crop, and how
To cure, and in capacious sacks infold,
I teach in verse Miltonian. Smile the muse,
And meditate an honour to that land
Where first I breath'd, and struggled into life,
Impatient, Cantium, to be call'd thy son.
Oh! cou'd I emulate Dan Sydney's Muse,

Thy Sydney, Cantium—He, from court retir'd,
In Penshurst's sweet Elysium sung delight,
Sung transport to the soft-responding streams
Of Medway, and enliven'd all her groves:
While ever near him, goddess of the green,
Fair Pembroke sat and smil'd immense applause.
With vocal fascination charm'd the Hours,
Unguarded left Heav'n's adamantine gate,
And to his lyre, swift as the winged sounds
That skim the air, danc'd unperceiv'd away.
Had I such pow'r, no peasants toil, no hops
Shou'd e'er debase my lay: far nobler themes,
The high achievements of thy warrior kings
Shou'd raise my thoughts, and dignify my song.
But I, young rustic, dare not leave my cot,
For so enlarg'd a sphere—ah! muse beware,
Lest the loud larums of the braying trump,
Lest the deep drum shou'd drown thy tender reed,
And mar its puny joints: me, lowly swain,
Every unshaven arboret, me the lawns,
Me the voluminous Medway's silver wave,
Content inglorious, and the hopland shades!
Yeomen and countrymen, attend my song:
Whether you shiver in the marshy Weald,
Egregious shepherds of unnumber'd flocks,
Whose fleeces, poison'd into purple, deck
All Europe's kings: or in fair Madum's vale
Imparadis'd, blest denizons, ye dwell;
Or Dorovernia's awful tow'rs ye love:
Or plough Tunbridgia's salutiferous hills
Industrious, and with draughts chalybiate heal'd,
Confess divine Hygeia's blissful seat;
The muse demands your presence, ere she tune
Her monitory voice; observe her well,
And catch the wholesome dictates as they fall.
   'Midst thy paternal acres, Farmer, say
Has gracious heav'n bestow'd one field, that basks

Its loamy bosom in the mid-day sun,
Emerging gently from the abject vale,
Nor yet obnoxious to the wind, secure
There shalt thou plant thy hop. This soil, perhaps,
Thou'lt say, will fill my garners. Be it so.
But Ceres, rural goddess, at the best
Meanly supports her vot'ry', enough for her,
If ill-persuading hunger she repell,
And keep the soul from fainting: to enlarge,
To glad the heart, to sublimate the mind,
And wing the flagging spirits to the sky,
Require th' united influence and aid
Of Bacchus, God of hops, with Ceres join'd.
'Tis he shall generate the buxom beer.
Then on one pedestal, and hand in hand,
Sculptur'd in Parian stone (so gratitude
Indites) let the divine co-partners rise.
Stands eastward in thy field a wood? tis well.
Esteem it as a bulwark of thy wealth,
And cherish all its branches; tho' we'll grant,
Its leaves umbrageous may intercept
The morning rays, and envy some small share
Of Sol's beneficence to th' infant germ.
Yet grutch not that: when whistling Eurus comes,
With all his worlds of insects in thy lands
To hyemate, and monarchize o'er all
Thy vegetable riches, then thy wood
Shall ope it's arms expansive, and embrace
The storm reluctant, and divert its rage.
Armies of animalc'les urge their way
In vain: the ventilating trees oppose
Their airy march. They blacken distant plains.

This site for thy young nursery obtain'd,
Thou hast begun auspicious, if the soil
(As sung before) be loamy; this the hop
Loves above others, this is rich, is deep,
Is viscous, and tenacious of the pole.

Yet maugre all its native worth, it may
Be meliorated with warm compost. See!
Yon craggy mountain, whose fastidious head
Divides the star-set hemisphere above,
And Cantium's plains beneath; the Appennine
Of a free Italy, whose chalky sides
With verdant shrubs dissimilarly gay,
Still captivate the eye, while at his feet
The silver Medway glides, and in her breast
Views the reflected landscape, charm'd she views
And murmurs louder ecstasy below.
Here let us rest a while, pleas'd to behold
Th' all beautiful horizon's wide expanse,
Far as the eagle's ken. Here tow'ring spires
First catch the eye, and turn the thoughts to heav'n.
The lofty elms in humble majesty
Bend with the breeze to shade the solemn groves,
And spread an holy darkness; Ceres there
Shines in her golden vesture. Here the meads
Enrich'd by Flora's dædal hand, with pride
Expose their spotted verdure. Nor are you,
Pomona, absent; you 'midst th' hoary leaves
Swell the vermilion cherry; and on yon trees
Suspend the pippin's palatable gold.
There old Sylvanus in that moss-grown grot
Dwells with his wood-nymphs: they with chaplets
      green
And russet mantles oft bedight, aloft
From yon bent oaks, in Medway's bosom fair
Wonder at silver bleak, and prickly pearch,
That swiftly thro' their floating forests glide.
Yet not even these—these ever varied scenes
Of wealth and pleasure can engage my eyes
T' o'erlook the lowly hawthorn, if from thence
The thrush, sweet warbler, chants th' unstudied lays
Which Phœbus' self, vaulting from yonder cloud
Refulgent, with enliv'ning ray inspires.

But neither tow'ring spires, nor lofty elms,
Nor golden Ceres, nor the meadows green,
Nor orchats, nor the russet mantled nymphs
Which to the murmurs of the Medway dance,
Nor sweetly warbling thrush, with half those charms
Attract my eyes, as yonder hop-land close,
Joint-work of Art and Nature, which reminds
The muse, and to her theme the wand'rer calls.

  Here then with pond'rous vehicles and teams
Thy rustics send, and from the caverns deep
Command them bring the chalk: thence to the kiln
Convey, and temper with Vulcanian fires.
Soon as 'tis form'd, thy lime with bounteous hand
O'er all thy lands disseminate; thy lands
Which first have felt the softening spade, and drank
The strength'ning vapours from nutricious marl.

  This done, select the choicest hop, t' insert
Fresh in the opening glebe. Say then, my muse,
Its various kinds, and from th' effete and vile,
The eligible separate with care.
The noblest species is by Kentish wights
The Master-hop yclep'd. Nature to him
Has giv'n a stouter stalk, patient of cold,
Or Phœbus ev'n in youth, his verdant blood
In brisk saltation circulates and flows
Indesinently vigorous: the next
Is arid, fetid, infecund, and gross,
Significantly styl'd the Fryar: the last
Is call'd the Savage, who in ev'ry wood,
And ev'ry hedge unintroduc'd intrudes.
When such the merit of the candidates,
Easy is the election; but, my friend,
Would'st thou ne'er fail, to Kent direct thy way,
Where no one shall be frustrated that seeks
Ought that is great or good. Hail, Cantium, hail!
Illustrious parent of the finest fruits,
Illustrious parent of the best of men!

For thee Antiquity's thrice sacred springs
Placidly stagnant at their fountain head,
I rashly dare to trouble (if from thence
If aught for thy util'ty I can drain)
And in thy towns adopt th' Ascræan muse.
Hail heroes, hail invaluable gems,
Splendidly rough within your native mines,
To luxury unrefined, better far
To shake with unbought agues in your weald,
Than dwell a slave to passion and to wealth,
Politely paralytic in the town.
Fav'rites of Heav'n! to whom the general doom
Is all remitted, who alone possess
Of Adam's sons fair Eden—rest ye here,
Nor seek an earthly good above the hop;
A good! untasted by your ancient kings,
And almost to your very sires unknown.
   In those blest days when great Eliza reign'd
O'er the adoring nation, when fair peace
Or spread an unstain'd olive round the land,
Or laurell'd war did teach our winged fleets
To lord it o'er the world, when our brave sires
Drank valour from uncauponated beer;
Then th' hop (before an interdicted plant,
Shun'd like fell aconite) began to hang
Its folded floscles from the golden vine,
And bloom'd a shade to Cantium's sunny shores
Delightsome, and in cheerful goblets laught
Potent, what time Aquarius' urn impends
To kill the dulsome day—potent to quench
The Syrian ardour, and autumnal ills
To heal with mild potations; sweeter far
Than those which erst the subtile Hengist mix'd
T' inthral voluptuous Vortigern. He, with love
Emasculate and wine, the toils of war
Neglected, and to dalliance vile and sloth
Emancipated, saw th' incroaching Saxons

147

With unaffected eyes; his hand which ought
T' have shook the spear of justice, soft and smooth,
Play'd ravishing divisions on the lyre:
This Hengist mark'd, and (for curs'd insolence
Soon fattens on impunity! and becomes
Briareus from a dwarf) fair Thanet gain'd.
Nor stopt he here; but to immense attempts
Ambition sky-aspiring led him on
Adventrous. He an only daughter rear'd,
Roxena, matchless maid! nor rear'd in vain.
Her eagle-ey'd callidity, grave deceit,
And fairy fiction rais'd above her sex,
And furnish'd her with thousand various wiles
Preposterous, more than female; wondrous fair
She was, and docile, which her pious nurse
Observ'd, and early in each female fraud
Her 'gan initiate: well she knew to smile,
Whene'er vexation gall'd her; did she weep?
'Twas not sincere, the fountains of her eyes
Play'd artificial streams, yet so well forc'd
They look'd like nature; for ev'n art to her
Was natural, and contrarieties
Seem'd in Roxena congruous and allied.
Such was she, when brisk Vortigern beheld,
Ill-fated prince! and lov'd her. She perceiv'd,
Soon she perceiv'd her conquest; soon she told,
With hasty joy transported, her old sire.
The Saxon inly smil'd, and to his isle
The willing prince invited, but first bad
The nymph prepare the potions; such as fire
The blood's meandering rivulets, and depress
To love the soul. Lo! at the noon of night
Thrice Hecate invok'd the maid—and thrice
The goddess stoop'd assent; forth from a cloud
She stoop'd, and gave the filters power to charm.
These in a splendid cup of burnish'd gold
The lovely sorceress mix'd, and to the prince

Health, peace and joy propin'd, but to herself
Mutter'd dire exorcisms, and wish'd effect
To th' love-creating draught: lowly she bow'd
Fawning insinuation bland, that might
Deceive Laertes' son; her lucid orbs
Shed copiously the oblique rays; her face
Like modest Luna's shone, but not so pale,
And with no borrow'd lustre; on her brow
Smil'd fallacy, while summoning each grace,
Kneeling she gave the cup. The prince (for who!
Who cou'd have spurn'd a suppliant so divine?)
Drank eager, and in ecstasy devour'd
Th' ambrosial perturbation; mad with love
He clasp'd her, and in Hymeneal bands
At once the nymph demanded and obtain'd.
Now Hengist, all his ample wish fulfill'd,
Exulted; and from Kent th' uxorious prince
Exterminated, and usurp'd his seat.
Long did he reign; but all-devouring time
Has raz'd his palace walls—Perchance on them
Grows the green hop, and o'er his crumbled bust
In spiral twines ascends the scancile pole.—
But now to plant, to dig, to dung, to weed;
Tasks how indelicate? demand the muse.

  Come, fair magician, sportive Fancy, come,
With thy unbounded imagery: child of thought,
From thy aerial citadel descend,
And (for thou canst) assist me. Bring with thee
Thy all-creative Talisman; with thee
The active spirits ideal, tow'ring flights,
That hover o'er the muse-resounding groves,
And all thy colourings, all thy shapes display.
Thou too be here, Experience, so shall I
My rules nor in low prose jejunely *say*,
Nor in smooth numbers musically err;
But vain is Fancy and Experience vain,
If thou, O Hesiod! Virgil of our land,

Or hear'st thou rather, Milton, bard divine,
Whose greatness who shalt imitate, save thee?
If thou, O Philips, fav'ring dost not hear
Me, inexpert of verse; with gentle hand
Uprear the unpinion'd Muse, high on the top
Of that immeasurable mount, that far
Exceeds thine own Plinlimmon, where thou tun'st
With Phœbus' self thy lyre. Give me to turn
Th' unwieldy subject with thy graceful ease,
Extol its baseness with thy art; but chief
Illumine, and invigorate with thy fire.
    When Phœbus looks thro' Aries on the spring,
And vernal flowers promise dulcet fruit,
Autumnal pride! delay not then thy setts
In Tellus' facile bosom to depose
Timely: if thou art wise the bulkiest chuse:
To every root three joints indulge, and form
The quincunx with well regulated hills.
Soon from the dung-enriched earth, their heads
Thy young plants will uplift, their virgin arms
They'll stretch, and, marriageable, claim the pole.
Nor frustrate thou their wishes, so thou may'st
Expect an hopeful issue, jolly Mirth,
Sister of taleful Jocus, tuneful Song,
And fat Good-nature with her honest face.
But yet in the novitiate of their love,
And tenderness of youth suffice small shoots
Cut from the widow'd willow, nor provide
Poles insurmountable as yet. 'Tis then
When twice bright Phœbus' vivifying ray,
Twice the cold touch of winter's icy hand,
They've felt; 'tis then we fell sublimer props.
'Tis then the sturdy woodman's axe from far
Resounds, resounds, and hark! with hollow groans
Down tumble the big trees, and rushing roll
O'er the crush'd crackling brake, while in his cave
Forlorn, dejected, 'midst the weeping dryads

Laments Sylvanus for his verdant care.
The ash, or willow for thy use select,
Or storm enduring chesnut; but the oak,
Unfit for this employ, for nobler ends
Reserve untouch'd; she when by time matur'd,
Capacious, of some British demi-god,
Vernon, or Warren, shall with rapid wing
Infuriate, like Jove's armour-bearing bird,
Fly on thy foes; they, like the parted waves,
Which to the brazen beak murmuring give way
Amazed and roaring, from the fight recede.—
In that sweet month, when to the list'ning swains
Fair Philomel sings love, and every cot
With garlands blooms bedight, with bandage meet
The tendrils bind, and to the tall poll tie,
Else soon, too soon their meretricious arms
Round each ignoble clod they'll fold, and leave
Averse the lordly prop. Thus, have I heard
Where there's no mutual tie, no strong connection
Of love-conspiring hearts, oft the young bride
Has prostituted to her slaves her charms,
While the infatuated lord admires
Fresh-budding sprouts, and issue not his own.
Now turn the glebe: soon with correcting hand,
When smiling June in jocund dance leads on
Long days and happy hours, from ev'ry vine
Dock the redundant branches, and once more
With the sharp spade thy numerous acres till.
The shovel next must lend its aid, enlarge
The little hillocks, and erase the weeds.
This in that month its title which derives
From great Augustus' ever sacred name!
Sovereign of science! master of the muse!
Neglected genius' firm ally! of worth
Best judge, and best rewarder, whose applause
To bards was fame and fortune! O! 'twas well,
Well did you too in this, all glorious heroes!

Ye Romans!—on Time's wing you've stamp'd his
    praise,
And time shall bear it to eternity.
    Now are our labours crown'd with their reward,
Now bloom the florid hops, and in the stream
Shine in their floating silver, while above
T' embow'ring branches culminate, and form
A walk impervious to the sun; the poles
In comely order stand; and while you cleave
With the small skiff the Medway's lucid wave,
In comely order still their ranks preserve,
And seem to march along th' extensive plain.
In neat arrangement thus the men of Kent,
With native oak at once adorn'd and arm'd,
Intrepid march'd; for well they knew the cries
Of dying Freedom, and Astræa's voice,
Who as she fled, to echoing woods complain'd
Of tyranny, and William; like a god,
Refulgent stood the conqueror, on his troops
He sent his looks enliv'ning as the sun's,
But on his foes frown'd agony, frown'd death.
On his left side in bright emblazonry
His falchion burn'd; forth from his sevenfold shield
A basilisk shot adamant; his brow
Wore clouds of fury!—on that with plumage crown'd
Of various hue sat a tremendous cone:
Thus sits high-canopied above the clouds,
Terrific beauty of nocturnal skies,
Northern Aurora; she thro' th' azure air
Shoots, shoots her trem'lous rays in painted streaks
Continual, while waving to the wind
O'er Night's dark veil her lucid tresses flow.
The trav'ler views th' unseemly day
Astound, the proud bend lowly to the earth,
The pious matrons tremble for the world.
But what can daunt th' insuperable souls
Of Cantium's matchless sons? On they proceed,

All innocent of fear; each face express'd
Contemptuous admiration, while they view'd
The well fed brigades of embroider'd slaves
That drew the sword for gain. First of the van,
With an enormous bough, a shepherd swain
Whistled with rustic notes; but such as show'd
A heart magnanimous: the men of Kent
Follow the tuneful swain, while o'er their heads
The green leaves whisper, and the big boughs bend.
'Twas thus the Thracian, whose-all quick'ning lyre
The floods inspir'd, and taught the rocks to feel,
Play'd before dancing Hæmus, to the tune,
The lute's soft tune! the fluttring branches wave,
The rocks enjoy it, and the rivulets hear,
The hillocks skip, emerge the humble vales,
And all the mighty mountain nods applause.
The conqueror view'd them, and as one that sees
The vast abrupt of Scylla, or as one
That from th' oblivious Lethaean streams
Has drank eternal apathy, he stood.
His host an universal panic seiz'd
Prodigious, inopine; their armour shook,
And clatter'd to the trembling of their limbs;
Some to the walking wilderness gan run
Confus'd, and in th' inhospitable shade
For shelter sought—Wretches! they shelter find,
Eternal shelter in the arms of death!
Thus when Aquarius pours out all his urn
Down on some lonesome heath, the traveller
That wanders o'er the wintry waste, accepts
The invitation of some spreading beech
Joyous; but soon the treacherous gloom betrays
Th' unwary visitor, while on his head
Th' enlarging drops in double show'rs descend.
    And now no longer in disguise the men
Of Kent appear; down they all drop their boughs,
And shine in brazen panoply divine.

O

Enough—great William (for full well he knew
How vain would be the conquest) to the sons
Of glorious Cantium gave their lives, and laws,
And liberties secure, and to the prowess
Of Kentish wights, like Cæsar, deign'd to yiel ¹.
Cæsar and William! hail immortal worthies,
Illustrious vanquish'd! Cantium, if to them,
Posterity with all her chiefs unborn,
Aught similar, aught second has to boast,
Once more (so prophesies the muse) thy sons
Shall triumph, emulous of their sires—till then
With olive, and with hop-garlands crown'd,
O'er all thy land reign Plenty, reign fair Peace.

BOOK THE SECOND

Omnia quæ multo ante memor provisa repones,
Si te digna manet divini gloria ruris.
Virg., Geor., lib. 1.

At length the muse her destin'd task resumes
With joy; agen o'er all her hop-land groves
She seeks t' expatiate free of wing. Long while
For a much-loving, much-lov'd youth she wept,
And sorrow'd silence o'er th' untimely urn.
Hush then, effeminate sobs; and thou, my heart,
Rebel to grief no more—And yet a while,
A little while, indulge the friendly tears.
O'er the wild world, like Noah's dove, in vain
I seek the olive peace, around me wide
See! see! the wat'ry waste—In vain forlorn
I call the Phoenix, fair Sincerity;
Alas!—extinguish'd to the skies she fled,
And left no heir behind her. Where is now
The eternal smile of goodness? Where is now
That all-extensive charity of soul,
So rich in sweetness, that the classic sounds
In elegance Augustan cloth'd, the wit
That flow'd perennial, hardly were observ'd,

154

Or, if observ'd, set off a brighter gem.
How oft, and yet how seldom did it seem!
Have I enjoy'd his converse?—When we met,
The hours how swift they sweetly fled, and till
Agen I saw him how they loiter'd. Oh!
Theophilus, thou dear departed soul,
What flattering tales thou told'st me? How thou'dst
        hail
My muse, and took'st imaginary walks
All in my hopland groves. Stay yet, oh stay!
Thou dear deluder, thou hast seen but half—
He's gone! and aught that's equal to his praise
Fame has not for me, tho' she prove most kind.
Howe'er this verse be sacred to thy name,
These tears, the last sad duty of a friend.
Oft I'll indulge the pleasurable pain
Of recollection; oft on Medway's banks
I'll muse on thee full pensive; while her streams
Regardful ever of my grief, shall flow
In sullen silence silverly along
The weeping shores—or else accordant with
My loud laments, shall ever and anon
Make melancholy music to the shades,
The hopland shades, that on her banks expose
Serpentine vines and flowing locks of gold.

  Ye smiling nymphs, th' inseparable train
Of saffron Ceres; ye, that gamesome dance,
And sing to jolly Autumn, while he stands
With his right hand poizing the scales of heav'n,
And while his left grasps Amalthea's horn:
Young chorus of fair Bacchanals, descend,
And leave awhile the sickle; yonder hill,
Where stand the loaded hop-poles, claims your care.
There mighty Bacchus stradling cross the bin,
Waits your attendance—There he glad reviews
His paunch, approaching to immensity
Still nearer, and with pride of heart surveys

Obedient mortals, and the world his own.
See! from the great metropolis they rush,
Th' industrious vulgar. They, like prudent bees,
In Kent's wide garden roam, expert to crop
The flow'ry hop, and provident to work,
Ere winter numb their sunburnt hands, and winds
Engaol them, murmuring in their gloomy cells.
From these, such as appear the rest t' excel
In strength and young agility, select.
These shall support with vigour and address
The bin-man's weighty office; now extract
From the sequacious earth the pole, and now
Unmarry from the closely clinging vine.
O'er twice three pickers, and no more, extend
The bin-man's sway; unless thy ears can bear
The crack of poles continual, and thine eyes
Behold unmoved the hurrying peasant tear
Thy wealth, and throw it on the thankless ground.
But first the careful planter will consult
His quantity of acres and his crop,
How many and how large his kilns; and then
Proportion'd to his wants the hands provide.
But yet of greater consequence and cost,
One thing remains unsung, a man of faith
And long experience, in whose thund'ring voice
Lives hoarse authority, potent to quell
The frequent frays of the tumultuous crew.
He shall preside o'er all thy hop-land store,
Severe dictator! His unerring hand,
And eye inquisitive, in heedful guise,
Shall to the brink the measure fill, and fair
On the twin registers the work record.
And yet I've known them own a female reign,
And gentle Mariane's soft Orphean voice
Has hymn'd sweet lessons of humanity
To the wild brutal crew. Oft her command
Has sav'd the pillars of the hop-land state,

The lofty poles from ruin, and sustain'd,
Like Anna, or Eliza, her domain,
With more than manly dignity. Oft I've seen,
Ev'n at her frown the boist'rous uproar cease,
And the mad pickers, tam'd to diligence,
Cull from the bin the sprawling sprigs, and leaves
That stain the sample, and its worth debase.
All things thus settled and prepar'd, what now
Can let the planter's purposes? Unless
The heav'ns frown dissent, and ominous winds
Howl thro' the concave of the troubled sky.
And oft, alas! the long experienc'd wights
(Oh! could they too prevent them) storms foresee.
For, as the storm rides on the rising clouds,
Fly the fleet wild-geese far away, or else
The heifer towards the zenith rears her head,
And with expanded nostrils snuffs the air:
The swallows too their airy circuits weave,
And screaming skim the brook; and fen bred frogs
Forth from their hoarse throats their old grutch recite:
Or from her earthly coverlets the ant
Heaves her huge eggs along the narrow way:
Or bends Thaumantia's variegated bow
Athwart the cope of heav'n: or sable crows
Obstreperous of wing, in crouds combine:
Besides, unnumber'd troops of birds marine,
And Asia's feather'd flocks, that in the muds
Of flow'ry edg'd Cayster wont to prey,
Now in the shallows duck their speckled heads,
And lust to lave in vain, their unctuous plumes
Repulsive baffle their efforts: Next heark
How the curs'd raven, with her harmful voice,
Invokes the rain, and croaking to herself,
Struts on some spacious solitary shore.
Nor want thy servants and thy wife at home
Signs to presage the show'r; for in the hall
Sheds Niobe her prescious tears, and warns

Beneath thy leaden tubes to fix the vase,
And catch the falling dew drops, which supply
Soft water and salubrious, far the best
To soak thy hops, and brew thy generous beer.
But tho' bright Phœbus smile, and in the skies
The purple-rob'd serenity appear;
Tho' every cloud be fled, yet if the rage
Of Boreas, or the blasting East prevail,
The planter has enough to check his hopes,
And in due bounds confine his joy; for see
The ruffian winds in their abrupt career,
Leave not a hop behind, or at the best
Mangle the circling vine, and intercept
The juice nutricious: fatal means, alas!
Their colour and condition to destroy.
Haste then, ye peasants; pull the poles, the hops;
Where are the bins? Run, run, ye nimble maids,
Move ev'ry muscle, ev'ry nerve extend,
To save our crop from ruin, and ourselves.

   Soon as bright Chanticleer explodes the night
With flutt'ring wings, and hymns the new-born day
The bugle-horn inspire, whose clam'rous bray
Shall rouse from sleep the rebel rout, and tune
To temper for the labours of the day.
Wisely the several stations of the bins
By lot determine. Justice this, and this
Fair prudence does demand; for not without
A certain method cou'dst thou rule the mob
Irrational, nor every where alike
Fair hangs the hop to tempt the picker's hand.

   Now see the crew mechanic might and main
Labour with lively diligence, inspir'd
By appetite of gain and lust of praise:
What mind so petty, servile, so debas'd,
As not to know ambition? Her great sway
From *Colin Clout* to emperors she exerts.
To err is human, human to be vain.

'Tis vanity, and mock desire of fame,
That prompts the rustic, on the steeple top
Sublime, to mark the outlines of his shoe,
And in the area to engrave his name.
With pride of heart the churchwarden surveys
High o'er the belfry, girt with birds and flow'rs,
His story wrote in capitals: "Twas I
That bought the font; and I repaired the pews.
With pride like this the emulating mob
Strive for the mastery—who first may fill
The bellying bin, and cleanest cull the hops.
Nor aught retards, unless invited out
By Sol's declining, and the evening's calm,
Leander leads Lætitia to the scene
Of shade and fragrance—Then th' exulting band
Of pickers male and female, seize the fair
Reluctant, and with boist'rous force and brute,
By cries unmov'd, they bury her i' th' bin.
Nor does thy youth escape—him too they seize,
And in such posture place as best may serve
To hide his charmer's blushes. Then with shouts
They rend the echoing air, and from them both
(So custom has ordain'd) a largess claim.

   Thus much be sung of picking—next succeeds
Th' important care of curing—Quit the field,
And at the kiln th' instructive muse attend.

   On your hair-cloth eight inches deep, nor more,
Let the green hops lie lightly; next expand
The smoothest surface with the toothy rake.
Thus far is just above; but more it boots
That charcoal flames burn equally below,
The charcoal flames, which from thy corded wood,
Or antiquated poles, with wond'rous skill,
The sable priests of Vulcan shall prepare.
Constant and moderate let the heat ascend;
Which to effect, there are, who with success
Place in the kiln the ventilating fan.

Hail, learned, useful man! whose head and heart
Conspire to make us happy, deign t' accept
One honest verse; and if thy industry
Has serv'd the hopland cause, the muse forebodes,
This sole invention, both in use and fame
The mystic fan of Bacchus shall exceed

When the fourth hour expires, with careful hand
The half-bak'd hops turn over. Soon as time
Has well exhausted twice two glasses more,
They'll leap and crackle with their bursting seeds,
For use domestic, or for sale mature.

There are, who in the choice of cloth t' enfold
Their wealthy crop, the viler, coarser sort,
With prodigal œconomy prefer:
All that is good is cheap, all dear that's base.
Besides the planter shou'd a bait prepare,
T' intrap the chapman's notice, and divert
Shrewd observation from her busy pry.

When in the bag thy hops the rustic treads,
Let him wear heel-less sandals; nor presume
Their fragrancy barefooted to defile:
Such filthy ways for slaves in Malaga
Leave we to practise—whence I've oft seen,
When beautiful Dorinda's iv'ry hand
Has built the pastry-fabric (food divine
For Christmas gambols and the hour of mirth)
As the dry'd foreign fruit, with piercing eye,
She cull'd suspicious—lo! she starts, she frowns
With indignation at a negro's nail.

Should'st thou thy harvest for the mart design,
Be thine own factor; nor employ those drones
Who've stings, but make no honey, selfish slaves!
That thrive and fatten on the planter's toil.

What then remains unsung? unless the care
To stack thy poles oblique in comely cones,
Lest rot or rain destroy them—'Tis a sight
Most seemly to behold, and gives, O Winter!

A landskip not unpleasing ev'n to thee.

   And now, ye rivals of the hopland state,
Madum and Dorovernia rejoice,
How great amidst such rivals to excel!
Let Grenovicum boast (for boast she may)
The birth of great Eliza.—Hail, my queen!
And yet I'll call thee by a dearer name,
My countrywoman, hail! Thy worth alone
Gives fame to worlds, and makes whole ages glorious!

   Let Sevenoaks vaunt the hospitable seat
Of Knoll most ancient: awefully, my muse,
These social scenes of grandeur and delight,
Of love and veneration, let me tread.
How oft beneath yon oak has amorous Prior
Awaken'd echo with sweet Chloe's name!
While noble Sackville heard, hearing approv'd,
Approving, greatly recompens'd. But he,
Alas! is number'd with th' illustrious dead,
And orphan merit has no guardian now!

   Next Shipbourne, tho' her precincts are confin'd
To narrow limits, yet can show a train
Of village beauties, pastorally sweet,
And rurally magnificent. Here Fairlawn
Opes her delightful prospects; dear Fairlawn
There, where at once at variance and agreed,
Nature and art hold dalliance. There where rills
Kiss the green drooping herbage, there where trees
The tall trees tremble at th' approach of heav'n,
And bow their salutation to the sun,
Who fosters all their foliage—These are thine,
Yes, little Shipbourne, boast that these are thine—
And if—but oh!—and if 'tis no disgrace,
The birth of him who now records thy praise.

   Nor shalt thou, Mereworth, remain unsung,
Where noble Westmoreland, his country's friend,
Bids British greatness love the silent shade,
Where piles superb, in classic elegance,

Arise, and all is Roman, like his heart.
  Nor Chatham, tho' it is not thine to show
The lofty forest or the verdant lawns,
Yet niggard silence shall not grutch thee praise.
The lofty forests by thy sons prepar'd
Becomes the warlike navy, braves the floods,
And gives Sylvanus empire in the main.
Oh that Britannia, in the day of war,
Wou'd not alone Minerva's valour trust,
But also hear her wisdom! Then her oaks
Shap'd by her own mechanics, wou'd alone
Her island fortify, and fix her fame;
Nor wou'd she weep, like Rachael, for her sons,
Whose glorious blood, in mad profusion,
In foreign lands is shed—and shed in vain.
Now on fair Dover's topmost cliffs I'll stand,
And look with scorn and triumph on proud France,
Of yore an isthmus jutting from this coast,
Join'd the Britannic to the Gallic shore;
But Neptune on a day with fury fir'd,
Rear'd his tremendous trident, smote the earth,
And broke th' unnatural union at a blow.—
''Twixt you and you, my servants and my sons,
Be there (he cried) eternal discord—France
Shall bow the neck to Cantium's peerless offspring,
And as the oak reigns lordly o'er the shrub,
So shall the hop have homage from the vine.'

PSO 1752

The Horatian Canons of Friendship

NAY, 'tis the same with all th' affected crew
Of singing men and singing women too:
Do they not set their catcalls up of course?
The King himself may ask them till he's hoarse;

But wou'd you crack their windpipes and their lungs,
The certain way's to bid them hold their tongues.
'Twas thus with *Minum—Minum* one wou'd think,
My Lord Mayor might have govern'd with a wink.
Yet did the Magistrate e'er condescend
To ask a song as kinsman or as friend,
The urchin coin'd excuses to get off,
'Twas—hem—the devil take this whoreson cough.
But wait awhile, and catch him in the glee,
He'd roar the Lion in the lowest key,
Or strain the Morning Lark quite up to G.
Act Beard, or Lowe, and show his tuneful art
From the plumb-pudding down to the desert.
Never on Earth was such a various elf,
He every day possess'd a different self;
Sometimes he'd scow'r along the streets like wind,
As if some fifty bailiffs were behind:
At other times he'd sadly saunt'ring crawl,
As tho' he led the hearse, or held the sable pall.
Now for promotion he was all on flame,
And ev'ry sentence from St. James's came.
He'd brag how Sir John **** met him in the Strand,
And how his Grace of ***** took him by the hand;
How the Prince saw him at the last review,
And ask'd who was that pretty youth in blue?
Now wou'd he praise the peaceful sylvan scene,
The healthful cottage, and the golden mean.
Now wou'd he cry, 'contented let me dwell
Safe in the harbour of my college cell;
No foreign cooks, nor livery'd servants nigh,
Let me with comfort eat my mutton pye;
While my pint-bottle, op'd by help of fork,
With wine enough to navigate a cork,
My sober solitary meal shall crown,
To study edge the mind, and drive the vapours down
Yet, strange to tell! this wond'rous student lay
Snoring in bed for all the livelong day;

163

Night was his time for labour—in a word,
Never was man so cleverly absurd.
But here a friend of mine turns up his nose,
'And you' (he cries) 'are perfect, I suppose:'
'Perfect! not I (pray, gentle sir, forbear)
In this good age, when vices are so rare,
I plead humanity, and claim my share.
Who has not faults? great MARLBOROUGH had one,
Nor CHESTERFIELD is spotless, nor the SUN.'
Grubworm was railing at his friend *Tom Queer*,
When *Witwoud* thus reproach'd him with a sneer,
'Have you no flaws, who are so prone to snub?'
'I have—but I forgive myself,' quoth *Grub*.
This is a servile selfishness, a fault
Which Justice scarce can punish, as she ought.
Blind as a poking, dirt-compelling mole,
To all that stains thy own polluted soul,
Yet each small failing spy'st in other men,
Spy'st with the quickness of an eagle's ken.
Tho' strong resentment rarely lag behind,
And all thy virulence be paid in kind.
Philander's temper's violent, nor fits
The wond'rous waggishness of modern wits;
His cap's awry, all ragged is his gown,
And (wicked rogue!) he wears his stockings down;
But h'as a soul ingenuous as his face,
To you a friend, and all the human race;
Genius, that all the depths of learning sounds,
And generosity, that knows no bounds.
In gems like these if the good youth excel,
Let them compensate for the awkward shell.
Sift then yourself, I say, and sift again,
Glean the pernicious tares from out the grain;
And ask thy heart, if Custom, Nature's heir,
Hath sown no undiscover'd fern-seed there;
This be our standard then, on this we rest,
Nor search the Casuists for another test.

THE HORATIAN CANONS OF FRIENDSHIP

Let's be like lovers gloriously deceiv'd,
And each good man a better still believ'd;
E'en Celia's wart Strephon will not neglect,
But praises, kisses, loves the dear defect.
Oh! that in friendship we were thus to blame,
And ermin'd candour, tender of our fame,
Wou'd cloath the honest errour with an honest name!
Be we then still to those we hold most dear,
Fatherly fond, and tenderly severe.
The sire, whose son squints forty thousand ways,
Finds in his features mighty room for praise:
'Ah! born' (he cries) 'to make the ladies sigh,
Jacky, thou hast an amorous cast o' th' eye.'
Another child's abortive—he believes
Nature most perfect in diminutives;
And men of ev'ry rank with one accord
Salute each crooked rascal with My Lord.
(For bandy legs, hump-back, and knocking knee,
Are all excessive signs of Q——ty.)
Thus let us judge our friends—if Scrub subsist
Too meanly, Scrub is an œconomist;
And if Tom Tinkle is full loud and pert,
He aims at wit, and does it to divert.
Largus is apt to bluster, but you'll find
'Tis owing to his magnitude of mind:
Lollius is passionate, and loves a whore,
Spirit and constitution!—nothing more—
Ned to a bullying peer is ty'd for life,
And in commendam holds a scolding wife;
Slave to a fool's caprice, and woman's will;
But patience, patience, is a virtue still!
Ask of Chamont a kingdom for a fish,
He'll give you three rather than spoil a dish;
Nor pride, nor luxury is in the case,
But hospitality—an't please your Grace.
Should a great gen'ral give a drab a pension—
Meanness!—the devil—'tis perfect condescension.

Such ways make many friends, and make friends
   long,
Or else my good friend Horace reasons wrong.
But we alas! e'en virtuous deeds invert,
And into vice misconstrue all desert.
See we a man of modesty and merit,
Sober and meek—we swear he has no spirit;
We call him stupid, who with caution breaks
His silence, and will think before he speaks.
Fidelio treads the path of life with care,
And eyes his footsteps; for he fears a snare.
His wary way still scandal misapplies,
And calls him subtle, who's no more than wise.
If any man is unconstrain'd and free,
As oft, my Lælius, I have been to thee,
When rudely to your room I chance to scowr,
And interrupt thee in the studious hour;
From Coke and Lyttleton thy mind unbend,
With more familiar nonsense of a friend;
Talk of my friendship, and of your desert,
Show thee my works, and candidly impart
At once the product of my head and heart,
Nasutus calls me fool, and clownish bear,
Nor (but for perfect candour) stops he there.
Ah! what unthinking, heedless things are men,
T' enact such laws as must themselves condemn?
In every human soul some vices spring
(For fair perfection is no mortal thing)
Whoe'er is with the fewest faults endu'd,
Is but the best of what cannot be good.
Then view me, friend, in an impartial light,
Survey the good and bad, the black and white;
And if you find me, Sir, upon the whole,
To be an honest and ingenuous soul,
By the same rule I'll measure you again,
And give you your allowance to a grain.
'Tis friendly and 'tis fair, on either hand,

To grant th' indulgence we ourselves demand.
If on your hump we cast a fav'ring eye,
You must excuse all those who are awry.
In short, since vice or folly, great or small,
Is more or less inherent in us all,
Whoe'er offends, our censure let us guide,
With a strong bias to the candid side;
Nor (as the stoics did in antient times)
Rank little foibles with enormous crimes.
If, when your butler, e'er he brings a dish,
Shou'd lick his fingers, or shou'd drop a fish,
Or from the side-board filch a cup of ale,
Enrag'd you send the puny thief to gaol;
You'd be (methinks) as infamous an oaf,
As that immense portentous scoundrel ——.
Yet worse by far (if worse at all can be)
In folly and iniquity is he,
Who, for some trivial, social, well-meant joke,
Which candour shou'd forget as soon as spoke,
Wou'd shun his friend, neglectful and unkind,
As if old parson Packthread was behind:
Who drags up all his visitors by force,
And, without mercy, reads them his discourse.
If sick at heart, and heavy at the head,
My drunken friend should reel betimes to bed;
And in the morn, with affluent discharge,
Should sign and seal his residence at large;
Or should he in some passionate debate,
By way of instance, break an earthen plate;
Wou'd I forsake him for a piece of delph?
No—not for China's wide domain itself.
If toys like these were cause of real grief,
What shou'd I do, or whither seek relief,
'Suppose him perjur'd faithless, pimp, or thief?'
Away—a foolish knavish tribe you are,
Who falsely put all vices on a par.
From this fair reason her assent withdraws,

167

E'en sordid Interest gives up the cause,
That mother of our customs and our laws.
When first yon golden Sun array'd the east,
Small was the difference 'twixt man and beast;
With hands, with nails, with teeth, with clubs they
    fought,
'Till malice was improv'd, and deadlier weapons
    wrought.
Language at length, and words experience found,
And sense obtain'd a vehicle in sound.
Then wholesome laws were fram'd, and towns were
    built,
And justice seiz'd the lawless vagrants guilt;
And theft, adultery, and fornication,
Were punish'd much, forsooth, tho' much in fashion:
For long before fair Helen's fatal charms
Had many a----------------------

------Hiatus magnus lacrymabilis
----
           set the world in arms.
But kindly kept by no historian's care,
They all, goodlack, have perish'd to an hair.
But be that as it may, yet in all climes,
There's diff'rent punishment for diff'rent crimes.
'Hold, blockhead, hold—this sure is not the way,
For all alike I'd slash, and all I'd slay,'
Cries W******N, 'if I had sovereign sway.'
Have sovereign sway, and in imperial robe,
With fury sultanate o'er half the globe.
Meanwhile, if I from each indulgent friend,
Obtain remission, when I chance t' offend,
Why, in return, I'll make the balance even,
And, for forgiving, they shall be forgiven.
With zeal I'll love, be courteous e'en to strife,
More blest than emperors in private life.

1750

The Hilliad

An epic poem.

—— Pallas te hoc vulnere, Pallas
Immolat, & pœnam scelerato ex sanguine sumit.
Virg.

THOU God of jest, who o'er th' ambrosial bowl,
Giv'st joy to Jove, while laughter shakes the pole;
And thou, fair Justice, of immortal line,
Hear, and assist the poet's grand design,
Who aims at triumph by no common ways,
But on the stem of dulness grafts the bays.
    O thou, whatever name delight thine ear,

NOTES VARIORUM

Thou god of jest,] As the design of heroic poetry is
to celebrate the virtues and noble achievements of
truly great personages, and conduct them through a
series of hardships to the completion of their wishes,
so the little epic delights in representing, with an ironi-
cal drollery, the mock qualities of those, who, for the
benefit of the laughing part of mankind, are pleased to
become egregiously ridiculous, in an affected imitation
of the truly renown'd worthies above-mentioned.
Hence our poet calls upon Momus, at the first open-
ing of his poem, to convert his hero into a jest. So that
in the present case, it cannot be said, *facit indignatio
versum*, but, if I may be allowed the expression, *facit
titillatio versum*; which may serve to show our author's
temper of mind is free from rancour, or ill-nature.
Notwithstanding the great incentives he has had to
prompt him to this undertaking, he is not actuated by
the spirit of revenge.

Grafts the bays.] Much puzzle hath been occasioned
among the naturalists concerning the engraftment here
mentioned. Hill's Natural History of Trees and Plants,

Pimp! Poet! Puffer! 'Pothecary! Play'r!
Whose baseless fame by vanity is buoy'd,

NOTES VARIORUM

vol. 52, page 336, saith, it has been frequently
attempted, but that the tree of dulness will not admit
any such inoculation. He adds in page 339, that he
himself tried the experiment for two years successively,
but that the twig of laurel, like a feather in the state of
electricity, drooped and died the moment he touched
it. Notwithstanding this authority, it is well known
that this operation has been performed by some choice
spirits. Erasmus in his encomium on folly shows how
it may be accomplished; in our own times Pope and
Garth found means to do the same: and in the sequel
of this work, we make no doubt but the stem here-
mentioned will bear some luxuriant branches, like the
tree in Virgil,

> Nec longum tempus, et ingens
> Exit ad Cœlum ramis felicibus arbos,
> Miraturque novas frondes et non sua Poma.

Poet,] Quinbus Flestrin saith, with his usual import-
ance, that this is the only piece of justice done to our
hero in this work. To this assents the widow at
Cuper's, who it seems is not a little proud of 'the
words by Dr. Hill, and the music by Lewis Granon,
esq.' This opinion is further confirmed by major Eng-
land, who admires the pretty turns on Kitty and Kate,
and Catherine and Katy, but from these venerable
authorities, judicious reader, you may boldly dissent
meo periculo.

Martinus Macularius

Puffer,] Of this talent take a specimen. In a letter
to himself he saith; 'you have discovered many of the
beauties of the ancients; they are obliged to you; we
are obliged to you; were they alive they would thank

Like the huge Earth, self-center'd in the void,
Accept one part'ner thy own worth t' explore,
And in thy praise be singular no more.

   Say, Muse, what Dæmon, foe to ease and truth,
First from the mortar dragg'd th' adventrous youth,
And made him, 'mongst the scribbling sons of men,
Change peace for war, the pestle for the pen?
'Twas on a day (O may that day appear
No more, but lose its station in the year,
In the new style be not its name enroll'd
But share annihilation in the old!)
A tawny Sybil, whose alluring song,
Decoy'd the 'prentices and maiden throng,
First from the counter young HILLARIO charm'd,

you; we who are alive do thank you.' His constant custom of running on in this manner, occasioned the following epigram,

> Hill puffs himself, forbear to chide;
>   An insect vile and mean,
> Must first, he knows, be magnify'd
>   Before it can be seen.

Like the huge Earth.] The allusion here seems to be taken from Ovid, who describes the Earth fixed in the air, by its own stupidity, or *vis inertiæ*:—

> Pendebat in aere tellus,
> Ponderibus librata suis.——

But, reader, dilate your imagination to take in the much greater idea our poet here presents to you: consider the immense inanity of space, and the comparative nothingness of the globe, and you may attain an adequate conception of our hero's reputation, and the mighty basis it stands upon.

   This note is partly by Macularius, and partly by Mr. Jinkyns, Philomath.

And first his unambitious soul alarm'd—
An old strip'd curtain cross her arms was flung,
And tatter'd tap'stry o'er her shoulders hung;
Her loins with patch-work cincture were begirt,
That more than spoke diversity of dirt;

NOTES VARIORUM

A tatter'd tap'stry] Our author has been extremely
negligent upon this occasion, and has indolently
omitted an opportunity of displaying his talent for
poetic imagery. Homer has described the shield of
Achilles with all the art of his imagination; Virgil has
followed him in this point, and indeed both he and
Ovid seem to be delighted when they have either a pic-
ture to describe, or some representation in the labours
of the loom. Hence arises a double delight; we admire
the work of the artificer, and the poet's account of it;
and this pleasure Mr. Smart might have impressed
upon his readers in this passage, as many things were
wrought into the tapestry here-mentioned. In one part
our hero was administering to a patient, 'and the fresh
vomit runs for ever green'. The theatre at May-fair
made a conspicuous figure in the piece—the pit seemed
to rise in an uproar—the gallery opened its rude
throats—and apples, oranges and half-pence flew
about our hero's ears.—The Mall in St. James's Park
was displayed in a beautiful vista, and you might per-
ceive Hillario with his janty air waddling along.—In
Mary-le-Bone Fields, he was dancing round a glow
worm, and finally the Rotunda at Ranelagh filled the
eye with its magnificence, and in a corner of it stood a
handsome young fellow holding a personage, dressed
in blue silk, by the ear; 'the very worsted still looked
black and blue'. There were many other curious
figures, but out of a shameful laziness has our poet
omitted them.

Polymetis Cantabrigiensis

172

With age her back was double and awry,
Twain were her teeth, and single was her eye,
Cold palsy shook her head—she seem'd at most
A living corpse, or an untimely ghost,
With voice far-fetch'd from hollow throat profound
And more than mortal was the infernal sound.
   'Sweet boy, who seem'st for glorious deeds
      design'd,
O come and leave that clyster pipe behind;
Cross this prophetic hand with silver coin,
And all the wealth and fame, I have, is thine'—
She said—he (for what stripling cou'd withstand?)
Straight with his ONLY six-pence grac'd her hand.
And now the prescious fury all her breast
At once invaded, and at once possess'd;
Her eye was fix'd in an extatic stare,
And on her head uprose th' astonish'd hair:
No more her colour, or her looks the same,
But moonstruck madness quite convuls'd her frame,
While, big with fate, again she silence broke,
And in few words voluminously spoke.
   'In these three lines athwart thy palm I see,
Either a tripod, or a triple-tree,
For, Oh! I ken by mysteries profound,
Too light to sink, thou never can'st be drown'd—
Whate'er thy end, the fates are now at strife,
Yet strange variety shall check thy life—
Thou grand dictator of each publick show,
Wit, moralist, quack, harlequin, and beau,
Survey man's vice, self-prais'd, and self preferr'd,
And be th' INSPECTOR of th' infected herd;

NOTES VARIORUM

Be th' Inspector, &c.] When the distemper first raged
among the horned cattle, the king and council ordered
a certain officer to superintend the beasts, and to direct
that such, as were found to be infected, should be

By any means aspire at any ends,
Baseness exalts, and cowardice defends,
The chequer'd world's before thee—go—farewell,
Beware of Irishmen—and learn to spell,'
Here from her breast th' inspiring fury flew:
She ceas'd—and instant from his sight withdrew.
Fir'd with his fate, and conscious of his worth,
The beardless wight prepar'd to sally forth.
But first ('twas just, 'twas natural to grieve)
He sigh'd and took a soft pathetic leave.
'Farewell, a long farewell to all my drugs,
My labell'd vials, and my letter'd jugs;
And you, ye bearers of no trivial charge,
Where all my Latin stands inscrib'd at large:
Ye jars, ye gallipots, and draw'rs adieu,
Be to my memory lost, as lost to view,
And ye, whom I so oft have joy'd to wipe,
Th' ear-sifting syringe, and back-piercing pipe,
Farewell—my day of glory's on the dawn,
And now,—Hillario's occupation's gone.'

    Quick with the word his way the hero made,
Conducted by a glorious cavalcade;
Pert Petulance the first attracts his eye,
And drowsy Dulness slowly saunters by,
With Malice old, and Scandal ever new,
And neutral Nonsense, neither false nor true.

NOTES VARIORUM

knocked on the head. This officer was called the In-
spector, and from thence I would venture to lay a
wager, our hero derived his title.

Bentley, Junior

Neutral Nonsense, &c.] It is not without propriety
that nonsense is introduced with the epithet, neutral;
nonsense being like a Dutchman, not only in an un-

Infernal Falsehold next approach'd the band
With *** and the Koran in her hand.
Her motley vesture with the leopard vies,
Stain'd with a foul variety of lies.
Next spiteful Enmity, gangren'd at heart,
Presents a dagger, and conceals a dart.
On th' earth crawls Flatt'ry with her bosom bare,
And Vanity sails over him in air.

   Such was the groupe—they bow'd and they ador'd,
And hail'd Hillario for their sovereign lord.
Flush'd with success, and proud of his allies,
Th' exulting hero thus triumphant cries.
'Friends, brethren, ever present, ever dear,

NOTES VARIORUM

meaning stupidity, but in the art of preserving a strict
neutrality.

Falsehood,] But why, exclaimeth a certain critic,
should falsehood be given to Hillario?—Because, re-
plieth Macularius, he has given many specimens of his
talent that way. Our hero took it into his head some
time since to tell the world that he caned a gentleman
whom he called by the name of Mario; what degree of
faith the town gave him upon that occasion, may be
collected from the two following lines, by a certain
wag who shall be nameless.

> To beat one man great Hill was fated;
> What man?—a man that he created.

The following epigram may be also properly in-
serted here.

> What H—ll one day says, he the next does deny,
> And candidly tells us—'tis all a damn'd lye:
> Dear doctor—this candour from you is not wanted;
> For why shou'd you own it? 'tis taken for granted.

Home to my heart, nor quit your title there,
While you approve, assist, instruct, inspire,
Heat my young blood, and set my soul on fire;
No foreign aid my daring pen shall chuse,
But boldly versify without a Muse,
I'll teach Minerva, I'll inspire the Nine,
Great Phœbus shall in consultation join,
And round my nobler brow his forfeit laurel twine.'

   He said—and Clamour, of Commotion born,
Rear'd to the skies her ear afflicting horn,
While Jargon grav'd his titles on a block,
And styl'd him M. D. Acad. Budig, Soc.

   But now the harbingers of fate and fame
Signs, omens, prodigies, and portents came.
Lo! (though mid-day) the grave Athenian fowl,
Eyed the bright Sun, and hail'd him with a howl,
Moths, mites, and maggots, fleas, (a numerous crew!)
And gnats and grubworms crouded on his view,
Insects! without the microscopic aid,
Gigantic by the eye of Dulness made!
And stranger still—and never heard before!

NOTES VARIORUM

Without a Muse, &c.] No the devil a bit!—I am the
only person that can do that!—My poems, written at
fifteen, were done without the assistance of any Muse,
and better than all Smart's poetry.—The Muses are
strumpets—they frequently give an intellectual gonor-
rhœa—Court debt not paid—I'll never be poet
laureate.—Coup de grace unanswerable—Our foes
shall knuckle—five pounds to any bishop that will
equal this—Gum guiacum for Latin lignum vitæ.
Adam the first Dutchman—victorious stroke for old
England—Tweedle-dum and tweedle-dee.

Oratory-Right-Reason-Chapel, Saturday
13th of January, and old style for ever.

176

A wooden lion roar'd, or seem'd to roar.
But (what the most his youthful bosom warm'd,
Heighten'd each hope and every fear disarm'd)
On an high dome a damsel took her stand,
With a well freighted Jordan in her hand,
Where curious mixtures strove on every side
And solids sound with laxer fluids vied—
Lo! on his crown the lotion choice and large,
She soused—and gave at once a full discharge.
Not Archimedes, when with conscious pride,
'I'VE FOUND IT OUT! I'VE FOUND IT OUT!' he cry'd,
Not costive bardlings, when a rhyme comes pat,
Not grave Grimalkin when she smells a rat:
Not the shrewd statesman when he scents a plot,
Not coy Prudelia, when she knows what's what,
Not our own hero, when (O matchless luck!)
His keen discernment found another Duck;
With such ecstatic transports did abound,
As what he smelt and saw, and felt and found.
'Ye gods, I thank ye, to profusion free,
Thus to adorn, and thus distinguish me,
And thou, fair Cloacina, whom I serve,
(If a desire to please is to deserve,)
To you I'll consecrate my future lays,
And on the smoothest paper print my soft essays.'
No more he spoke; but slightly slid along,
Escorted by the miscellaneous throng.
  And now, thou goddess, whose fire-darting eyes
Defy all distance and transpierce the skies,
To men the councils of the gods relate,
And faithfully describe the grand debate.
  The cloud-compelling thund'rer, at whose call
The gods assembled in th' etherial hall,
From his bright throne the deities addrest:
'What impious noise disturbs our awful rest,
With din prophane assaults immortal ears,
And jars harsh discord to the tuneful spheres?

177

Nature, my hand-maid, yet without a stain,
Has never once productive prov'd in vain,
'Till now—luxuriant and regardless quite
Of her divine, eternal rule of right,
On mere privation sh'as bestow'd a frame,
And dignify'd a nothing with a name,
A wretch devoid of use, of sense and grace,
Th' insolvent tenant of encumber'd space.

   'Good is his cause, and just is his pretence,'
(Replies the god of theft and eloquence.)
'A hand mercurial, ready to convey,
E'en in the presence of the garish day,
The work an English classic late has writ,
And by adoption be the sire of wit
Sure to be this is to be something—sure,
Next to perform, 'tis glorious to procure.
Small was th' exertion of my god-like soul,
When privately Apollo's herd I stole,
Compar'd to him, who braves th' all-seeing sun,
And boldly bids th' astonish'd world look on.'

   Her approbation Venus next exprest,
And on Hillario's part the throne addrest,
'If there be any praise the nails to pare,
And in soft ringlets wreathe th' elastic hair,
In talk and tea to trifle time away,
The mien so easy and the dress so gay!
Can my Hillario's worth remain unknown,
With whom coy Sylvia trusts herself alone.
With whom, so pure, so innocent his life,
The jealous husband leaves his buxom wife?
What tho' he ne'er assume the post of Mars;
By me disbanded from all amorous wars;
His fancy (if not person) he employs,
And oft ideal countesses enjoys—
Tho' hard his heart, yet beauty shall controul,
And sweeten all the rancour of his soul,
While his black self, Florinda ever near,

Shews like a diamond in an Æthiop's ear.'
   When Pallas—thus—'Cease—ye immortals—cease,
Nor rob serene stupidity of peace—
Should Jove himself in calculation mad
Still negatives to blank negations add,
How could the barren cyphers ever breed,
But nothing still from nothing would proceed?
Raise or depress—or magnify—or blame,
Inanity will ever be the same.'

NOTES VARIORUM

Diamond in an Æthiop's ear,] There is neither morality, nor integrity, nor unity, nor universality in this poem.—The author of it is a Smart; I hope to see a Smartead published; I had my pocket picked the other day, as I was going through Paul's Church-yard, and I firmly believe it was this little author, as the man who can pun, will also pick a pocket.

John Dennis, Junior

Inanity will ever be, &c.] Our author does not here mean to list himself among the disputants concerning pure space, but the doctrine he would advance, is, that nothing can come from nothing. In so unbelieving an age as this, it is possible this tenet may not be received, but if the reader has a mind to see it handled at large, he may find it in Rumgurtius, vol. 16, pagina 1001. De hac re multum et turpiter hallucinantur scriptores tam exteri quam domestici. Spatium enim absolutum et relativum debent distingui, priusquam distincta esse possunt; neque ulla alia regula ad normam rei metaphysicæ quadrabit, quam triplex consideratio de substantiâ inanitatis, sive entitate nihili, quæ quidem consideratio triplex ad unam reduci potest necessitatem; nempe idem spatium de quo jam satis dictum est. This opinion is further corroborated by the tracts of the society of Bourdeaux. Selon la distinction entre les

'Not so' (says Phœbus) 'my celestial friend,
E'en blank privation has its use and end—
How sweetly shadows recommend the light,
And darkness renders my own beams more bright!
How rise from filth the violet and rose!
From emptiness how softest music flows!

NOTES VARIORUM

choses, qui n'ont pas de différence, il nous faut absolu-
ment agréer, que les idées, qui ont frappé l'imagina-
tion, peuvent bien être effacées, pourvu qu'on ne
s'avise pas d'oublier cet espace immense, qui en-
vironne toute la nature, et le systême des étoiles.
Among our countrymen, I do not know any body that
has handled this subject so well as the accurate Mr.
Fielding, in his Essay upon Nothing, which the reader
may find in the first volume of his Miscellanies; but
with all due deference to his authority, we beg leave to
dissent from one assertion in the said essay; the resi-
dence of nothing might in his time have been in a
critic's head, and we are apt to believe that there is a
something like nothing in most critic's heads to this-
day, and this false appearance misled the excellent
metaphysician just quoted; for nothing, in its *puris
naturalibus*, as Gravesend describes it in his experi-
mental philosophy, does subsist no where so properly
at present as in the pericranium of our hero.

Mart. Macularius

Music flows,] 'Persons of most genius,' says the
Inspector, Friday Jan. 26, Number 587, 'have in
general been the fondest of music; sir Isaac Newton
was remarkable for his affection for harmony; he was
scarce ever missed at the beginning of any perform-
ance, but was seldom seen at the end of it.' And indeed
of this opinion is M. Macularius; and he further adds,
that if sir Isaac was still living, it is probable he would

How absence to possession adds a grace,
And modest vacancy to all gives place?
Contrasted when fair Nature's works we spy,
More they allure the mind and more they charm the
    eye.
So from Hillario some effect may spring,
E'en him—that slight Penumbra of a thing.'
Morpheus at length in the debate awoke,
And drowsily a few dull words he spoke—
Declar'd Hillario was the friend of ease,
And had a soporific pow'r to please,
Once more Hillario he pronounc'd with pain,
But at the very sound was lull'd to sleep again.

NOTES VARIORUM

be at the beginning of the Inspector's next song at
Cuper's, but that he would not be at the end of it, may
be proved to a mathematical demonstration, though
Hillario takes so much pleasure in beating time to
them himself, and though he so frequently exclaims,
very fine!—O fine!—vastly fine!

Lull'd to sleep again.] The hypnotic, or soporiferous
quality of Hillario's pen is manifest from the following
asseveration, which was published in the New Crafts-
man, and is a letter from a tradesman in the city.

'Sir,

'From a motive of gratitude, and for the sake of
those of my fellow-creatures, who may unhappily be
afflicted, as I have been for some time past, I beg leave,
through the channel of your paper, to communicate
the disorder I have laboured under, and the extra-
ordinary cure I have lately met with. I have had for
many months successively a slow nervous fever, with
a constant flutter on my spirits, attended with per-
tinacious watchings, twitchings of the nerves, and
other grievous symptoms, which reduced me to a mere

Momus the last of all, in merry mood,
As moderator in th' assembly stood.
'Ye laughter-loving pow'rs, ye Gods of mirth,
What not regard my deputy on Earth?
Whose chymic skill turns brass to gold with ease,
And out of Cibber forges Socrates?
Whose genius makes consistencies to fight,
And forms an union betwixt wrong and right?
Who (five whole days in senseless malice past)
Repents, and is religious at the last?
A paltry play'r, that in no parts succeeds,
A hackney writer, whom no mortal reads.
The trumpet of a base deserted cause,

NOTES VARIORUM

shadow. At length, by the interposition of divine
Providence, a friend who had himself experienced it,
advised me to have recourse to the reading of the In-
spectors. I accordingly took one of them, and the effect
it had upon me was such that I fell into a profound
sleep, which lasted near six and thirty hours. By this I
have attained a more composed habit of body, and I
now doze away almost all my time, but for fear of a
lethargy, am ordered to take them in smaller quanti-
ties. A paragraph at a time now answers my purpose,
and under Heaven I owe my sleeping powers to the
above-mentioned Inspectors. I look upon them to be a
grand soporificum mirabile, very proper to be had in
all families. He makes great allowance to those who
buy them to sell again, or to send abroad to the planta-
tions; and the above fact I am ready to attest whenever
called upon. Given under my hand this 4th day of
January, 1753.

The trumpet, &c.] In a very pleasant account of the
riots in Drury-lane play-house, by Henry Fielding,
esq. we find the following humorous description of

Damn'd to the scandal of his own applause;
While thus he stands a general wit confest,
With all these titles, all these talents blest,
Be he by Jove's authority assign'd,
The UNIVERSAL BUTT of all mankind.'

So spake and ceas'd the joy-exciting god,
And Jove immediate gave th' assenting nod,
When Fame her adamantine trump uprear'd,
And thus th' irrevocable doom declar'd.

'While in the vale perennial fountains flow,
And fragrant Zephyrs musically blow,
While the majestic sea from pole to pole,
In horrible magnificence shall roll,

NOTES VARIORUM

our hero in the character of a trumpeter. 'They all ran away except the trumpeter, who having an empyema in his side, as well as several dreadful bruises on his breech, was taken. When he was brought before Garrick to be examined, he said the ninnies, to whom he had the honour to be trumpeter, had resented the use made of the monsters by Garrick. That it was unfair, that it was cruel, that it was inhuman to employ a man's own subjects against him. That Rich was lawful sovereign over all the monsters in the universe, with much more of the same kind; all which Garrick seemed to think unworthy of an answer; but when the trumpeter challenged him as his acquaintance, the chief with great disdain turned his back, and ordered the fellow to be dismissed with full power of trumpeting again on what side he pleased.' Hillario has since trumpeted in the cause of pantomime, the gaudy scenery of which with great judgment he dismisses from the Opera-house, and saith, it is now fixed in its proper place in the theatre. On this occasion, Macularius cannot help exclaiming, 'O Shakespear! O Jonson! rest, rest, perturbed spirits.'

183

While yonder glorious canopy on high
Shall overhang the curtains of the sky,
While the gay seasons their due course shall run,
Ruled by the brilliant stars and golden sun,
While wit and fool antagonists shall be,
And sense and taste and nature shall agree,
While love shall live, and rapture shall rejoice,
Fed by the notes of Handel, Arne and Boyce,
While with joint force o'er humour's droll domain,
Cervantes, Fielding, Lucian, Swift shall reign,
While thinking figures from the canvas start,
And Hogarth is the Garrick of his art.
So long in gross stupidity's extreme,
Shall H-ll th' ARCH-DUNCE remain o'er every dunce
     supreme.'

1753

OCCASIONAL
POEMS

On seeing Miss H—— P——t in an Apothecary's Shop

FALLACIOUS Nymph, who here by Stealth
Would seem to be the Goddess HEALTH!
Mask'd with that divine Disguise,
Think'st thou to scape Poetick Eyes?
Back, Siren—for, I know, thou stray'd
From the harmonious Ambuscade,
Where many a Traveller that took
The Invitation of thy Look,
Has felt the Coz'nage of thy Charms,
Tickled to Death within thine Arms.
Know, that I saw you yester Night,
At once with Horror and Delight,
Drag *Luna* from her heavenly Frame,
And outshine her when she came.
Yes, Inchantress, I can tell
How by the Virtue of a Spell,
Cloath'd like Cherub-Innocence,
Here you fix your Residence,
That securely you may mix
Your Philtres in the Streams of Styx;
And have at Hand, in every Part,
Materials for your magic Art;
Fossils, Fungus's, and Flow'rs,
With all the fascinating Pow'rs.—
God of the prescribing Trade,
Doctor *Phœbus*, lend thine Aid;
If thou'lt some antidote devise,
I'll call thee *Harvey* of the Skies;
Or (for at one Glance thou can'st see
All that is, or that shall be,
Intentions ripening into Act,
And Plans emerging up to Fact,)

187

Look in her Eyes, and thence explain
All the Mischief that they mean.
Say in what Grove, and near what Trees
Will she seek th' Hippomanes;
There, there I'll meet her,—there I'll try
Th' asswasive Pow'r of Harmony.
I think, I've got an Amulet,
That will her Rage a while abate.
No—all resistance is in vain—
Charmer, I yield—I hug my Chain—
Alas!—I see 'tis to no End
With such Puissance to contend;
For since continually you dwell
In that Apothecary's Cell,
And While so studiously you pry
Into the sage Dispensary,
And read so many Doctor's Bill,
You learn infallibly to kill.--

The Museum 1746

Lovely Harriote

A crambo ballad.

GREAT *Phœbus* in his vast Career,
Who forms the self-succeeding Year,
    Thron'd in his Amber Chariot;
Sees not an Object half so bright,
Nor gives such Joy, such Life, such Light,
    As dear delicious *Harriote*.

Pedants of dull phlegmatic Turns,
Whose Pulse not beats, whose Blood not burns,
    Read *Malebranche*, *Boyle* and *Marriot*;

LOVELY HARRIOTE

I scorn their Philosophic Strife,
And study Nature from the Life,
   (Where most she shines) in *Harriote*.

When she admits another Wooer,
I rave like *Shakespeare's* jealous *Moor*,
   And am, as ranting *Barry* hot;
True, virtuous, lovely, was his Dove,
But Virtue, Beauty, Truth and Love,
   Are other Names for *Harriote*.

Ye honest Members who oppose,
And fire both Houses with your Prose,
   Though never can you carry aught;
You might command the Nations Sense,
And without Bribery convince,
   Had you the voice of *Harriote*.

You of the Musick common weal,
Who borrow, beg, compose, or steal,
   Cantata, Air, or Ariet;
You'd burn your cumb'rous Works in score;
And sing, compose, and play no more,
   If once you heard my *Harriote*.

Were there a Wretch who durst essay,
Such wond'rous Sweetness to betray,
   I'd call him an *Iscariot*;
But her e'vn Satyrs can't annoy,
So strictly chaste, tho' kindly coy,
   Is fair angelic *Harriote*.

While Sultans, Emperors, and Kings,
(Mean Appetite of earthly Things)
   In all the Waste of War riot;
Love's softer Duel be my Aim,
Praise, Honour, Glory, Conquest, Fame,
   Are center'd all in *Harriote*.

I swear by *Hymen* and the pow'rs
That haunt Love's ever-blushing Bow'rs,
    So sweet a Nymph to marry ought:
Then may I hug her silken Yoke,
And give the last, the final Stroke,
    T' accomplish lovely *Harriote*.

                                    Md 1751

To Miss H——, with some Musick

Written by a Poet outragiously in love.

INCOMPARABLE *Harriot*, loveliest fair,
That e'er breath'd sweetness on the vital air,
Whose matchless form to us below is giv'n,
As a bright pattern of the rest of heav'n,
Blest with a face, a temper, and a mind
To please, to sooth, and to instruct mankind!
Accept these notes—the warbling song begin,
And with your voice compleat the cherubin;
Swift with your iv'ry fingers wake the keys,
And make e'en ——'s desolation please.
O wou'd some God but listen to my pray'r,
And waft me to thee thro' the fields of air,
Thrown at thy feet a suppliant I'd reveal
Each wish, each anguish, that my thoughts conceal,
In whisp'ring kisses I'd confess the whole,
And musically murmur out my soul.
May all the pow'rs that on fair virgins wait,
Heap on thee all that's happy, good and great,
All that of earthly bliss you can conceive,
Your hopes can image, or your faith believe!
But vain are pray'rs, and all my wishes vain,
You are already all that I can feign.
With that sweet mind, to that fair body giv'n,
You must be blest, for all are blest in heav'n.

190

But you from *Time* th' improving form receive,
And he, alas! can take as well as give,
But that exalted soul which you enjoy,
Is what nor *Time* can give—nor can destroy.

GM 1754

Ode to Lady Harriot

To Harriot all accomplish'd fair,
Begin, ye Nine, a grateful air;
Ye Graces join her worth to tell,
And blazon what you can't excell.

Let Flora rifle all her bow'rs,
For fragrant shrubs, and painted flow'rs,
And, in her vernal robes array'd,
Present them to the noble maid.

Her breath shall give them new perfume,
Her blushes shall their dyes outbloom;
The lily now no more shall boast
Its whiteness, in her bosom lost.

See yon delicious woodbines rise
By oaks exalted to the skies,
So view in Harriot's matchless mind
Humility and greatness join'd.

To paint her dignity and ease,
Form'd to command, and form'd to please,
In wreaths expressive be there wove
The birds of Venus and of Jove.

There where th' immortal laurel grows,
And there, where blooms the crimson rose,
Be with this line the chaplet bound,
That beauty is with virtue crown'd.

Md 1751

Lines with a Pocket Book

OF all returns in man's advice
'Tis gratitude that makes the price,
And what sincerity designs
Is richer than Peruvian mines.
Thus estimate the heart's intent,
In what the faithful hands present.
This volume soon shall worth derive
From what your industry shall hive,
And then in every line produce
The tale of industry and use.
Here too let your appointments be,
And set down many a day for me;
O may the year we now renew
Be stor'd with happiness for you;
With all the wealth your friends would choose,
And all the praise which you refuse;
With love, sweet inmate of the breast,
And meekness, while in blessing, blest.
Privileges of the University of Cambridge

To Miss A——n

LONG, with undistinguish'd Flame,
I lov'd each fair, each witty Dame.
My Heart the Belle-Assembly gain'd,
And all an equal Sway maintain'd.

But when you came, you stood confest
Sole Sultana of my Breast;
For you eclips'd, supremely fair,
All the whole Seraglio there.

In this her Mien, in that her Grace,
In a third I lov'd a Face;
192

But you in ev'ry Feature shine,
Universally divine.

What can those tumid Paps excel,
Do they sink, or do they swell?
While those lovely wanton Eyes
Sparkling meet them, as they rise.

Thus is silver Cynthia seen,
Glist'ning o'er the glassy Green,
While attracted swell the Waves,
Emerging from their inmost Caves.

When to sweet Sounds your Steps you suit,
And weave the Minuet to the Lute,
Heav'ns! how you glide!—her Neck—her Chest—
Does she move, or does she rest?

As those roguish Eyes advance,
Let me catch their side-long Glance,
Soon—or they'll elude my Sight,
Quick as Lightning and as bright.

Thus the bashful Pleiad cheats,
Charms her moment, and retreats,
Then peeps again—then skulks unseen,
Veil'd behind the azure Skreen.

Like the ever-toying Dove,
Smile Immensity of Love;
Be *Venus* in each outward Part,
And wear the Vestal in your Heart.

When I ask a Kiss, or so—
Grant it with a begging no,
And let each Rose that decks your Face
Blush assent to my Embrace.

Md 1750

To Miss * * * *

One of the Chichester Graces. —Written in Goodwood
Gardens, September, 1750.

'YE Hills that overlook the plains,
Where Wealth and Gothic Greatness reigns,
Where Nature's hand by Art is check'd,
And Taste herself is architect;
Ye fallows gray, ye forests brown,
And seas that the vast prospect crown,
Ye freight the soul with fancy's store,
Nor can she one idea more!'

I said—when dearest of her kind
(Her form, the picture of her mind)
CHLORIS approach'd—the landscape flew.
All nature vanish'd from my view!
She seem'd all nature to comprize,
Her lips! her beauteous breasts! her eyes!
That rous'd, and yet abash'd desire,
With liquid, languid, living fire!

But then—her voice!—how fram'd t' endear!
The music of the Gods to hear!
Wit that so pierc'd, without offence!
So brac'd by the strong nerves of sense!
PALLAS with VENUS play'd her part,
To rob me of an honest heart;
Prudence and passion jointly strove,
And reason was th' ally of love.

Ah me! thou sweet, delicious maid,
From whence shall I solicit aid?
Hope and despair alike destroy,
One kills with grief, and one with joy.

194

Celestial CHLORIS! Nymph divine!
To save me, the dear task be thine.
Though conquest be the woman's care,
The angel's glory is to spare.

St 1751

To Jenny Gray

BRING, Phœbus, from Parnassian bow'rs,
A chaplet of poetic flowers,
　　That far outbloom the May;
Bring verse so smooth, and thoughts so free,
And all the Muses heraldry,
　　To blazon Jenny Gray.

Observe yon almond's rich perfume,
Presenting Spring with early bloom,
　　In ruddy tints how gay!
Thus, foremost of the blushing fair,
With such a blithsome, buxom air,
　　Blooms lovely Jenny Gray.

The merry, chirping, plumy throng,
The bushes and the twigs among
　　That pipe the sylvan lay,
All hush'd at her delightful voice
In silent ecstacy rejoice,
　　And study Jenny Gray.

Ye balmy odour-breathing gales,
That lightly sweep the green rob'd vales,
　　And in each rose-bush play;
I know you all, you're arrant cheats,
And steal your more than natural sweets,
　　From lovely Jenny Gray.

Pomona and that Goddess bright,
The florist's and the maid's delight,
    In vain their charms display;
The luscious nectarine, juicy peach,
In richness, nor in sweetness reach
    The lips of Jenny Gray.

To the sweet knot of Graces three,
Th' immortal band of bards agree,
    A tuneful tax to pay;
There yet remains a matchless worth,
There yet remains a lovelier fourth,
    And she is Jenny Gray.

R 1791

Epithalamium on a Late Happy Marriage

WHEN *Hymen* once the mutual Bands has wove,
Exchanging Heart for Heart, and Love for Love,
The happy Pair, with mutual Bliss elate,
Own to be single's an imperfect State.
But when two Hearts united thus agree
With equal sense, and equal Constancy,
This, HAPPINESS, is thy extreamest Goal,
'Tis Marriage both of Body, and of Soul,
'Tis making Heav'n below with matchless Love,
And's a fair Step to reach the Heav'n above.

Md 1752

To Miss Kitty Bennet, and Her Cat Crop

FULL many a Heart, that now is free,
May shortly, fair one, beat for thee,
    And court thy pleasing Chain;
Then prudent hear a Friend's Advice,
And learn to guard, by Conduct nice,
    The Conquests you shall gain.

When *Tabby Tom* your *Crop* pursues,
How many a Bite and many a Bruise
    The amorous Swain endures?
E'er yet one favouring Glance he catch,
What frequent Squalls, how many a Scratch
    His Tenderness procures?

Tho' this, 'tis own'd, be somewhat rude,
And Puss by nature be a Prude,
    Yet hence you may improve,
By decent Pride, and Dint of Scoff,
Keep caterwauling Coxcombs off,
    And ward th' Attacks of Love.

Your *Crop* a mousing when you see,
She teaches you *Œconomy*
    Which makes the Pot to boil:
And when she plays with what she gains,
She shows you Pleasure springs from Pains,
    And Mirth's the Fruit of Toil.

Md 1752

To Ethelinda

On her doing my verses the honour of wearing them
in her bosom.—Written at thirteen.

HAPPY verses! that were prest
In fair Ethelinda's breast!
Happy Muse, that didst embrace
The sweet, the heav'nly-fragrant place!
Tell me, is the omen true,
Shall the bard arrive there too?

Oft thro' my eyes my soul has flown,
And wanton'd on that ivory throne:
There with extatic transport burn'd,
And thought it was to heav'n return'd.
Tell me, is the omen true,
Shall the body follow too?

When first at nature's early birth,
Heav'n sent a man upon the Earth,
Ev'n Eden was more fruitful found,
When Adam came to till the ground:
Shall then those breasts be fair in vain,
And only rise to fall again?

No, no, fair nymph—for no such end
Did Heav'n to thee its bounty lend;
That breast was ne'er design'd by fate
For verse, or things inanimate;
Then throw them from that downy bed,
And take the poet in their stead.

PSO 1752

Epithalamium

DESCEND, descend, ye sweet Aonian maids,
    Leave the Parnassian shades,
    The joyful Hymeneal sing,
    And to a lovelier Belle
Than fiction can devise, or eloquence can tell,
    Your vocal tributes bring.
And you, ye winged choristers, that fly
In all the pensile gardens of the sky,
    Chant thro' th' enamel'd grove,
Stretch from the trembling twigs your little throats,
With all the wild variety of artless notes,
    But let each note be love.
    Fragrant Flora, queen of May,
    All bedight with garlands gay,
    Where in the smooth-shaven green
    The spangled cowslips variegate the scene,
    And the rivulet between,
    Whispers, murmurs, sings,
    As it stops, or falls, or springs;
There spread a sofa of thy softest flowers,
    There let the bridegroom stay,
There let him hate the light, and curse the day,
    And dun the tardy hours.

But see the bride—she comes with silent pace,
    Full of majesty and love;
    Not with a nobler grace
    Look'd the imperial wife of Jove,
    When erst ineffably she shone
In Venus' irresistible, inchanting zone.
  Phœbus, great god of verse, the nymph observe,
    Observe her well;
Then touch each sweetly-trem'lous nerve
    Of thy resounding shell:

Her like huntress-Dian paint,
Modest, but without restraint;
From Pallas take her decent pace,
With Venus sweeten all her face,
From the Zephyrs steal her sighs,
From thyself her sun-bright eyes;
Then baffled, thou shalt see,
That as did Daphne thee,
Her charms thy genius' force shall fly,
And by no soft persuasive sounds be brib'd
To come within INVENTION's narrow eye;
But all indignant shun its grasp, and scorn to be
describ'd.

Now see the bridegroom rise,
Oh! how impatient are his joys!
Bring zephyrs to depaint his voice,
But lightning for his eyes.
He leaps, he springs, he flies into her arms,
With joy intense,
Feeds ev'ry sense,
And sultanates o'er all her charms.
Oh! had I Virgil's comprehensive strain,
Or sung like Pope, without a word in vain,
Then should I hope my numbers might contain,
Egregious nymph, thy boundless happiness,
How arduous to express!
Such may it last to all eternity:
And may thy Lord with thee,
Like two coeval pines in Ida's grove,
That interweave their verdant arms in love,
Each mutual office cheerfully perform,
And share alike the sunshine, and the storm;
And ever, as you flourish hand in hand,
Both shade the shepherd and adorn the land,
Together with each growing year arise,
Indissolubly link'd, and climb at last the skies.

An Ode on the 26th of January

Being the Birth-Day of a Young Lady.

ALL hail, and welcome joyous Morn,
  Welcome to th' infant Year;
Whether smooth Calms thy Face adorn,
  Or lowring Clouds appear;
Tho' Billows lash the sounding Shore,
And Tempests thro' the Forests roar,
  Sweet *Nancy's* Voice shall soothe the Sound;
Tho' Darkness shou'd invest the Skies,
New Day shall beam from *Nancy's* Eyes,
  And bless all Nature round.

Let but those Lips their Sweets disclose,
  And rich Perfumes exhale,
We shall not want the fragrant Rose,
  Nor miss the southern Gale.
Then loosely to the Winds unfold,
Those radiant Locks of burnish'd Gold,
  Or on thy Bosom let them rove;
His Treasure-house there *Cupid* keeps,
And hoards up, in two snowy heaps,
  His stores of choicest Love.

This Day each warmest Wish be paid
  To thee the Muse's Pride,
I long to see the blooming Maid
  Chang'd to the blushing Bride.
So shall thy Pleasure and thy Praise
Increase with the increasing Days.
  And present Joys exceed the past;
To give and to receive Delight,
Shall be thy Task both Day and Night,
  While Day and Night shall last.

Md 1752

The Lass with the Golden Locks

No more of my Harriot, of Polly no more,
Nor all the bright beauties that charm'd me before;
My heart for a slave to gay Venus I've sold,
And barter'd my freedom for ringlets of gold:
I'll throw down my pipe, and neglect all my flocks,
And will sing to my lass with the golden locks.

Tho' o'er her white forehead the gilt tresses flow,
Like the rays of the sun on a hillock of snow;
Such painters of old drew the Queen of the Fair,
'Tis the taste of the antients, 'tis classical hair:
And though witlings may scoff, and though raillery
    mocks,
Yet I'll sing to my lass with the golden locks.

To live and to love, to converse and be free,
Is loving, my charmer, and living with thee:
Away go the hours in kisses and rhime,
Spite of all the grave lectures of old father Time;
A fig for his dials, his watches and clocks,
He's best spent with the lass of the golden locks.

Than the swan in the brook she's more dear to my
    sight,
Her mien is more stately, her breast is more white,
Her sweet lips are rubies, all rubies above,
Which are fit for the language or labour of love;
At the park in the mall, at the play in the box,
My lass bears the bell with her golden locks.

Her beautiful eyes, as they roll or they flow,
Shall be glad for my joy, or shall weep for my woe;
She shall ease my fond heart, and shall sooth my soft
    pain;

While thousands of rivals are sighing in vain;
Let them rail at the fruit they can't reach, like the fox,
While I have the lass with the golden locks.

PSO 1752

On the Fifth of December

Being the birth-day of a very beautiful young lady.

HAIL, eldest of the monthly train,
    Sire of the winter drear,
DECEMBER, in whose iron reign
    Expires the chequer'd year.
Hush all the blust'ring blasts that blow,
And proudly plum'd in silver snow,
    Smile gladly on this blest of days.
The livery'd clouds shall on thee wait,
And PHŒBUS shine in all his state
    With more than summer rays,

Tho' jocund JUNE may justly boast
    Long days and happy hours,
Tho' AUGUST be POMONA's host,
    And MAY be crown'd with flow'rs;
Tell JUNE, his fire and crimson dies,
By HARRIOT's blush and HARRIOT's eyes,
    Eclips'd and vanquish'd, fade away:
Tell AUGUST, thou canst let him see
A richer, riper fruit than he,
    A sweeter flow'r than MAY.

St 1750

203

To Miss S—— P——e

FAIR partner of my *Nancy's* heart,
Who feel'st, like me, love's poignant dart;
Who at a frown can'st pant for pain,
And at a smile revive again;
Who doat'st to that severe degree,
You're jealous, e'en of constancy;
Born hopes and fears and doubts to prove,
And each vicissitude of love!
To this my humble suit attend,
And be my advocate and friend,
So may just heav'n your goodness bless;
Successful ev'n in my success!
Oft at the silent hour of night,
When bold intrusion wings her flight,
My fair, from care and bus'ness free,
Unbosoms all her soul to thee,
Each hope with which her bosom heaves,
Each tender wish her heart receives
To thee are intimately known,
And all her thoughts become thy own:
Then take the blessed blissful hour,
To try love's sweet infectious pow'r;
And let your sister souls conspire
In love's, as friendship's calmer fire.
So may thy transport equal mine,
Nay—every joy be doubly thine!
So may the youth, whom you prefer,
Be all I wish to be to her.

R 1791

204

On My Wife's Birth-Day

'Tis *Nancy's* birth-day—raise your strains,
Ye nymphs of the Parnassian plains,
And sing with more than usual glee
To *Nancy*, who was born for me.

Tell the blithe Graces as they bound
Luxuriant in the buxom round;
They're not more elegantly free,
Than *Nancy*, who was born for me.

Tell royal *Venus*, though she rove,
The queen of the immortal grove;
That she must share her golden fee
With *Nancy*, who was born for me.

Tell *Pallas*, though th' Athenian school,
And ev'ry trite pedantic fool,
On her to place the palm agree,
'Tis *Nancy's*, who was born for me.

Tell spotless *Dian*, though she range,
The regent of the up-land grange,
In chastity she yields to thee,
O, *Nancy*, who wast born for me.

Tell *Cupid*, *Hymen*, and tell *Jove*,
With all the pow'rs of life and love,
That I'd disdain to breathe or *be*,
If *Nancy* was not born for me.

GM 1754

205

To the Rev. Mr. P[owel]l

On the non-performance of a promise he made the author
of a hare.

FRIEND, with regard to this same Hare,
Am I to hope, or to despair?
By punctual Post the Letter came,
With P***l's Hand, and P***l's Name:
Yet there appear'd, for Love or Money,
Nor Hare, nor Leveret, nor Coney.
Say, my dear *Morgan*, has my Lord,
Like other great Ones kept his Word?
Or have you been deceiv'd by 'squire?
Or has your Poacher lost his Wire,
Or in some unpropitious Hole,
Instead of Puss, trepann'd a Mole?
Thou valiant Son of great *Cadwallader*,
Hast thou a Hare, or hast thou swallow'd her?

But, now, methinks I hear you say,
(And shake your Head) 'Ah, well-a-day!
Painful Pre-eminence to be wise,
We WITS have such short Memories.
Oh, that the Act was not in Force!
A Horse!—my Kingdom for a Horse!
To love—yet be deny'd the Sport!
Oh! for a Friend or two at Court!
God knows, there's scarce a Man of Quality
In all our peerless Principality—'

But hold—for on his Country joking,
To a warm *Welchman's* most provoking.
As for poor Puss, upon my Honour,
I never set my Heart upon her.
But any Gift from Friend to Friend,
Is pleasing in it's Aim and End.
I, like the Cock, wou'd spurn a Jewel,
Sent by th' unkind, th' unjust, or cruel.
But honest P***el!——Sure from him

A Barley-corn wou'd be a Gem.
Pleas'd therefore had I been, and proud,
And prais'd thy generous Heart aloud,
If 'stead of Hare (but do not blab it)
You'd send me only a *Welch* Rabbit.

Md 1752

To my Worthy Friend Mr. T. B.

One of the people called Quakers. —Written in his Garden,
July, 1752.

FREE from the proud, the pompous, and the vain,
How simply neat, and elegantly plain
Thy rural Villa lifts its modest Head,
Where fair Convenience reigns in Fashion's stead;
Where sober Plenty does its Bliss impart,
And glads thine hospitable, honest Heart.
Mirth without Vice, and Rapture without Noise,
And all the decent, all the manly Joys!
Beneath a shadowy Bow'r, the Summer's Pride,
Thy darling *Tullia* sitting by thy Side;
Where Light and Shade in varied Scenes display
A Contrast sweet, like friendly *yea* and *nay*.
My Hand, the Secretary of my Mind,
Left thee these Lines upon the *poplar's* Rind.

Md 1752

Epistle to Dr. Nares

SMART sends his compliments and pray'rs
Health and long life to Dr. Nares—
But the chief business of the Card,
Is 'Come to dinner with the bard',

207

Who makes a mod'rate share of wit
Put on the pot, and turn the spit.
'Tis said the Indians teach their sons
The use of bows instead of guns;
And ere the striplings dare to dine,
They shoot their victuals off a pine.
The Public is as kind to me,
As to his child a Cherokee;
And if I chance to hit my aim,
I chuse to feast upon the game;
For panegyric or abuse
Shall make the quill produce the goose,
With apple-sauce and Durham mustard,
And cooling-pie o'er-laid with custard.
Pray please to signify with this
My love to Madam, Bob, and Miss,
Likewise to Nurse and little Poll—
Whose praise so justly you extol.

P.S. I have (don't think it a chimaera)
Some good sound Port and right Madeira.
                                    Notes and Queries, 1866

An Invitation to Mrs. Tyler

A clergyman's lady, to dine upon a couple of ducks on the
anniversary of the author's wedding-day.

HAD I the pen of sir John Suckling,
And could find out a rhyme for duckling,
Why, dearest madam, in that case,
I would invite you to a brace.
Haste, gentle shepherdess, away,
To morrow is the gaudy day,
That day, when to my longing arms,
Nancy resign'd her golden charms,

And set my am'rous inclination
Upon the bus'ness of the nation.
Industrious Moll, with many a pluck,
Unwings the plumage of each duck;
And as she sits a brooding o'er,
You'd think she'd hatch a couple more.
Come, all ye Muses, come and sing,—
Shall we then roast them on a string?
Or shall we make our dirty jilt run,
To beg a roast of Mrs. Bilton?
But to delight you more with these,
We shall provide a dish of pease:
On ducks alone we'll not regale you,
We'll wine, we'll punch you, and we'll ale you.
To morrow is the gaudy day,
Haste, gentle shepherdess, away.

GM 1754

Epistle to Mrs. Tyler

IT ever was allow'd, dear Madam,
Ev'n from the days of father Adam,
Of all perfection flesh is heir to,
Fair patience is the gentlest virtue;
This is a truth our grandames teach,
Our poets sing, and parsons preach;
Yet after all, dear Moll, the fact is
We seldom put it into practice;
I'll warrant (if one knew the truth)
You've call'd me many an idle youth,
And styled me rude ungrateful bear,
Enough to make a parson swear.

I shall not make a long oration
In order for my vindication,

209

For what the plague can I say more
Than lazy dogs have done before;
Such stuff is nought but mere tautology,
And so take that for my apology.

First then for custards, my dear Mary,
The produce of your dainty dairy,
For stew'd, for bak'd, for boil'd, for roast,
And all the teas and all the toast;
With thankful tongue and bowing attitude,
I here present you with my gratitude:
Next for your apples, pears and plumbs
Acknowledgment in order comes;
For wine, for ale, for fowl, for fish—for
Ev'n all one's appetite can wish for:
But O ye pens, and O ye pencils,
And all ye scribbling utensils,
Say in what words and in what metre,
Shall unfeign'd admiration greet her,
For that rich banquet so refin'd
Her conversation gave the mind;
The solid meal of sense and worth,
Set off by the desert of mirth;
Wit's fruit and pleasure's genial bowl,
And all the joyous flow of soul;
For these, and every kind ingredient
That form'd your love—your most obedient.

                                        R 1791

An Epistle to John Sherratt, Esq.

Haec mihi erunt imis infixa medullis,
Perpetuusque ANIMI debitor HUJUS ero.
Ovid, de Trist., Eleg. iv.

OF all the offrings thanks can find,
None equally delights the mind;
Or charms so much, or holds so long.
As gratitude express'd in song.
We reckon all the BOOK of GRACE
By verses, as the source we trace,
And in the spirit all is great
By number, melody and weight.
By nature's light each heathen sage,
Has thus adorn'd th' immortal page;
Demosthenes and Plato's prose,
From skill in mystic measure flows;
And ROLT's sublime, historic stile,
Is better than the Muses smile.
Take then from heartiness profest,
What in the bard's conceit is best;
The golden sheaf desertion gleans
For want of better helps and means.

Well nigh seven years had fill'd their tale,
From Winter's urn to Autumn's scale,
And found no friend to grief and *Smart*,
Like Thee and Her, thy sweeter part;
Assisted by a friendly pair
That chose the side of CHRIST and PRAY'R,
To build the great foundation laid,
By one sublime, transcendent maid.
'Tis well to signalize a deed,
And have no precedent to plead;
'Tis blessing as by God we're told,
To come and visit friends in hold;

211

Which skill is greater in degree,
If goodness set the pris'ner free.
'Tis you that have in my behalf,
Produc'd the robe and kill'd the calf;
Have hail'd the *restoration day*,
And bid the loudest music play.
If therefore there is yet a note
Upon the lyre, that I devote,
To gratitude's divinest strains,
One gift of love for thee remains;
One gift above the common cast,
Of making fair memorials last.

Not He whose highly finish'd piece,
Outshone the chissel'd forms of Greece;
Who found with all his art and fame,
A partner in the house I claim;
Not he that pencils CHARLOTTE'S eyes,
And boldly bids for ROMNEY'S prize;
Not both the seats, where arts commune
Can blazon like a word in tune;
But this our young scholasticks con,
As warrant from th' *Apulian* Swan.
Then let us frame our steps to climb,
Beyond the sphere of chance and time,
And raise our thought on HOLY WRIT,
O'er mortal works and human wit.
The lively acts of CHRISTIAN LOVE,
Are treasur'd in the rolls above;
Where Archangelic concerts ring,
And God's accepted poets sing.
So Virtue's plan to parry praise,
Cannot obtain in after days,
Atchievements in the Christian cause,
Ascend to vast and sure applause;
Where Glory fixes to endure
All precious, permanent and pure.

Of such a class in such a sphere,
Shall thy distinguish'd deed appear;
Whose spirit open and avow'd
Array'd itself against the croud,
With chearfulness so much thine own,
And all thy motive God alone;
To run thy keel across the boom,
And save my vessel from her doom,
And cut her from the pirate's port,
Beneath the cannon of the fort,
With colours fresh and sails unfurl'd,
Was nobly dar'd to beat the world;
And stands for ever on record,
IF TRUTH AND LIFE BE GOD AND LORD.

P 1763

Munificence and Modesty

A Poem; The Hint from a Painting of Guido.

O VOICE OF APPROBATION, bless
The spirits still demanding less,
The more their natures have to need,
The more their services can plead;
The more their mighty merits claim—
The voice of Approbation came.

Fair MODESTY, divinely sweet,
With garb prepared, and lamp replete,
Lamented still from sun to sun
So much received, and nothing done.
Her abstinence was insincere,
Her studies not enough severe;
Her thoughts at fault and still to seek,
Her words inadequate and weak;
Her actions wretched and restrain'd,

Her passions neither balk'd nor rein'd.
Her head she waved in meek distrust,
Her eyes were fix'd to reach the dust;
Her cheeks were tinctured to receive
The blushes of the crimson eve,
Prophetic of a better day,
When thus she framed her hymn to pray.
'O Thou whose bounties never fail,
Who smil'st upon the lowly vale,
And giv'st fertility and peace
Their flow'ry lawn and golden fleece;
Who send'st the spirit of the breeze,
To bend the heads of stately trees,
Till pines with all their state and rank,
Bow like the bulrush on the bank.
Who bid'st the little brook flow on,
And warbling sooth the silent swan,
And spreading form the shaded lake,
Untill th' emerging rays retake
The transcript of the scene to Thee,
O FATHER of SIMPLICITY.
As this thy glossy turf I press,
And prostrate on my forehead bless,
Consider for the poor infirm,
The harmless sheep, th' obnoxious worm,
The stooping yoke that turn the soil,
And all the children of thy toil.
In fine, of all the num'rous race,
Of all that crowd and ought to grace
Thy vast immeasurable board,
To me the lowest lot afford.'

SHE bow'd, she sigh'd, and made her pause:
And instantly th' immense applause
Of thunder in the height was heard,
And all the host of Heav'n appear'd.
And thro' the great and glorious throng,

Of Seraphims, ten thousand strong
Came down that prince of high degree,
Th' archangel LIBERALITY.
A crown of Beryls graced his head,
His wings were closed, his hands were spread;
His stature nobler than the rest,
A sun and belt adorn'd his breast;
His voice was rapture to the ears,
His look like GRANBY in his geers;
When lighting on the dewy sod,
Thus spake the Almoner of God.
'Survey these scenes from east to west,
All earth in bloom and verdure drest;
Those olives planted by the line,
That forrest after God's design.
Those naked rocks that rise to bound,
The vine-infested elms around;
The golden meads that far extend,
And to the silver streams descend.
Those fields of corn in youthful green,
Where larks prepare the nest unseen.
Or turn your eyes, immortal Fair,
To yon gay walks of art and care,
Where the throng'd hive their sweets augment,
And murmur not, but thro' content.
That long canal so clear and deep,
Unmov'd but by the Crusion's leap;
That Grotto, which from Gani's mines,
And Ocean's ransack'd bosom shines.
I, whose commission's to dispense
The meed of God's munificence,
To thy undoubted worth resign,
These joys of thought and sense, as thine.'

I ASK not (MODESTY replied)
For wealthy regions far and wide;
I rest content, if but you spare,

What is the utmost of my pray'r;
A little cot my frame to house,
With room enough to pay my vows.
'Then take a view of yonder tow'rs,
Where Fortune deals her gifts in flow'rs;
Where that vast bulwark's proud disdain
Runs a long terras on the main;
Whose strong foundation Ocean laves,
And bustles with officious waves,
To bring with many a thousand sail,
Whate'er refinement can regale;
Rich fruits of oriental zest,
Perfumes of ARABY the blest,
With precious ornaments to wear,
Upon thy hands, thy neck, thy hair:
O Queen of the transcendent few,
All decoration is thy due.'
Remote from cities and their noise
Serenity herself enjoys,
And free from grandeur and expense,
Had best be cloth'd with innocence.
'If such thine elevated mind,
Chuse pleasures for thy sex design'd;
A blooming youth I will provide,
To make thee a transported bride;
To give each day some new delight,
And bless the soft connubial night.'
I may not act a double part,
And offer a divided heart;
Let other nymphs their swains endear,
For my affections are not here.
'Accomplish then that great desire,
To which the wise and good aspire;
A name that no distraction knows,
Whose fragrance is as SHARON's rose;
Which makes the highest flight of fame,
By vast and popular acclaim.'

O rather may I still refrain,
Nor run the risk of being vain;
To peace and silence let me cleave,
And *give* the glory—not receive.
'Yet, yet accept a gift of love,
The royal Sceptre and the Dove;
All things on earth thou shalt command,
Whatever heart, whatever hand;
Why are those charming looks aground?
Arise, aspire, thou shalt be crown'd.'
Talk not of crowns—I have no will,
No power, no thought.—'No more, be still.
Who's there?' The vast Cherubic flight,
Of thousand thousands on the right.
'Who's there?' The ORIEL and his SONG,
Full eighty thousand legions strong.—
'Hand from the nether zenith down
The chariot with the emeral'd crown
By Phœnix drawn.—Lo! this is SHE,
Which has achieved the first degree;
And scorning MAMMON and his leav'n,
Has one Eternity and Heav'n.'

PSO 1764

RELIGIOUS AND
DEVOTIONAL POEMS

To the Reverend and Learned Dr. Webster

Occasioned by his Dialogues on Anger and Forgiveness.

'TWAS when the omniscient creative pow'r
　　Display'd his wonders by a mortal's hand,
And, delegated at th' appointed hour,
　　　　Great MOSES led away his chosen band;
　　When ISRAEL's host, with all their stores,
　　Past thro' the ruby-tinctur'd crystal shores,
The wilderness of waters and of land:
　　Then persecution rag'd in heav'n's own cause,
　　And right or neighbouring kingdoms to infringe,
　　Strict justice for the breach of Nature's laws,
　　Strict justice, who's full sister to revenge:
　　The legislator held the scythe of fate,
　　　　Where'er his legions chanc'd to stray,
　　　　Death and destruction mark'd their bloody way;
Immoderate was their rage, for mortal was their hate.

But when the king of righteousness arose,
　　And on the illumin'd East serenely smil'd,
He shone with meekest mercy on his foes,
　　　　Bright as the sun, but as the moon-beams mild;
　　　　From anger, fell revenge, and discord free,
　　　　　　He bad war's hellish clangour cease,
　　　　　　In pastoral simplicity and peace,
And show'd to men that face, which MOSES could not
　　　　see.

Well hast thou, WEBSTER, pictur'd Christian love,
　　And copied our great master's fair design,
But livid Envy would the light remove,
　　　　Or croud thy portrait in a nook malign—
　　The Muse shall hold it up to popular view—
　　Where the more candid and judicious few

221

Shall think the bright original they see,
The likeness nobly lost in the identity.

Oh hadst thou liv'd in better days than these,
  E'er to excel by all was deem'd a shame!
Alas! thou hast no modern arts to please,
  And to deserve is all thy empty claim.
Else thou'dst been plac'd, by learning, and by wit,
There, where thy dignify'd inferiours sit—
  Oh *they* are in their generations wise,
Each path of interest *they* have sagely trod,—
  To live—to thrive—to rise—and still to rise—
Better to bow to men, than kneel to God.

Behold where poor unmansion'd Merit stands,
  All cold, and crampt with penury and pain;
Speechless thro' want, she rears th' imploring hands,
  And begs a little bread, but begs in vain;
While Bribery and Dulness, passing by,
Bid her, in sounds barbarian, starve and die.
      'Away' (they cry) 'we never saw thy name
        Or in Preferment's list, or that of Fame;
      Away—nor here the fate thou earn'st bewail,
Who canst not buy a vote, nor hast a soul for sale.'

Oh Indignation, wherefore wert thou given,
  If drowsy Patience deaden all thy rage?—
Yet we must *bear*—such is the will of heaven;
  And, WEBSTER, so prescribes thy candid page.
Then let us hear thee preach seraphic love,
Guide our disgusted thoughts to things above;
  So our free souls, fed with divine repast,
    (Unmindful of low mortals mean employ)
  Shall taste the present, recollect the past,
    And strongly hope for every future joy.

St 1751

On the Eternity of the Supreme Being

HAIL, wond'rous Being, who in pow'r supreme
Exists from everlasting, whose great Name
Deep in the human heart, and every atom
The Air, the Earth or azure Main contains,
In undecypher'd characters is wrote—
INCOMPREHENSIBLE!—O what can words
The weak interpreters of mortal thoughts,
Or what can thoughts (tho' wild of wing they rove
Thro' the vast Concave of th' ætherial round)
If to the Heav'n of Heavens they'd win their way
Advent'rous, like the birds of night they're lost,
And delug'd in the flood of dazling day.—

May then the youthful, uninspired Bard
Presume to hymn th' Eternal; may he soar
Where seraph, and where Cherubin on high
Resound th' unceasing plaudits, and with them
In the grand Chorus mix his feeble voice?

He may—if Thou, who from the witless babe
Ordainest honor, glory, strength and praise,
Uplift th' unpinion'd Muse, and deign t' assist,
GREAT POET of the UNIVERSE, his song.

Before this earthly Planet wound her course
Round Light's perennial fountain, before Light
Herself 'gan shine, and at th' inspiring word
Shot to existence in a blaze of day,
Before 'the Morning-Stars together sang'
And hail'd Thee Architect of countless worlds—
Thou art—all glorious, all-beneficent,
All Wisdom and Omnipotence thou art.

But is the Era of Creation fix'd
At when these Worlds began? Cou'd aught retard
Goodness, that knows no bounds, from blessing ever,
Or keep th' immense Artificer in sloth?
Avaunt the dust-directed crawling thought,

223

That Puissance immeasurably vast,
And Bounty inconceivable cou'd rest
Content, exhausted with one week of action—
No—in th' exertion of thy righteous pow'r,
Ten thousand times more active than the Sun,
Thou reign'd, and with a mighty hand compos'd
Systems innumerable, matchless all,
All stampt with thine uncounterfeited seal.

But yet (if still to more stupendous heights
The Muse unblam'd her aching sense may strain)
Perhaps wrapt up in contemplation deep,
The best of beings on the noblest theme
Might ruminate at leisure, Scope immense
Th' eternal Pow'r and Godhead to explore,
And with itself th' omniscient mind replete.
This were enough to fill the boundless All,
This were a Sabbath worthy the Supreme!
Perhaps enthron'd amidst a choicer few,
Of Sp'rits inferior, he might greatly plan
The two Prime Pillars of the Universe,
Creation and Redemption—and a while
Pause—with the grand presentiments of glory.

Perhaps—but all's conjecture here below,
All ignorance, and self-plum'd vanity—
O Thou, whose ways to wonder at's distrust,
Whom to describe's presumption (all we can, —
And all we may—) be glorified, be prais'd.

A Day shall come when all this Earth shall perish,
Nor leave behind ev'n Chaos; it shall come
When all the armies of the elements
Shall war against themselves, and mutual rage
To make Perdition triumph; it shall come,
When the capacious atmosphere above
Shall in sulphureous thunders groan, and die,
And vanish into void; the earth beneath
Shall sever to the center, and devour
Th' enormous blaze of the destructive flames.—

Ye rocks, that mock the raving of the floods,
And proudly frown upon th' impatient deep,
Where is your grandeur now? Ye foaming waves,
That all along th' immense Atlantic roar,
In vain ye swell; will a few drops suffice
To quench the inextinguishable fire?
Ye mountains, on whose cloud-crown'd tops the
    cedars
Are lessen'd into shrubs, magnific piles,
That prop the painted chambers of the heav'ns
And fix the earth continual; Athos, where;
Where, Tenerif's thy stateliness to day?
What, Ætna, are thy flames to these?—No more
Than the poor glow-worm to the golden Sun.

  Nor shall the verdant vallies then remain
Safe in their meek submission; they the debt
Of nature and of justice too must pay.
Yet I must weep for you, ye rival fair,
Arno and Andalusia; but for thee
More largely and with filial tears must weep,
O Albion, O my country; thou must join,
In vain dissever'd from the rest, must join
The terrors of th' inevitable ruin.

  Nor thou, illustrious monarch of the day;
Nor thou, fair queen of night; nor you, ye stars,
Tho' million leagues and million still remote,
Shall yet survive that day; Ye must submit
Sharers, not bright spectators of the scene.

  But tho' the earth shall to the center perish,
Nor leave behind ev'n Chaos; tho' the air
With all the elements must pass away,
Vain as an ideot's dream; tho' the huge rocks,
That brandish the tall cedars on their tops,
With humbler vales must to perdition yield;
Tho' the gilt Sun, and silver-tressed Moon
With all her bright retinue, must be lost;
Yet thou, Great Father of the world, surviv'st

Eternal, as thou wert: Yet still survives
The soul of man immortal, perfect now,
And candidate for unexpiring joys.

   He comes! He comes! the awful trump I hear;
The flaming sword's intolerable blaze
I see; He comes! th' Archangel from above.
'Arise, ye tenants of the silent grave,
Awake incorruptible and arise;
From east to west, from the antarctic pole
To regions hyperborean, all ye sons,
Ye sons of Adam, and ye heirs of Heav'n—
Arise, ye tenants of the silent grave,
Awake incorruptible and arise.'

   'Tis then, nor sooner, that the restless mind
Shall find itself at home; and like the ark
Fix'd on the mountain-top, shall look aloft
O'er the vague passage of precarious life;
And, winds and waves and rocks and tempests past,
Enjoy the everlasting calm of heav'n:
'Tis then, nor sooner, that the deathless soul
Shall justly know its nature and its rise:
'Tis then the human tongue new-tun'd shall give
Praises more worthy the eternal ear.
Yet what we can, we ought;—and therefore, Thou,
Purge thou my heart, Omnipotent and Good!
Purge thou my heart with hyssop, lest like Cain
I offer fruitless sacrifice, with gifts
Offend, and not propitiate the Ador'd.
Tho' gratitude were bless'd with all the pow'rs
Her bursting heart cou'd long for, tho' the swift,
The firey-wing'd imagination soar'd
Beyond ambition's wish—yet all were vain
To speak Him as he is, who is INEFFABLE.
Yet still let reason thro' the eye of faith
View him with fearful love; let truth pronounce,
And adoration on her bended knee
With heav'n directed hands confess His reign,

And let th' Angelic, Archangelic band
With all the Hosts of Heav'n, cherubic Forms,
And forms Seraphic, with their silver trumps
And golden lyres attend:—'For Thou art holy,
For thou art One, th' Eternal, who alone
Exerts all goodness, and transcends all praise.'

1750

On the Immensity of the Supreme Being

ONCE more I dare to rouse the sounding string,
The poet of my God—Awake my glory,
Awake my lute and harp—my self shall wake,
Soon as the stately night-exploding bird
In lively lay sings welcome to the dawn.

   List ye! how Nature with ten thousand tongues
Begins the grand thanksgiving, Hail, all hail,
Ye tenants of the forest and the field!
My fellow subjects of th' eternal King,
I gladly join your Mattins, and with you
Confess his presence, and report his praise.

   O thou, who or the Lambkin, or the Dove,
When offer'd by the lowly, meek, and poor,
Prefer'st to Pride's whole hecatomb, accept
This mean Essay, nor from thy treasure-house
Of Glory' immense, the orphan's mite exclude.

   What tho' th' Almighty's regal throne be rais'd
High o'er yon azure heav'n's exalted dome
By mortal eye unken'd—where East nor West
Nor South, nor blust'ring North has breath to blow;
Albeit He there with Angels, and with Saints
Hold conference, and to his radiant host
Ev'n face to face stand visibly confest:
Yet know that nor in Presence or in Pow'r
Shines He less perfect here; 'tis Man's dim eye

227

That makes th' obscurity. He is the same,
Alike in all his Universe the same.

   Whether the mind along the spangled sky
Measures her pathless walk, studious to view
Thy works of vaster fabric, where the Planets
Weave their harmonious rounds, their march directing
Still faithful, still inconstant to the Sun;
Or where the Comet thro' space infinite
(Tho' whirling worlds oppose, and globes of fire)
Darts, like a javelin, to his destin'd goal.
Or where in Heav'n above the Heav'n of Heav'ns
Burn brighter suns, and goodlier planets roll
With Satellits more glorious—Thou art there.

   Or whether on the Ocean's boist'rous back
Thou ride triumphant, and with out-stretch'd arm
Curb the wild winds and discipline the billows,
The suppliant sailor finds Thee there, his chief,
His only help—when Thou rebuk'st the storm—
It ceases—and the vessel gently glides
Along the glassy level of the calm.

   Oh! cou'd I search the bosom of the sea,
Down the great depth descending; there thy works
Wou'd also speak thy residence; and there
Wou'd I thy servant, like the still profound,
Astonish'd into silence muse thy praise!
Behold! behold! th' unplanted garden round
Of vegetable coral, sea-flow'rs gay,
And shrubs of amber from the pearl-pav'd bottom
Rise richly varied, where the finny race
In blithe security their gambols play:
While high above their heads Leviathan
The terror and the glory of the main
His pastime takes with transport, proud to see
The ocean's vast dominion all his own.

   Hence thro' the genial bowels of the earth
Easy may fancy pass; till at thy mines,
Gani, or *Raolconda*, she arrive,

And from the adamant's imperial blaze
Form weak ideas of her maker's glory.
Next to *Pegu* or *Ceylon* let me rove,
Where the rich ruby (deem'd by sages old
Of sovereign virtue) sparkles ev'n like Sirius
And blushes into flames. Thence will I go
To undermine the treasure-fertile womb
Of the huge *Pyrenean*, to detect
The Agat and the deep-intrenched gem
Of kindred Jasper—Nature in them both
Delights to play the Mimic on herself;
And in their veins she oft pourtrays the forms
Of leaning hills, of trees erect, and streams
Now stealing softly on, now thund'ring down
In desperate cascade, with flow'rs and beasts
And all the living landskip of the vale.
In vain thy pencil, *Claudio*, or *Poussin*,
Or thine, immortal *Guido*, wou'd essay
Such skill to imitate—it is the hand
Of God himself—for God himself is there.

Hence with the ascending springs let me advance,
Thro' beds of magnets, minerals and spar,
Up to the mountain's summit, there t' indulge
Th' ambition of the comprehensive eye,
That dares to call th' Horizon all her own.
Behold the forest, and th' expansive verdure
Of yonder level lawn, whose smooth-shorn sod
No object interrupts, unless the oak
His lordly head uprears, and branching arms
Extends—Behold in regal solitude,
And pastoral magnificence he stands
So simple! and so great! the under-wood
Of meaner rank an awful distance keep.
Yet Thou art there, yet God himself is there
Ev'n on the bush (tho' not as when to Moses
He shone in burning Majesty reveal'd)
Nathless conspicuous in the linnet's throat

Is his unbounded goodness—Thee her Maker,
Thee her Preserver chants she in her song;
While the all emulative vocal tribe
The grateful lesson learn—no other voice
Is heard, no other sound—for in attention
Buried, ev'n babbling *Echo* holds her peace.
   Now from the plains, where th' unbounded prospect
Gives liberty her utmost scope to range,
Turn we to yon enclosures, where appears
Chequer'd variety in all her forms,
Which the vague mind attract and still suspend
With sweet perplexity. What are yon tow'rs
The work of lab'ring man and clumsy art
Seen with the ring-dove's nest—on that tall beech
Her pensile house the feather'd Artist builds—
The rocking winds molest her not; for see,
With such due poize the wond'rous fabrick's hung,
That, like the compass in the bark, it keeps
True to itself and stedfast ev'n in storms.
Thou ideot, that asserts there is no God,
View and be dumb for ever—
Go bid *Vitruvios* or *Palladio* build
The bee his mansion, or the ant her cave—
Go call *Correggio*, or let *Titian* come
To paint the hawthorn's bloom, or teach the cherry
To blush with just vermilion—hence away—
Hence ye prophane! for God himself is here.
Vain were th' attempt, and impious to trace
Thro' all his works th' Artificer Divine—
And tho' nor shining sun, nor twinkling star
Bedeck'd the crimson curtains of the sky;
Tho' neither vegetable, beast, nor bird
Were extant on the surface of this ball,
Nor lurking gem beneath; tho' the great sea
Slept in profound stagnation, and the air
Had left no thunder to pronounce its maker;
Yet man at home, within himself, might find

ON THE OMNISCIENCE OF THE SUPREME BEING

The Deity immense, and in that frame
So fearfully, so wonderfully made,
See and adore his providence and pow'r—
I see, and I adore—O God most bounteous!
O infinite of Goodness and of Glory!
The knee, that Thou hast shap'd, shall bend to Thee,
The tongue, which Thou has tun'd, shall chant thy
    praise,
And thine own image, the immortal soul,
Shall consecrate herself to Thee for ever.

                         1751

On the Omniscience of the Supreme Being

ARISE, divine Urania, with new strains
To hymn thy God, and thou, immortal Fame,
Arise, and blow thy everlasting trump.
All glory to th' Omniscient, and praise,
And pow'r, and domination in the height!
And thou, cherubic Gratitude, whose voice
To pious ears sounds silverly so sweet,
Come with thy precious incense, bring thy gifts,
And with thy choicest stores the altar crown.
Thou too, my Heart, whom he, and he alone,
Who all things knows, can know, with love replete,
Regenerate, and pure, pour all thyself
A living sacrifice before his throne:
And may th' eternal, high mysterious tree,
That in the center of the arched Heav'ns
Bears the rich fruit of knowledge, with some branch
Stoop to my humble reach, and bless my toil!
    When in my mother's womb conceal'd I lay
A senseless embryo, then my soul thou knewst,
Knewst all her future workings, every thought,
And every faint idea yet unform'd.

When up the imperceptible ascent
Of growing years, led by thy hand, I rose,
Perception's gradual light, that ever dawns
Insensibly to day, thou didst vouchsafe,
And teach me by that reason thou inspir'dst,
That what of knowledge in my mind was low,
Imperfect, incorrect—in thee is wonderous,
Uncircumscrib'd, unsearchably profound,
And estimable solely by itself.

What is that secret pow'r, that guides the brutes,
Which ignorance calls instinct? 'Tis from thee,
It is the operation of thine hands,
Immediate, instantaneous; 'tis thy wisdom,
That glorious shines transparent thro' thy works.
Who taught the pye, or who forewarn'd the jay
To shun the deadly nightshade? tho' the cherry
Boasts not a glossier hue, nor does the plumb
Lure with more seeming sweets the amorous eye,
Yet will not the sagacious birds, decoy'd
By fair appearance, touch the noxious fruit,
They know to taste is fatal, whence alarm'd
Swift on the winnowing winds they work their way.
Go to, proud reas'ner, philosophic man,
Hast thou such prudence, thou such knowledge?—No.
Full many a race has fall'n into the snare
Of meretricious looks, of pleasing surface,
And oft in desert isles the famish'd pilgrim
By forms of fruit, and luscious taste beguil'd,
Like his forefather Adam, eats and dies.
For why? his wisdom on the leaden feet
Of slow experience, dully tedious, creeps,
And comes, like vengeance, after long delay.

The venerable sage, that nightly trims
The learned lamp, t' investigate the pow'rs
Of plants medicinal, the earth, the air,
And the dark regions of the fossil world,
Grows old in following, what he ne'er shall find;

Studious in vain! till haply, at the last
He spies a mist, then shapes it into mountains,
And baseless fabric from conjecture builds.
While the domestic animal, that guards
At midnight hours his threshold, if oppress'd
By sudden sickness, at his master's feet
Begs not that aid his services might claim,
But is his own physician, knows the case,
And from th' emetic herbage works his cure.
Hark, from afar the feather'd matron screams,
And all her brood alarms, the docile crew
Accept the signal one and all, expert
In th' art of nature and unlearn'd deceit:
Along the sod, in counterfeited death,
Mute, motionless they lie; full well appriz'd,
That the rapacious adversary's near.
But who inform'd her of the approaching danger,
Who taught the cautious mother that the hawk
Was hatcht her foe, and liv'd by her destruction?
Her own prophetic soul is active in her,
And more than human providence her guard.

    When Philomela, e'er the cold domain
Of cripled winter 'gins t' advance, prepares
Her annual flight, and in some poplar shade
Takes her melodious leave, who then's her pilot?
Who points her passage thro' the pathless void
To realms from us remote, to us unknown?
Her science is the science of her God.
Not the magnetic index to the North
E'er ascertains her course, nor buoy, nor beacon,
She Heav'n-taught voyager, that sails in air,
Courts nor coy West nor East, but instant knows
What Newton, or not sought, or sought in vain.

    Illustrious name, irrefragable proof
Of man's vast genius, and the soaring soul!
Yet what wert thou to him, who knew his works,
Before creation form'd them, long before

He measur'd in the hollow of his hand
Th' exulting ocean, and the highest heav'ns
He comprehended with a span, and weigh'd
The mighty mountains in his golden Scales:
Who shone supreme, who was himself the light,
E'er yet Refraction learn'd her skill to paint,
And bend athwart the clouds her beauteous bow.

When Knowledge at her father's dread command
Resign'd to Israel's king her golden key,
Oh to have join'd the frequent auditors
In wonder and delight, that whilom heard
Great Solomon descanting on the brutes!
Oh how sublimely glorious to apply
To God's own honour, and good will to man,
That wisdom he alone of men possess'd
In plenitude so rich, and scope so rare!
How did he rouse the pamper'd silken sons
Of bloated ease, by placing to their view
The sage industrious ant, the wisest insect,
And best œconomist of all the field!
Tho' she presumes not by the solar orb
To measure time and seasons, nor consults
Chaldean calculations, for a guide;
Yet conscious that December's on the march
Pointing with icie hand to want and woe,
She waits his dire approach, and undismay'd
Receives him as a welcome guest, prepar'd
Against the churlish winter's fiercest blow.
For when, as yet the favourable Sun
Gives to the genial earth th' enlivening ray,
Not the poor suffering slave, that hourly toils
To rive the groaning earth for ill-sought gold,
Endures such trouble, such fatigue, as she;
While all her subterraneous avenues,
And storm-proof cells, with management most meet
And unexampled housewifry, she forms,
Then to the field she hies, and on her back,

234

Burden immense! she bears the cumbrous corn.
Then many a weary step, and many a strain,
And many a grievous groan subdued, at length
Up the huge hill she hardly heaves it home:
Nor rests she here her providence, but nips
With subtle tooth the grain, lest from her garner
In mischievous fertility it steal,
And back to day-light vegetate its way.
Go to the ant, thou sluggard, learn to live,
And by her wary ways reform thine own.
But, if thy deaden'd sense, and listless thought
More glaring evidence demand; behold,
Where you pellucid populous hive presents
A yet uncopied model to the world!
There Machiavel in the reflecting glass
May read himself a fool. The Chemist there
May with astonishment invidious view
His toils outdone by each plebeian Bee,
Who, at the royal mandate, on the wing
From various herbs, and from discordant flow'rs
A perfect harmony of sweets compounds.

  Avaunt Conceit, Ambition take thy flight
Back to the prince of vanity and air!
Oh! 'tis a thought of energy most piercing,
Form'd to make pride grow humble; form'd to force
Its weight on the reluctant mind, and give her
A true but irksome image of herself.
Woful vicissitude! when Man, fall'n Man,
Who first from Heav'n, from gracious God himself,
Learn'd knowledge of the Brutes, must know by
      Brutes
Instructed and reproach'd, the scale of being;
By slow degrees from lowly steps ascend,
And trace Omniscience upwards to its spring!
Yet murmur not, but praise—for tho' we stand
Of many a Godlike privilege amerc'd
By Adam's dire transgression, tho' no more

Is Paradise our home, but o'er the portal
Hangs in terrific pomp the burning blade;
Still with ten thousand beauties blooms the Earth,
With pleasures populous, and with riches crown'd.
Still is there scope for wonder and for love
Ev'n to their last exertion—show'rs of blessings
Far more than human virtue can deserve,
Or hope expect, or gratitude return.
Then, O ye people, O ye Sons of Men,
Whatever be the colour of your lives,
Whatever portion of itself his Wisdom
Shall deign t' allow, still patiently abide,
And praise him more and more; nor cease to chant
ALL GLORY TO THE OMNISCIENT, AND PRAISE,
AND POW'R, AND DOMINATION IN THE HEIGHT!
And thou, cherubic Gratitude, whose voice
To pious ears sounds silverly so sweet.
Come with the precious incense, bring thy gifts,
And with the choicest stores the altar crown.
TΩ ΘΕΩ ΔΟΞΑ.

1752

On the Power of the Supreme Being

' TREMBLE, thou Earth!' th' anointed poet said,
'At God's bright presence, tremble, all ye mountains,
And all ye hillocks on the surface bound.'
Then once again, ye glorious thunders roll,
The Muse with transport hears ye, once again
Convulse the solid continent, and shake,
Grand music of omnipotence, the isles.
'Tis thy terrific voice, thou God of power,
'Tis thy terrific voice; all Nature hears it
Awaken'd and alarm'd; she feels its force,
In every spring she feels it, every wheel,

And every movement of her vast machine.
Behold! quakes Apennine, behold! recoils
Athos, and all the hoary-headed Alps
Leap from their bases at the godlike sound.
But what is this, celestial though the note,
And proclamation of the reign supreme,
Compar'd with such as, for a mortal ear
Too great, amaze the incorporeal worlds?
Shou'd ocean to his congretated waves
Call in each river, cataract, and lake,
And with the watery world down a huge rock
Fall headlong in one horrible cascade,
'Twere but the echo of the parting breeze,
When Zephyr faints upon the lilly's breast,
'Twere but the ceasing of some instrument,
When the last ling'ring undulation
Dies on the doubting ear, if nam'd with sounds
So mighty! so stupendous! so divine!
    But not alone in the aërial vault
Does he the dread theocracy maintain;
For oft, enrag'd with his intestine thunders,
He harrows up the bowels of the earth,
And shocks the central magnet—Cities then
Totter on their foundations, stately columns,
Magnific walls, and heav'n-assaulting spires.
What tho' in haughty eminence erect
Stands the strong citadel, and frowns defiance
On adverse hosts, though many a bastion jut
Forth from the ramparts elevated mound,
Vain the poor providence of human art,
And mortal strength how vain! while underneath
Triumphs his mining vengeance in th' uproar
Of shatter'd towers, riven rocks, and mountains,
With clamour inconceivable uptorn,
And hurl'd adown th' abyss. Sulphureous pyrites
Bursting abrupt from darkness into day,
With din outrageous and destructive ire

Augment the hideous tumult, while it wounds
Th' afflicted ear, and terrifies the eye
And rends the heart in twain. Twice have we felt,
Within Augusta's walls, twice have we felt
Thy tnreaten'd indignation, but ev'n Thou,
Incens'd Omnipotent, art gracious ever,
Thy goodness infinite but mildly warn'd us
With mercy-blended wrath: O spare us still,
Nor send more dire conviction: we confess
That thou art He, th' Almighty: we believe:
For at thy righteous power whole systems quake,
For at thy nod tremble ten thousand worlds.

   Hark! on the winged whirlwind's rapid rage,
Which is and is not in a moment—hark!
On the hurricane's tempestuous sweep he rides
Invincible, and oaks and pines and cedars
And forests are no more. For, conflict dreadful!
The West encounters East, and Notus meets
In his career the Hyperborean blast.
The lordly lions shudd'ring seek their Dens,
And fly like tim'rous deer; the king of birds,
Who dar'd the solar ray, is weak of wing
And faints and falls and dies;—while He supreme
Stands stedfast if in the center of the storm.

   Wherefore, ye objects terrible and great,
Ye thunders, earthquakes, and ye fire-fraught wombs
Of fell volcanoes, whirlwinds, hurricanes,
And boiling billows hail! in chorus join
To celebrate and magnify your Maker,
Who yet in works of a minuter mould
Is not less manifest, is not less mighty.

   Survey the magnet's sympathetic love,
That wooes the yielding needle; contemplate
Th' attractive amber's power, invisible
Ev'n to the mental eye; or when the blow
Sent from th' electric sphere assaults thy frame,
Shew me the hand, that dealt it!—baffled here

By his omnipotence, Philosophy
Slowly her thoughts inadequate revolves,
And stands, with all his circling wonders round her,
Like heavy Saturn in th' etherial space
Begirt with an inexplicable ring.

   If such the operations of his power,
Which at all seasons and in ev'ry place
(Rul'd by establish'd laws and current nature)
Arrest th' attention! Who? O Who shall tell
His acts miraculous, when by his own decrees
Repeals he, or suspends, when by the hand
Of Moses or of Joshua, or the mouths
Of his prophetic seers, such deeds he wrought,
Before th' astonish'd Sun's all-seeing eye,
That Faith was scarce a virtue. Need I sing
The fate of Pharaoh and his numerous band
Lost in the reflux of the watry walls,
That melted to their fluid state again?
Need I recount how Sampson's warlike arm
With more than mortal nerves was strung t' o'erthrow
Idolatrous Philistia? Shall I tell
How David triumph'd, and what Job sustain'd?
—But, O supreme, unutterable mercy!
O love unequal'd, mystery immense,
Which angels long t'unfold! 'tis man's redemption
That crowns thy glory, and thy pow'r confirms,
Confirms the great, th' uncontroverted claim.
When from the Virgin's unpolluted womb,
Shone forth the Sun of Righteousness reveal'd
And on benighted reason pour'd the day;
'Let there be peace' (he said) and all was calm
Amongst the warring world—calm as the sea,
When 'O, be still, ye boisterous winds,' he cry'd,
And not a breath was blown, nor murmur heard.
His was a life of miracles and might,
And charity and love, ere yet he taste
The bitter draught of death, ere yet he rise

Victorious o'er the universal foe,
And Death, and Sin and Hell in triumph lead.
His by the right of conquest is mankind,
And in sweet servitude and golden bonds
Were ty'd to him for ever.—O how easy
Is his ungalling Yoke, and all his burdens
'Tis ecstacy to bear! Him, blessed Shepherd,
His flocks shall follow through the maze of life,
And shades that tend to Day-spring from on high;
And as the radiant roses, after fading,
In fuller foliage and more fragrant breath
Revive in smiling spring, so shall it fare
With those that love him—for sweet is their savour,
And all eternity shall be their spring.
Then shall the gates and everlasting doors,
At which the *King of Glory* enters in,
Be to the saints unbarr'd: and there, where pleasure
Boasts an undying bloom, where dubious hope
Is certainty, and grief-attended love
Is freed from passion—there we'll celebrate
With worthier numbers, him, who is, and was,
And in immortal prowess King of Kings
Shall be the Monarch of all worlds for ever.

1754

On the Goodness of the Supreme Being

ORPHEUS, for so the Gentiles call'd thy name,
Israel's sweet psalmist, who alone could wake
Th' inanimate to motion; who alone
The joyful hillocks, the applauding rocks,
And floods with musical persuasion drew;
Thou, who to hail and snow gav'st voice and sound,
And mad'st the mute melodious!—greater yet
Was thy divinest skill, and rul'd o'er more

Than art or nature; for thy tuneful touch
Drove trembling Satan from the heart of Saul,
And quell'd the evil Angel:—in this breast
Some portion of thy genuine spirit breathe,
And lift me from myself; each thought impure
Banish; each low idea raise, refine,
Enlarge, and sanctify;—so shall the muse
Above the stars aspire, and aim to praise
Her God on earth, as he is prais'd in heaven.

Immense Creator! whose all-pow'rful hand
Fram'd universal Being, and whose Eye
Saw like thyself, that all things form'd were good;
Where shall the tim'rous bard thy praise begin,
Where end the purest sacrifice of song,
And just thanksgiving?—The thought-kindling light,
Thy prime production, darts upon my mind
Its vivifying beams, my heart illumines,
And fills my soul with gratitude and Thee.
Hail to the chearful rays of ruddy morn,
That paint that streaky East, and blithsome rouse
The birds, the cattle, and mankind from rest!
Hail to the freshness of the early breeze,
And Iris dancing on the new-fall'n dew!
Without the aid of yonder golden globe
Lost were the garnet's lustre, lost the lilly,
The tulip and auricula's spotted pride;
Lost were the peacock's plumage, to the sight
So pleasing in its pomp and glossy glow.
O thrice-illustrious! were it not for thee
Those pansies, that reclining from the bank,
View through th' immaculate, pellucid stream
Their portraiture in the inverted heaven,
Might as well change their triple boast, the white,
The purple, and the gold, that far outvie
The Eastern monarch's garb, ev'n with the dock,
Ev'n with the baneful hemlock's irksome green.
Without thy aid, without thy gladsome beams

The tribes of woodland warblers wou'd remain
Mute on the bending branches, nor recite
The praise of him, who, e'er he form'd their lord,
Their voices tun'd to transport, wing'd their flight,
And bade them call for nurture, and receive;
And lo! they call; the blackbird and the thrush,
The woodlark, and the redbreast jointly call;
He hears and feeds their feather'd families,
He feeds his sweet musicians,—nor neglects
Th' invoking ravens in the greenwood wide;
And though their throats coarse ruttling hurt the ear,
They mean it all for music, thanks and praise
They mean, and leave ingratitude to man,—
But not to all,—for hark the organs blow
Their swelling notes round the cathedral's dome,
And grace th' harmonious choir, celestial feast
To pious ears, and med'cine of the mind;
The thrilling trebles and the manly base
Join in accordance meet, and with one voice
All to the sacred subject suit their song.
While in each breast sweet melancholy reigns
Angelically pensive, till the joy
Improves and purifies;—the solemn scene
The Sun through storied panes surveys with awe,
And bashfully with-holds each bolder beam.
Here, as her home, from morn to eve frequents
The cherub Gratitude;—behold her eyes!
With love and gladness weepingly they shed
Extatic smiles; the incense, that her hands
Uprear, is sweeter than the breath of May
C ught from the nectarine's blossom, and her voice
Is more than voice can tell; to him she sings,
To him who feeds, who clothes and who adorns,
Who made and who preserves, whatever dwells
In air, in steadfast earth, or fickle sea.
O he is good, he is immensely good!
Who all things form'd, and form'd them all for man;

242

ON THE GOODNESS OF THE SUPREME BEING

Who mark'd the climates, varied every zone,
Dispensing all his blessings for the best
In order and in beauty:—raise, attend,
Attest, and praise, ye quarters of the world!
Bow down, ye elephants, submissive bow
To him, who made the mite; though Asia's pride,
Ye carry armies on your tow'r-crown'd backs,
And grace the turban'd tyrants, bow to him
Who is as great, as perfect and as good
In his less-striking wonders, till at length
The eye's at fault and seeks the assisting glass.
Approach and bring from Araby the blest
The fragrant cassia, frankincense and myrrh,
And meekly kneeling at the altar's foot
Lay all the tributary incense down.
Stoop, sable Africa, with rev'rence stoop,
And from thy brow take off the painted plume;
With golden ingots all thy camels load
T' adorn his temples, hasten with thy spear
Reverted, and thy trusty bow unstrung,
While unpursu'd thy lions roam and roar,
And ruin'd tow'rs, rude rocks and caverns wide
Remurmur to the glorious, surly sound.
And thou, fair India, whose immense domain
To counterpoise the Hemisphere extends,
Haste from the West, and with thy fruits and flow'rs;
Thy mines and med'cines, wealthy maid, attend.
More than the plenteousness so fam'd to flow
By fabling bards from Amalthea's horn
Is thine; thine therefore be a portion due
Of thanks and praise: come with thy brilliant crown
And vest of furr, and from thy fragrant lap
Pomegranates and the rich ananas pour.
But chiefly thou, Europa, seat of grace
And christian excellence, his goodness own,
Forth from ten thousand temples pour his praise;
Clad in the armour of the living God

Approach, unsheath the spirit's flaming sword;
Faith's shield, Salvation's glory-compass'd helm
With fortitude assume, and o'er your heart
Fair truth's invulnerable breast-plate spread;
Then join the general chorus of all worlds,
And let the song of charity begin
In strains seraphic, and melodious pray'r.
'O all-sufficient, all beneficent,
Thou God of goodness and of glory, hear!
Thou, who to lowliest minds dost condescend,
Assuming passions to enforce thy laws,
Adopting jealousy to prove thy love:
Thou, who resign'd humility uphold,
Ev'n as the florist props the drooping rose,
But quell tyrannic pride with peerless pow'r,
Ev'n as the tempest rives the stubborn oak,
O all-sufficient, all-beneficent,
Thou God of goodness and of glory, hear!
Bless all mankind, and bring them in the end
To Heav'n, to immortality, and THEE!'

1756

Hymn to the Supreme Being

On recovery from a dangerous fit of illness.

WHEN *Israel's* ruler on the royal bed
  In anguish and in perturbation lay,
The down reliev'd not his anointed head,
  And rest gave place to horror and dismay.
Fast flow'd the tears, high heav'd each gasping sigh
When God's own prophet thunder'd—MONARCH,
    THOU MUST DIE.

'And must I go,' th' illustrious mourner cry'd,
  'I who have serv'd thee still in faith and truth,

Whose snow-white conscience no foul crime has died
   From youth to manhood, infancy to youth,
Like *David*, who have still rever'd thy word
The sovereign of myself and servant of the Lord!'

The judge Almighty heard his suppliant's moan,
   Repeal'd his sentence, and his health restor'd;
The beams of mercy on his temples shone,
   Shot from that heaven to which his sighs had soar'd;
The Sun retreated at his maker's nod
And miracles confirm the genuine work of God.

But, O immortals! What had I to plead
   When death stood o'er me with his threat'ning
     lance,
When reason left me in the time of need,
   And sense was lost in terror or in trance,
My sick'ning soul was with my blood inflam'd,
   And the celestial image sunk, defac'd and maim'd.

I sent back memory, in heedful guise,
   To search the records of preceding years;
Home, like the raven to the ark, she flies,
   Croaking bad tidings to my trembling ears.
O Sun, again that thy retreat was made,
And threw my follies back into the friendly shade!

But who are they, that bid affliction cease!—
   Redemption and forgiveness, heavenly sounds!
Behold the dove that brings the branch of peace,
   Behold the balm that heals the gaping wounds—
Vengeance divine's by penitence supprest—
She struggles with the angel, conquers, and is blest.

Yet hold, presumption, nor too fondly climb,
   And thou too hold, O horrible despair!
In man humility's alone sublime,
   Who diffidently hopes he's *Christ's* own care—

O all-sufficient Lamb! in death's dread hour
Thy merits who shall slight, or who can doubt thy
    power?

But soul-rejoicing health again returns,
    The blood meanders gentle in each vein,
The lamp of life renew'd with vigour burns,
    And exil'd reason takes her seat again—
Brisk leaps the heart, the mind's at large once more,
To love, to praise, to bless, to wonder and adore.

The virtuous partner of my nuptial bands,
    Appear'd a widow to my frantic sight;
My little prattlers lifting up their hands,
    Beckon me back to them, to life, and light;
I come, ye spotless sweets! I come again,
Nor have your tears been shed, nor have ye knelt in
    vain.

All glory to th' ETERNAL, to th' IMMENSE,
    All glory to th' OMNISCIENT and GOOD,
Whose powr's uncircumscrib'd, whose love's intense,
    But yet whose justice ne'er could be withstood.
Except thro' him—thro' him, who stands alone,
Of worth, of weight allow'd for all Mankind t' atone!

He rais'd the lame, the lepers he made whole,
    He fix'd the palsied nerves of weak decay,
He drove out Satan from the tortur'd soul,
    And to the blind gave or restor'd the day,—
Nay more,—far more unequal'd pangs sustain'd,
Till his lost fallen flock his taintless blood regain'd.

My feeble feet refus'd my body's weight,
    Nor wou'd my eyes admit the glorious light,
My nerves convuls'd shook fearful of their fate,
    My mind lay open to the powers of night.

246

HYMN TO THE SUPREME BEING

He pitying did a second birth bestow
A birth of joy--not like the first of tears and woe.

Ye strengthen'd feet, forth to his altar move;
   Quicken, ye new-strung nerves, th' enraptur'd lyre;
Ye heav'n-directed eyes, o'erflow with love;
   Glow, glow, my soul, with pure seraphic fire;
Deeds, thoughts, and words no more his mandates
    break,
But to his endless glory work, conceive, and speak.

O! penitence, to virtue near allied,
   Thou can'st new joys e'en to the blest impart;
The list'ning angels lay their harps aside
   To hear the music of thy contrite heart;
And heav'n itself wears a more radiant face,
When charity presents thee to the throne of grace.

Chief of metallic forms is regal gold;
   Of elements, the limpid fount that flows;
Give me 'mongst gems the brilliant to behold;
   O'er *Flora's* flock imperial is the rose;
Above all birds the sov'reign eagle soars;
And monarch of the field the lordly lion roars.

What can with great *Leviathan* compare,
   Who takes his pastime in the mighty main?
What, like the *Sun*, shines thro' the realms of air,
   And gilds and glorifies th' ethereal plain—
Yet what are these to man, who bears the sway;
For all was made for him—to serve and to obey.

Thus in high heaven charity is great,
   Faith, hope, devotion hold a lower place;
On her the cherubs and the seraphs wait,
   Her, every virtue courts, and every grace;

See! on the right, close by th' Almighty's throne,
In him she shines confest, who came to make her
    known.

Deep-rooted in my heart then let her grow,
    That for the past the future may atone;
That I may act what thou hast giv'n to know,
    That I may live for THEE and THEE alone,
And justify those sweetest words from Heav'n,
'THAT HE SHALL LOVE THEE MOST TO WHOM THOU'ST
    MOST FORGIVEN.'

                                 1756

Jubilate Agno

Roman numerals indicate the pages of the manuscript.

I

REJOICE in God, O ye Tongues; give the glory to the Lord, and the Lamb.   1

Nations, and languages, and every Creature, in which is the breath of Life.

Let man and beast appear before him, and magnify his name together.

Let Noah and his company approach the throne of Grace, and do homage to the Ark of their Salvation.

Let Abraham present a Ram, and worship the God of his Redemption.   5

Let Isaac, the Bridegroom, kneel with his Camels, and bless the hope of his pilgrimage.

Let Jacob, and his speckled Drove adore the good Shepherd of Israel.

Let Esau offer a scape Goat for his seed, and rejoice in the blessing of God his father.

Let Nimrod, the mighty hunter, bind a Leopard to the altar, and consecrate his spear to the Lord.

Let Ishmael dedicate a Tyger, and give praise for the liberty, in which the Lord has set him at large.   10

Let Balaam appear with an Ass, and bless the Lord his people and his creatures for a reward eternal.

Let Anah, the son of Zibion, lead a Mule to the temple, and bless God, who amerces the consolation of the creature for the service of Man.

Let Daniel come forth with a Lion, and praise God with all his might through faith in Christ Jesus.

Let Naphthali with an Hind give glory in the goodly words of Thanksgiving.

15 Let Aaron, the high priest, sanctify a Bull, and let
   him go free to the Lord and Giver of Life.

Let the Levites of the Lord take the Beavers of the
   brook alive into the Ark of the Testimony.

Let Eleazar with the Ermine serve the Lord decently
   and in purity.

Let Ithamar minister with a Chamois, and bless the
   name of Him, which cloatheth the naked.

Let Gershom with an Pygarg bless the name of Him,
   who feedeth the hungry.

20 Let Merari praise the wisdom and power of God with
   the Coney, who scoopeth the rock, and archeth in
   the sand.

Let Kohath serve with the Sable, and bless God in
   the ornaments of the Temple.

Let Jehoiada bless God with an Hare, whose mazes
   are determined for the health of the body and to
   parry the adversary.

Let Ahitub humble himself with an Ape before
   Almighty God, who is the maker of variety and
   pleasantry.

Let Abiathar with a Fox praise the name of the Lord,
   who ballances craft against strength and skill
   against number.

25 Let Moses, the Man of God, bless with a Lizard, in
   the sweet majesty of good-nature, and the mag-
   nanimity of meekness.

II

1 Let Joshua praise God with an Unicorn—the swift-
   ness of the Lord, and the strength of the Lord, and
   the spear of the Lord mighty in battle.

Let Caleb with an Ounce praise the Lord of the Land
   of beauty and rejoice in the blessing of his good
   Report.

Let Othniel praise God with the Rhinoceros, who put
   on his armour for the reward of beauty in the Lord.

Let Tola bless with the Toad, which is the good
creature of God, tho' his virtue is in the secret, and
his mention is not made.

Let Barak praise with the Pard—and great is the 5
might of the faithful and great is the Lord in the
nail of Jael and in the sword of the Son of Abinoam.

Let Gideon bless with the Panther—the Word of the
Lord is invincible by him that lappeth from the
brook.

Let Jotham praise with the Urchin, who took up his
parable and provided himself for the adversary to
kick against the pricks.

Let Boaz, the Builder of Judah, bless with the Rat,
which dwelleth in hardship and peril, that they may
look to themselves and keep their houses in order.

Let Obed-Edom with a Dormouse praise the Name of
the Lord God his Guest for increase of his store
and for peace.

Let Abishai bless with the Hyæna—the terror of the 10
Lord, and the fierceness of his wrath against the
foes of the King and of Israel.

Let Elthan praise with the Flea, his coat of mail, his
piercer, and his vigour, which wisdom and provi-
dence have contrived to attract observation and to
escape it.

Let Heman bless with the Spider, his warp and his
woof, his subtlety and industry, which are good.

Let Chalcol praise with the Beetle, whose life is
precious in the sight of God, tho' his appearance is
against him.

Let Darda with a Leech bless the Name of the
Physician of body & soul.

Let Mahol praise the Maker of Earth and Sea with 15
the Otter, whom God has given to dive and to bur-
row for his preservation.

Let David bless with the Bear—The beginning of vic-
tory to the Lord—to the Lord the perfection of

excellence—Hallelujah from the heart of God, and
from the hand of the artist inimitable, and from the
echo of the heavenly harp in sweetness magnifical
and mighty.

Let Solomon praise with the Ant and give the glory
to the Fountain of all Wisdom.

Let Romamti—ezer bless with the Ferret—The Lord
is a rewarder of them, that diligently seek him.

Let Samuel, the Minister from a child, without ceas-
ing praise with the Porcupine, which is the creature
of defence and stands upon his arms continually.

20 Let Nathan with the Badger bless God for his retired
fame, and privacy inaccessible to slander.

Let Joseph, who from the abundance of his blessing
may spare to him, that lacketh, praise with the
Crocodile, which is pleasant and pure, when he is
interpreted, tho' his look is of terror and offence.

Let Esdras bless Christ Jesus with the Rose and his
people, which is a nation of living sweetness.

Let Mephibosheth with the Cricket praise the God of
chearfulness, hospitality, and gratitude.

Let Shallum with the Frog bless God for the
meadows of Canaan, the fleece, the milk and the
honey.

25 Let Hilkiah praise with the Weasel, which sneaks for
his prey in craft, and dwelleth at ambush.

Let Job bless with the Worm—the life of the Lord is
in Humiliation, the Spirit also and the truth.

Let Elihu bless with the Tortoise, which is food for
praise and thanksgiving.

Let Hezekiah praise with the Dromedary—the zeal
for the glory of God is excellence, and to bear his
burden is grace.

Let Zadoc worship with the Mole—before honour is
humility, and he that looketh low shall learn.

30 Let Gad with the Adder bless in the simplicity of the
preacher and the wisdom of the creature.

252

III

Let Tobias bless Charity with his Dog, who is faith- 1
    ful, vigilant, and a friend in poverty.

Let Anna bless God with the Cat, who is worthy to
    be presented before the throne of grace, when he
    has trampled upon the idol in his prank.

Let Benaiah praise with the Asp—to conquer malice
    is nobler, than to slay the lion.

Let Barzillai bless with Snail—a friend in need is as
    the balm of Gilead, or as the slime to the wounded
    bark.

Let Joab with the Horse worship the Lord God of 5
    Hosts

Let Shemaiah bless God with the Caterpiller—the
    minister of vengeance is the harbinger of mercy.

Let Ahimelech with the Locust bless God from the
    tyranny of numbers.

Let Cornelius with the Swine bless God, which puri-
    fyeth all things for the poor.

Let Araunah bless with the Squirrel, which is a gift
    of homage from the poor man to the wealthy and
    increaseth goodwill.

Let Bakbakkar bless with the Salamander, which 10
    feedeth upon ashes as bread, and whose joy is at
    the mouth of the furnace.

Let Jabez bless with Tarantula, who maketh his bed
    in the moss, which he feedeth, that the pilgrim may
    take heed to his way.

Let Jakim with the Satyr bless God in the dance.

Let Iddo praise the Lord with the Moth—the writings
    of man perish as the garment, but the Book of God
    endureth for ever.

Let Nebuchadnezzar bless with the Grasshopper—the
    pomp and vanities of the World are as the herb of
    the field, but the glory of the Lord increaseth for
    ever.

15 Let Naboth bless with the Canker-worm—envy is
    cruel and killeth & preyeth upon that which God
    has given to aspire and bear fruit.

    Let Lud bless with the Elk, the strenuous asserter of
    his liberty, and the maintainer of his ground.

    Let Obadiah with the Palmer-worm bless God for the
    remnant that is left.

    Let Agur bless with the Cockatrice—The consolation
    of the world is deceitful, and temporal honour the
    crown of him that creepeth.

    Let Ithiel bless with the Baboon, whose motions are
    regular in the wilderness, and who defendeth him-
    self with a staff against the assailant.

20 Let Ucal bless with the Cameleon, which feedeth on
    the Flowers and washeth himself in the dew.

    Let Lemuel bless with the Wolf, which is a dog with-
    out a master, but the Lord hears his cries and feeds
    him in the desert.

    Let Hananiah bless with the Civet, which is pure
    from benevolence.

    Let Azarias bless with the Reindeer, who runneth
    upon the waters, and wadeth thro' the land in snow.

    Let Mishael bless with the Stoat—the praise of the
    Lord gives propriety to all things.

25 Let Savaran bless with the Elephant, who gave his life
    for his country that he might put on immortality.

    Let Nehemiah the imitator of God bless with the
    Monkey, who is workd down from Man.

    Let Manasses bless with the Wild-Ass—liberty beget-
    teth insolence, but necessity is the mother of
    prayer.

    Let Jebus bless with the Camelopard, which is good
    to carry and to parry and to kneel.

    Let Huz bless with the Polypus—lively subtlety is
    acceptable to the Lord.

30 Let Buz bless with the Jackall—but the Lord is the
    Lion's provider.

IV

Let Meshullam bless with the Dragon, who maketh   1
his den in desolation and rejoiceth amongst the
ruins.

Let Enoch bless with the Rackoon, who walked with
God as by the instinct.

Let Hashbadana bless with the Catamountain, who
stood by the Pulpit of God against the dissensions
of the Heathen.

Let Ebed-Melech bless with the Mantiger, the blood
of the Lord is sufficient to do away the offence of
Cain, and reinstate the creature which is amerced.

Let A Little Child with a Serpent bless Him, who   5
ordaineth strength in babes to the confusion of the
Adversary.

Let Huldah bless with the Silkworm—the orna-
ments of the Proud are from the bowells of their
Betters.

Let Susanna bless with the Butterfly—beauty hath
wings, but chastity is the Cherub.

Let Sampson bless with the Bee, to whom the Lord
hath given strength to annoy the assailant and wis-
dom to his strength.

Let Amasiah bless with the Chaffer—the top of tree is
for the brow of the champion, who has given the
glory to God.

Let Hashum bless with the Fly, whose health is the   10
honey of the air, but he feeds upon the thing
strangled, and perisheth.

Let Malchiah bless with the Gnat—it is good for man
and beast to mend their pace.

Let Pedaiah bless with the Humble-Bee, who loves
himself in solitude and makes his honey alone.

Let Maaseiah bless with the Drone, who with the
appearance of a Bee is neither a soldier nor an
artist, neither a swordsman nor smith.

Let Urijah bless with the Scorpion, which is a scourge against the murmurers—the Lord keep it from our coasts.

15 Let Anaiah bless with the Dragon-fly, who sails over the pond by the wood-side and feedeth on the cressies.

Let Zorobabel bless with the Wasp, who is the Lord's architect, and buildeth his edifice in armour.

Let Jehu bless with the Hornet, who is the soldier of the Lord to extirpate abomination and to prepare the way of peace.

Let Mattithiah bless with the Bat, who inhabiteth the desolations of pride and flieth amongst the tombs.

Let Elias which is the innocency of the Lord rejoice with the Dove.

20 Let Asaph rejoice with the Nightingale—The musician of the Lord! and the watchman of the Lord!

Let Shema rejoice with the Glowworm, who is the lamp of the traveller and mead of the musician.

Let Jeduthun rejoice with the Woodlark, who is sweet and various.

Let Chenaniah rejoice with Chloris, in the vivacity of his powers and the beauty of his person.

Let Gideoni rejoice with the Goldfinch, who is shrill and loud, and full withal.

25 Let Giddalti rejoice with the Mocking-bird, who takes off the notes of the Aviary and reserves his own.

Let Jogli rejoice with the Linnet, who is distinct and of mild delight.

Let Benjamin bless and rejoice with the Redbird, who is soft and soothing.

Let Dan rejoice with the Blackbird, who praises God with all his heart, and biddeth to be of good cheer.

V

Let Elizur rejoice with the Partridge, who is a   1
prisoner of state and is proud of his keepers.

Let Shedeur rejoice with Pyrausta, who dwelieth in
a medium of fire, which God hath adapted for
him.

Let Shelumiel rejoice with Olor, who is of a goodly
savour, and the very look of him harmonizes the
mind.

Let Jael rejoice with the Plover, who whistles for his
live, and foils the marksmen and their guns.

Let Raguel rejoice with the Cock of Portugal—God   5
send good Angels to the allies of England!

Let Hobab rejoice with Necydalus, who is the Greek
of a Grub.

Let Zurishaddai with the Polish Cock rejoice—The
Lord restore peace to Europe.

Let Zuar rejoice with the Guinea Hen—The Lord add
to his mercies in the WEST!

Let Chesed rejoice with Strepsiceros, whose weapons
are the ornaments of his peace.

Let Hagar rejoice with Gnesion, who is the right sort   10
of eagle, and towers the highest.

Let Libni rejoice with the Redshank, who migrates
not but is translated to the upper regions.

Let Nahshon rejoice with the Seabreese, the Lord
give the sailors of his Spirit.

Let Helon rejoice with the Woodpecker—the Lord
encourage the propagation of trees!

Let Amos rejoice with the Coote——prepare to meet
thy God, O Israel.

Let Ephah rejoice with Buprestis, the Lord endue us   15
with temperance & humanity, till every cow have
her mate!

Let Sarah rejoice with the Redwing, whose harvest is
in the frost and snow.

Let Rebekah rejoice with Iynx, who holds his head on
one side to deceive the adversary.

Let Shuah rejoice with Boa, which is the vocal serpent.

Let Ehud rejoice with Onocrotalus, whose braying is
for the glory of God, because he makes the best
musick in his power.

20 Let Shamgar rejoice with Otis, who looks about him
for the glory of God, & sees the horizon compleat
at once.

Let Bohan rejoice with the Scythian Stag—he is beef
and breeches against want & nakedness.

Let Achsah rejoice with the Pigeon who is an anti-
dote to malignity and will carry a letter.

Let Tohu rejoice with the Grouse—the Lord further
the cultivating of heaths the peopling of deserts.

Let Hilleb rejoice with Ammodytes, whose colour is
deceitful and he plots against the pilgrim's feet.

25 Let Eli rejoice with Leucon·—he is an honest fellow,
which is a rarity.

Let Jemuel rejoice with Charadrius, who is from the
HEIGHT & the sight of him is good for the jaundice.

Let Pharaoh rejoice with Anataria, whom God per-
mits to prey upon the ducks to check their increase.

Let Lotan rejoice with Sauterelle. Blessed be the
name of the Lord from the Lote-tree to the Palm.

Let Dishon rejoice with the Landrail, God give his
grace to the society for preserving the game.

30 Let Hushim rejoice with the King's Fisher, who is of
royal beauty, tho' plebeian size.

Let Machir rejoice with Convolvulus, from him to the
ring of Saturn, which is the girth of Job; to the sight
of God from Job & his daughters BLESSED BE JESUS.

Let Atad bless with Eleos, the nightly Memorialist
ελεησον κυριε.

Let Jamim rejoice with the Bittern blessed be the
name of Jesus for Denver Sluice, Ruston, & the
draining of the fens.

258

Let Ohad rejoice with Byturos who eateth the vine
    and is a minister of temperance.

Let Zohar rejoice with Cychramus who cometh with   35
    the quails on a particular affair.

Let Serah, the daughter of Asher, rejoice with Ceyx,
    who maketh his cabin in the Halcyon's hold.

Let Magdiel rejoice with Ascarides, which is the
    life of the bowels—the worm hath a part in our
    frame.

Let Becher rejoice with Oscen who terrifies the
    wicked, as trumpet and alarm the coward.

Let Shaul rejoice with Circos, who hath clumsy
    legs, but he can wheel it the better with his
    wings.

Let Hamul rejoice with the Crystal, who is pure and   40
    translucent.

Let Ziphien rejoice with the Tit-Lark, who is a
    groundling, but he raises the spirits.

Let Mibzar rejoice with the Cadess, as is there num-
    ber, so are their names, blessed be the Lord Jesus
    for them all.

Let Jubal rejoice with Cæcilia, the woman and the
    slowworm praise the name of the Lord.

Let Arodi rejoice with the Royston Crow, there is a
    society of them at Trumpington & Cambridge.

Let Areli rejoice with the Criel, who is a dwarf that   45
    towereth above others.

Let Phuvah rejoice with Platycerotes, whose weapons
    of defence keep them innocent.

Let Shimron rejoice with the Kite, who is of more
    value than many sparrows.

Let Sered rejoice with the Wittal—a silly bird is wise
    unto his own preservation.

Let Elon rejoice with Attelabus, who is the Locust
    without wings.

Let Jahleel rejoice with the Woodcock, who liveth   50
    upon suction and is pure from his diet.

Let Shuni rejoice with the Gull, who is happy in not
being good for food.

Let Ezbon rejoice with Musimon, who is from the
ram and she-goat.

Let Barkos rejoice with the Black Eagle, which is the
least of his species and the best-natured.

Let Bedan rejoice with Ossifrage—the bird of prey
and the man of prayer.

55 Let Naomi rejoice with Pseudosphece, who is be-
tween a wasp and a hornet.

Let Ruth rejoice with the Tumbler—it is a pleasant
thing to feed him and be thankful.

Let Ram rejoice with the Fieldfare, who is a good
gift from God in the season of scarcity.

Let Manoah rejoice with Cerastes, who is a Dragon
with horns.

Let Talmai rejoice with Alcedo, who makes a cradle
for its young, which is rock'd by the winds.

60 Let Bukki rejoice with the Buzzard, who is clever,
with the reputation of a silly fellow.

Let Michal rejoice with Leucocruta who is a mixture
of beauty and magnanimity.

Let Abiah rejoice with Morphnus who is a bird of
passage to the Heavens.

Let Hur rejoice with the Water-wag-tail, who is a
neighbour, and loves to be looked at.

Let Dodo rejoice with the purple Worm, who is
cloathed sumptuously, tho' he fares meanly.

65 Let Ahio rejoice with the Merlin who is a cousin
german of the hawk.

Let Joram rejoice with the Water Rail, who takes his
delight in the river.

Let Chileab rejoice with Ophion who is clean made,
less than an hart, and a Sardinian.

Let Shephatiah rejoice with the little Owl, which is
the wingged Cat.

Let Ithream rejoice with the great Owl, who under-
standeth that which he professes.
Let Abigail rejoice with Lethophagus God be graci-
ous to the widows indeed.   70

VI

Let Anathoth bless with Saurix, who is a bird of   1
melancholy.
Let Shammua rejoice with the Vultur who is strength
and fierceness.
Let Shobab rejoice with Evech who is of the goat
kind which is meditation and pleasantry.
Let Ittai the Gittite rejoice with the Gerfalcon
amicus certus in re incertâ cernitur.
Let Ibhar rejoice with the Pochard a child born in   5
prosperity is the chiefest blessing of peace.
Let Elishua rejoice with Cantharis God send bread
and milk to the children.
Let Chimham rejoice with Drepanis who is a passen-
ger from the sea to heaven.
Let Toi rejoice with Percnopteros which haunteth the
sugar-fens.
Let Nepheg rejoice with Cenchris which is the spotted
serpent.
Let Japhua rejoice with Buteo who hath three   10
testicles.
Let Gibeon rejoice with the Puttock, who will shift
for himself to the last extremity.
Let Elishama rejoice with Mylæcos $I\varsigma\chi\varepsilon\tau\varepsilon\ \chi\varepsilon\iota\rho\alpha$
$\mu\upsilon\lambda\alpha\iota\upsilon\upsilon\ \alpha\lambda\iota\tau\rho\iota\delta\varepsilon\varsigma.\ \varepsilon\upsilon\delta\varepsilon\tau\varepsilon\ \mu\alpha\varkappa\rho\alpha.$
Let Elimelech rejoice with the Horn-Owl who is of
gravity and amongst my friends in the tower.
Let Eliada rejoice with the Gier-eagle who is swift
and of great penetration.
Let Eliphalet rejoice with Erodius who is God's good 15
creature, which is sufficient for him.

Let Jonathan, David's nephew, rejoice with Ori-
pelargus who is noble by his ascent.

Let Sheva rejoice with the Hobby, who is the service
of the great.

Let Ahimaaz rejoice with the Silver-Worm who is a
living mineral.

Let Shobi rejoice with the Kastrel blessed be the
name JESUS in falconry and in the MALL.

20 Let Elkanah rejoice with Cymindis the Lord illumin-
ate us against the powers of darkness.

Let Ziba rejoice with Glottis, whose tongue is
wreathed in his throat.

Let Micah rejoice with the spotted Spider, who
counterfeits death to effect his purposes.

Let Rizpah rejoice with the Eyed Moth who is beau-
tiful in corruption.

Let Naharai, Joab's armour-bearer [rejoice] with
Rock who is a bird of stupendous magnitude.

25 Let Abiezer, the Anethothite, rejoice with Phrynos
who is the scaled frog.

Let Nachon rejoice with Parcas who is a serpent
more innocent than others.

Let Lapidoth with Percnos the Lord is the builder of
the wall of CHINA—REJOICE.

Let Ahinoam rejoice with Prester—The seed of the
woman hath bruised the serpent's head.

Let Phurah rejoice with Penelopes the servant of
Gideon with the fowl of the brook.

30 Let Jether, the son of Gideon, rejoice with Ecchetœ
which are musical grashoppers.

Let Hushai rejoice with the Ospray who is able to
parry the eagle.

Let Eglah rejoice with Phalaris who is a pleasant
object upon the water.

Let Haggith rejoice with the white Weasel who
devoureth the honey and it's maker.

Let Abital rejoice with Ptyas who is arrayed in green
and gold.

Let Maacah rejoice with Dryophyte who was blessed   35
of the Lord in the valley.

Let Zabud Solomon's friend rejoice with Oryx who is
a frolicksome mountaineer.

Let Adoniram the receiver general of the excise
rejoice with Hypnale the sleepy adder.

Let Pedahel rejoice with Pityocampa who eateth his
house in the pine.

Let Ibzam rejoice with the Brandling the Lord
further the building of bridges & making rivers
navigable.

Let Gilead rejoice with the Gentle the Lord make me   40
a fisher of men.

Let Zelophehad rejoice with Ascalabotes who casteth
not his coat till a new one is prepared for him.

Let Mahlah rejoice with Pellos who is a tall bird and
stately.

Let Tirzah rejoice with Tylus which is the Cheeslip
and food for the chicken.

Let Hoglah rejoice with Leontophonos who will kill
the lion, if he is eaten.

Let Milcah rejoice with the Horned Beetle, who will   45
strike a man in the face.

Let Noah rejoice with Hibris who is from a wild boar
and a tame sow.

Let Abdon rejoice with the Glede who is very vora-
cious & may not himself be eaten.

Let Zuph rejoice with Dipsas, whose bite causeth
thirst.

Let Shechem of Manasseh rejoice with the Green
Worm whose livery is of the field.

Let Gera rejoice with the Night Hawk blessed are   50
those who watch when others sleep.

Let Anath rejoice with Rauca who inhabiteth the root
of the oak.

Let Cherub rejoice with the Cherub who is a bird and
a blessed Angel.

LET PETER rejoice with the MOONFISH who keeps up
the life in the waters by night.

Let Andrew rejoice with the Whale, who is arrayd in
beauteous blue & is a combination of bulk &
activity.

55 Let James rejoice with the Skuttle-Fish, who foils his
foe by the effusion of his ink.

Let John rejoice with Nautilus who spreads his sail &
plies his oar, and the Lord is his pilot.

Let Philip rejoice with Boca, which is a fish that can
speak.

Let Bartholemew rejoice with the Eel, who is pure in
proportion to where he is found & how he is used.

Let Thomas rejoice with the Sword-Fish, whose aim
is perpetual & strength insuperable.

60 Let Matthew rejoice with Uranoscopus, whose eyes
are lifted up to God.

Let James the less, rejoice with the Haddock, who
brought the piece of money for the Lord and Peter.

Let Jude bless with the Bream, who is of melancholy
from his depth and serenity.

Let Simon rejoice with the Sprat, who is pure and
innumerable.

Let Matthias rejoice with the Flying-Fish, who has a
part with the birds, and is sublimity in his conceit.

65 Let Stephen rejoice with Remora—The Lord remove
all obstacles to his glory.

Let Paul rejoice with the Seale, who is pleasant &
faithfull, like God's good ENGLISHMAN.

Let Agrippa, which is Agricola, rejoice with Elops,
who is a choice fish.

Let Joseph rejoice with the Turbut, whose capture
makes the poor fisher-man sing.

Let Mary rejoice with the Maid—blessed be the name
of the immaculate CONCEPTION.

Let John, the Baptist, rejoice with the Salmon— 70
blessed be the name of the Lord Jesus for infant
Baptism.

Let Mark rejoice with the Mullet, who is John Dore,
God be gracious to him & his family.

Let Barnabas rejoice with the Herring—God be
gracious to the Lord's fishery.

Let Cleopas rejoice with the Mackerel, who cometh
in a shoal after a leader.

Let Abiud of the Lord's line rejoice with Murex, who
is good and of a precious tincture.

Let Eliakim rejoice with the Shad, who is contemned 75
in his abundance.

Let Azor rejoice with the Flounder, who is both of
the sea and of the river.

Let Sadoc rejoice with the Bleak, who playeth upon
the surface in the Sun.

Let Achim rejoice with the Miller's Thumb, who is a
delicious morsel for the waterfowl.

Let Eliud rejoice with Cinædus, who is a fish yellow
all over.

Let Eleazar rejoice with the Grampus, who is a 80
pompous spouter.

VII

For I am not without authority in my jeopardy, 1
which I derive inevitably from the glory of the
name of the Lord.

For I bless God whose name is Jealous—and there is
a zeal to deliver us from everlasting burnings.

For in my existimation is good even amongst the
slanderers and my memory shall arise for a sweet
savour unto the Lord.

For I bless the PRINCE of PEACE and pray that all the
guns may be nail'd up, save such are for the rejoic-
ing days.

5 For I have abstained from the blood of the grape and
    that even at the Lord's table.

  For I have glorified God in GREEK and LATIN, the
    consecrated languages spoken by the Lord on
    earth.

  For I meditate the peace of Europe amongst family
    bickerings and domestic jars.

  For the HOST is in the WEST—The Lord make us
    thankful unto salvation.

  For I preach the very GOSPEL of CHRIST without
    comment & with this weapon shall I slay
    envy.

10 For I bless God in the rising generation, which is on
    my side.

  For I have translated in the charity, which makes
    things better & I shall be translated myself at the
    last.

  For he that walked upon the sea, hath prepared the
    floods with the Gospel of peace.

  For the merciful man is merciful to his beast, and to
    the trees that give them shelter.

  For he hath turned the shadow of death into the
    morning, the Lord is his name.

15 For I am come home again, but there is nobody to
    kill the calf or to pay the musick.

  For the hour of my felicity, like the womb of Sarah,
    shall come at the latter end.

  For I shou'd have avail'd myself of waggery, had not
    malice been multitudinous.

  For there are still serpents that can speak—God bless
    my head, my heart & my heel.

  For I bless God that I am of the same seed with
    Ehud, Mutius Scævola, and Colonel Draper.

20 For the word of God is a sword on my side—no
    matter what other weapon a stick or a straw.

  For I have adventured myself in the name of the
    Lord, and he hath mark'd me for his own.

For I bless God for the Postmaster general & all con-
veyancers of letters under his care especially Allen
& Shelvock.

For my grounds in New Canaan shall infinitely com-
pensate for the flats & maynes of Staindrop Moor.

For the praise of God can give to a mute fish the
notes of a nightingale.

For I have seen the White Raven & Thomas Hall of   25
Willingham & am myself a greater curiosity than
both.

For I look up to heaven which is my prospect to
escape envy by surmounting it.

For if Pharaoh had known Joseph, he woud have
blessed God & me for the illumination of the
people.

For I pray God to bless improvements in gardening
till London be a city of palm-trees.

For I pray to give his grace to the poor of England,
that Charity be not offended & that benevolence
may increase.

For in my nature I quested for beauty, but God, God   30
hath sent me to sea for pearls.

For there is a blessing from the STONE of JESUS which
is founded upon hell to the precious jewell on the
right hand of God.

For the nightly Visitor is at the window of the im-
penitent, while I sing a psalm of my own composing.

For there is a note added to the scale, which the Lord
hath made fuller, stronger & more glorious.

For I offer my goat as he browses the vine, bless the
Lord from chambering & drunkeness.

For there is a traveling for the glory of God without   35
going to Italy or France.

For I bless the children of Asher for the evil I did them
& the good I might have received at their hands.

For I rejoice like a worm in the rain in him that
cherishes and from him that tramples.

For I am ready for the trumpet & alarm to fight to
die & to rise again.

For the banish'd of the Lord shall come about again,
for so he hath prepared for them.

40 For sincerity is a jewel which is pure & transparent,
eternal & inestimable.

For my hands and my feet are perfect as the
sublimity of Naphtali and the felicity of Asher.

For the names and number of animals are as the
names and number of the stars.

For I pray the Lord Jesus to translate my MAGNIFICAT
into verse and represent it.

For I bless the Lord Jesus from the bottom of
Royston Cave to the top of King's Chapel.

45 For I am a little fellow, which is intitled to the great
mess by the benevolence of God my father.

For I this day made over my inheritance to my
mother in consideration of her infirmities.

For I this day made over my inheritance to my
mother in consideration of her age.

For I this day made over my inheritance to my
mother in consideration of her poverty.

For I bless the thirteenth of August, in which I had
the grace to obey the voice of Christ in my con-
science.

50 For I bless the thirteenth of August, in which I was
willing to run all hazards for the sake of the name
of the Lord.

For I bless the thirteenth of August, in which I was
willing to be called a fool for the sake of Christ.

For I lent my flocks and my herds and my lands at
once unto the Lord.

For nature is more various than observation tho'
observers be innumerable.

For Agricola is Γεωργος.

55 For I pray God to bless POLLY in the blessing of
Naomi and assign her to the house of DAVID,

For I am in charity with the French who are my foes
and Moabites because of the Moabitish woman.

For my Angel is always ready at a pinch to help me
out and to keep me up.

For CHRISTOPHER must slay the Dragon with a
PAEON's head.

For they have seperated me and my bosom, whereas
the right comes by setting us together.

For Silly fellow! Silly fellow! is against me and   60
belongeth neither to me nor my family.

For he that scorneth the scorner hath condescended
to my low estate.

For Abiah is the father of Joab and Joab of all
Romans and English Men.

For they pass by me in their tour, and the good
Samaritan is not yet come.

For I bless God in the behalf of TRINITY COLLEGE in
CAMBRIDGE & the society of PURPLES in LONDON.

For I have a nephew CHRISTOPHER to whom I implore 65
the grace of God.

For I pray God bless the CAM—Mr. HIGGS & Mr. &
Mrs. WASHBOURNE as the drops of the dew.

For I pray God bless the king of Sardinia and make
him an instrument of his peace.

For I am possessed of a cat, surpassing in beauty,
from whom I take occasion to bless Almighty God.

For I pray God for the professors of the University
of Cambridge to attend & to amend.

For the Fatherless Children and widows are never   70
deserted of the Lord.

VIII

For I pray God be gracious to the house of Stuart   1
and consider their afflictions.

For I pray God be gracious to the seed of Virgil to
Mr. GOODMAN SMITH of King's and Joseph STUD.

For I give God the glory that I am a son of ABRAHAM
a PRINCE of the house of my fathers.

For my brethren have dealt deceitfully as a brook,
and as the stream of brooks that pass away.

For I bless God for my retreat at CANBURY, as it was
the place of the nativity of my children.

5 For I pray God to give them the food which I cannot
earn for them any otherwise than by prayer.

For I pray God bless the Chinese which are of
ABRAHAM and the Gospel grew with them at the
first.

For I bless God in the honey of the sugar-cane and
the milk of the cocoa.

For I bless God in the libraries of the learned & for
all the booksellers in the world.

10 For I bless God in the strength of my loins and for
the voice which he hath made sonorous.

For tis no more a merit to provide for oneself, but to
quit all for the sake of the Lord.

For there is no invention but the gift of God, and no
grace like the grace of gratitude.

For grey hairs are honourable and tell every one of
them to the glory of God.

For I bless the Lord Jesus for the memory of GAY,
POPE and SWIFT.

15 For all good words are from GOD and all others are
cant.

For I am enobled by my ascent and the Lord haith
raised me above my Peers.

For I pray God bless my Lord CLARENDON and his
seed for ever.

For there is silver in my mines and I bless God that
it is rather there than in my coffers.

For I blessed God in St. James's Park till I routed all
the company.

20 For the officers of the peace are at variance with me
and the watchman smites me with his staff.

For I am the seed of the WELCH WOMAN and speak
the truth from my heart.

For they lay wagers touching my life.——God be
gracious to the winners.

For the piety of Rizpah is imitable in the Lord—
wherefore I pray for the dead.

For the Lord is my ROCK and I am the bearer of his
CROSS.

For I am like a frog in the brambles, but the Lord   25
hath put his whole armour upon me.

For I was a Viper-catcher in my youth and the Lord
delivered me from his venom.

For I rejoice that I attribute to God, what others
vainly ascribe to feeble man.

For I am ready to die for his sake—who lay down his
life for all mankind.

For the son of JOSHUA shall prevail against the ser-
vant of Gideon—Good men have their betters.

For my seed shall worship the Lord JESUS as numer-   30
ous & musical as the grashoppers of Paradise.

For I pray God to turn the council of Ahitophel into
foolishness.

For the learning of the Lord increases daily, as the
sun is an improving angel.

For I pray God for a reformation amongst the
women and the restoration of the veil.

For beauty is better to look upon than to meddle
with and tis good for a man not to know a
woman.

For the Lord Jesus made him a nosegay and blessed   35
it & he blessed the inhabitants of flowers.

For a faithful friend is the medicine of life, but a
neighbour in the Lord is better than he.

For I stood up betimes in behalf of LIBERTY,
PROPERTY and NO EXCISE.

For they began with grubbing up my trees & now
they have excluded the planter.

271

For I am the Lord's builder and free & accepted
MASON in CHRIST JESUS.

40 For I bless God in all gums & balsams & every thing
that ministers relief to the sick.

For the Sun's at work to make me a garment & the
Moon is at work for my wife.

For tali and stately are against me, but humiliation
on humiliation is on my side.

For I have a providential acquaintance with men who
bear the names of animals.

For I bless God to Mr. Lion Mr. Cock Mr. Cat Mr.
Talbot Mr. Hart Mrs. Fysh Mr. Grub, and Miss
Lamb.

45 For they throw my horns in my face and reptiles
make themselves wings against me.

For I bless God for the immortal soul of Mr. Pigg of
DOWNHAM in NORFOLK.

For I fast this day even the 31st of August N.S. to
prepare for the SABBATH of the Lord.

For the bite of an Adder is cured by it's greese & the
malice of my enemies by their stupidity.

For I bless God in SHIPBOURNE FAIRLAWN the
meadows the brooks and the hills.

50 For the adversary hath exasperated the very birds
against me, but the Lord sustain'd me.

For I bless God for my Newcastle friends the voice of
the raven and heart of the oak.

For I bless God for every feather from the wren in
the sedge to the CHERUBS & their MATES.

FOR I pray the Lord JESUS that cured the LUNATICK to
be merciful to all my brethren and sisters in these
houses.

For they work me with their harping-irons, which is a
barbarous instrument, because I am more un-
guarded than others.

55 For the blessing of God hath been on my epistles,
which I have written for the benefit of others.

For I bless God that the CHURCH OF ENGLAND is one
of the SEVEN evn the candlestick of the Lord.

For the ENGLISH TONGUE shall be the language of the
WEST.

For I pray Almighty CHRIST to bless the MAGDALEN
HOUSE & to forward a National purification.

For I have the blessing of God in the three POINTS
of manhood, of the pen, of the sword, & of
chivalry.   60

For I am inquisitive in the Lord, and defend the
philosophy of the scripture against vain deceit.

For the nets come down from the eyes of the Lord to
fish up men to their salvation.

For I have a greater compass both of mirth and
melancholy than another.

For I bless the Lord JESUS in the innumerables, and
for ever & ever.

For I am redoubted, and redoubtable in the Lord, as
is THOMAS BECKET my father.   65

For I have had the grace to GO BACK, which is my
blessing unto prosperity.

For I paid for my seat in St. PAUL's, when I was six
years old & took possession against the evil day.

For I am descended from the steward of the island
blessed be the name of the Lord Jesus king of
England.

For the poor gentleman is the first object of the
Lord's charity & he is the most pitied who hath
lost the most.

For I am in twelve HARDSHIPS, but he that was born
of a virgin shall deliver me out of all.   70

For I am safe, as to my head, from the female dancer
and her admirers.

For I pray for CHICHESTER to give the glory to God,
and to keep the adversary at bay.

For I am making to the shore day by day, the Lord
Jesus take me.

For I bless the Lord JESUS upon RAMSGATE PIER—the
Lord forward the building of harbours.

For I bless the Lord JESUS for his very seed, which is
in my body.

75 For I pray for R and his family, I pray for Mr.
Becher, and I bean for the Lord JESUS.

For I pray to God for Nore, for the Trinity house,
for all light-houses, beacons and buoys.

For I bless God that I am not in a dungeon, but am
allowed the light of the Sun.

For I pray God for the PYGMIES against their
featherd adversaries, as a deed of charity.

For I pray God for all those, who have defiled them-
selves in matters inconvenient.

80 For I pray God be gracious to CORNELIUS MATTHEWS
name & connection.

IX

1 For I am under the same accusation with my Saviour
—for they said, he is besides himself.

For I pray God for the introduction of new creatures
into this island.

For I pray God for the ostriches of Salisbury Plain,
the beavers of the Medway & silver fish of Thames.

For Charity is cold in the multitude of possessions, &
the rich are covetous of their crumbs.

5 For I pray to be accepted as a dog without offence,
which is best of all.

For I wish to God and desire towards the most High,
which is my policy.

For the tides are the life of God in the ocean, and he
sends his angel to trouble the great DEEP.

For he hath fixed the earth upon arches & pillars, and
the flames of hell flow under it.

For the grosser the particles the nearer to the sink, &
the nearer to purity, the quicker the gravitation.

274

For MATTER is the dust of the Earth, every atom of   10
which is the life.

For MOTION is as the quantity of life direct, & that
which hath not motion, is resistance.

For Resistance is not of GOD, but he—hath built his
works upon it.

For the Centripetal and Centrifugal forces are GOD
SUSTAINING and DIRECTING.

For Elasticity is the temper of matter to recover its
place with vehemence.

For Attraction is the earning of parts, which have a   15
similitude in the life.

For the Life of God is in the Loadstone, and there is
a magnet, which pointeth due EAST.

For the Glory of God is always in the East, but can-
not be seen for the cloud of the crucifixion.

For due East is the way to Paradise, which man
knoweth not by reason of his fall.

For the Longitude is (nevertheless) attainable by
steering angularly notwithstanding.

For Eternity is a creature & is built upon Eternity   20
καταβολη επι τη διαβολη.

For Fire is a mixed nature of body & spirit, & the
body is fed by that which hath not life.

For Fire is exasperated by the Adversary, who is
Death, unto the detriment of man.

For an happy Conjecture is a miraculous cast by the
Lord Jesus.

For a bad Conjecture is a draught of stud and mud.

For there is a Fire which is blandishing, and which is   25
of God direct.

For Fire is a substance and distinct, and purifyeth
evn in hell.

For the Shears is the first of the mechanical powers,
and to be used on the knees.

For if Adam had used this instrument right, he would
not have fallen.

For the power of the Shears is direct as the life.

30 For the power of the WEDGE is direct as it's altitude
    by communication of Almighty God.

For the Skrew, Axle & Wheel, Pulleys, the Lever &
    inclined Plane are known in the Schools.

For the Centre is not known but by the application of
    the members to matter.

For I have shown the Vis Inertiæ to be false, and
    such is all nonsense.

For the Centre is the hold of the Spirit upon the
    matter in hand.

35 For FRICTION is inevitable because the Universe is
    FULL of God's works.

For the PERPETUAL MOTION is in all the works of
    Almighty GOD.

For it is not so in the engines of man, which are made
    of dead materials, neither indeed can be.

For the Moment of bodies, as it is used, is a false
    term—bless God ye Speakers on the Fifth of
    November.

For Time and Weight are by their several estimates.

40 For I bless GOD in the discovery of the LONGITUDE
    direct by the means of GLADWICK.

For the motion of the PENDULUM is the longest in
    that it parries resistance.

For the WEDDING GARMENTS of all men are prepared
    in the SUN against the day of acceptation.

For the Wedding Garments of all women are prepared
    in the MOON against the day of their purification.

For CHASTITY is the key of knowledge as in Esdras,
    Sir Isaac Newton & now, God be praised, in me.

45 For Newton nevertheless is more of error than of the
    truth, but I am of the WORD of GOD.

For WATER is not of solid constituents, but is dis-
    solved from precious stones above.

For the life remains in its dissolvent state, and that in
    great power.

For WATER is condensed by the Lord's FROST, tho' not
by the FLORENTINE experiment.

For GLADWICK is a substance growing on hills in the
East, candied by the sun, and of diverse colours.

For it is neither stone nor metal but a new creature, 50
soft to the ax, but hard to the hammer.

For it answers sundry uses, but particularly it sup-
plies the place of Glass.

For it giveth a benign light without the fragility,
malignity or mischief of Glass.

For it attracteth all the colours of the GREAT BOW
which is fixed in the EAST.

For the FOUNTAINS and SPRINGS are the life of the
waters working up to God.

For they are in SYMPATHY with the waters above the 55
Heavens, which are solid.

For the Fountains, springs and rivers are all of them
from the sea, whose water is filtrated and purified
by the earth.

For is Water above the visible surface in a spiritualiz-
ing state, which cannot be seen but by application
of a CAPILLARY TUBE.

For the ASCENT of VAPOURS is the return of thanks-
giving from all humid bodies.

For the RAIN WATER kept in a reservoir at any alti-
tude, suppose of a thousand feet will make a
fountain from a spout of ten feet of the same
height.

For it will ascend in a stream two thirds of the way 60
and afterwards prank itself into ten thousand
agreeable forms.

For the SEA is a seventh of the Earth—the spirit of
the Lord by Esdras.

For MERCURY is affected by the AIR because it is of a
similar subtlety.

For the rising in the BAROMETER is not effected by
pressure but by sympathy.

For it cannot be seperated from the creature with
which it is intimately & eternally connected.

65 For where it is stinted of air there it will adhere
together & stretch on the reverse.

For it works by ballancing according to the hold of
the spirit.

For QUICK-SILVER is spiritual and so is the AIR to all
intents and purposes.

For the AIR-PUMP weakens & dispirits but cannot
wholly exhaust.

For SUCKTION is the withdrawing of the life, but life
will follow as fast as it can.

70 For there is infinite provision to keep up the life in
all the parts of Creation.

For the AIR is contaminated by curses and evil
language.

X

1 For poysonous creatures catch some of it & retain it
or ere it goes to the adversary.

For IRELAND was without these creatures, till of late,
because of the simplicity of the people.

For the AIR is purified by prayer which is made aloud
and with all our might.

For loud prayer is good for weak lungs and for a
vitiated throat.

5 For SOUND is propagated in the spirit and in all
directions.

For the VOICE of a figure compleat in all its parts.

For a man speaks HIMSELF from the crown of his head
to the sole of his feet.

For a LION roars HIMSELF compleat from head to tail.

For all these things are seen in the spirit which makes
the beauty of prayer.

10 For all whispers and unmusical sounds in general are
of the Adversary.

278

For 'I will hiss saith the Lord' is God's denunciation
of death.

For applause or the clapping of the hands is the
natural action of a man on the descent of the glory
of God.

For EARTH which is an intelligence hath a voice and a
propensity to speak in all her parts.

For ECHO is the soul of the voice exerting itself in
hollow places.

For ECHO cannot act but when she can parry the   15
adversary.

For ECHO is greatest in Churches and where she can
assist in prayer.

For a good voice hath its Echo with it and it is
attainable by much supplication.

For the VOICE is from the body and the spirit—and is
a body and a spirit.

For the prayers of good men are therefore visible to
second-sighted persons.

For HARPSICHORDS are best strung with gold wire.   20

For HARPS and VIOLS are best strung with Indian
weed.

For the GERMAN FLUTE is an indirect—the common
flute good, bless the Lord Jesus BENJAMIN HALLET.

For the feast of TRUMPETS should be kept up that
being the most direct & acceptable of all instru-
ment.

For the TRUMPET of God is a blessed intelligence & so
are all the instruments in HEAVEN.

For GOD the father Almighty plays upon the HARP of   25
stupendous magnitude and melody.

For innumerable Angels fly out at every touch and
his tune is a work of creation.

For at that time malignity ceases and the devils
themselves are at peace.

For this time is perceptible to man by a remarkable
stillness and serenity of soul.

For the Æolian harp is improveable into regularity.
30 For when it is so improved it will be known to be the
SHAWM.
For it woud be better if the LITURGY were musically
performed.
For the strings of the SHAWM were upon a cylinder
which turned to the wind.
For this was spiritual musick altogether, as the wind
is a spirit.
For there is nothing but it may be played upon in
delight.
35 For the flames of fire may be blown thro musical pipes.
For it is so higher up in the vast empyrean.
For [nothing] is so real as that which is spiritual.
For an IGNIS FATUUS is either the fool's conceit or a
blast from the adversary.
For SHELL-FIRE or ELECTRICAL is the quick air when it
is caught.
40 For GLASS is worked in the fire till it partakes of its
nature.
For the electrical fire is easily obtain'd by the working
of glass.
For all spirits are of fire and the air is a very benign
one.
For the MAN in VACUO is a flat conceit of preposterous
folly.
For the breath of our nostrils is an electrical spirit.
45 For an electrical spirit may [be] exasperated into a
malignant fire.
For it is good to quicken in paralytic cases being the
life applied unto death.
For the method of philosophizing is in a posture of
Adoration.
For the School-Doctrine of Thunder & Lightning is a
Diabolical Hypothesis.
For it is taking the nitre from the lower regions and
directing it against the Infinite of Heights.

For THUNDER is the voice of God direct in verse and   50
musick.

For LIGHTNING is a glance of the glory of God.

For the Brimstone that is found at the times of
thunder & lightning is worked up by the Adver-
sary.

For the voice is always for infinite good which he
strives to impede.

For the Devil can work coals into shapes to afflict
the minds of those that will not pray.

For the coffin and the cradle and the purse are all   55
against a man.

For the coffin is for the dead and death came by dis-
obedience.

For the cradle is for weakness and the child of man
was originally strong from the womb.

For the purse is for money and money is dead matter
with the stamp of human vanity.

For the adversary frequently sends these particular
images out of the fire to those whom they concern.

For the coffin is for me because I have nothing to do   60
with it.

For the cradle is for me because the old Dragon
attacked me in it & [I] overcame in Christ.

For the purse is for me because I have neither money
nor human friends.

For LIGHT is propagated at all distances in an instant
because it is actuated by the divine conception.

For the Satellites of the planet prove nothing in this
matter but the glory of Almighty God.

For the SHADE is of death and from the adversary.   65

For Solomon said vanity of vanities vanity of vanities
all is vanity.

For Jesus says verity of verities, verity of verities all is
verity.

For Solomon said THOU FOOL in malice from his own
vanity.

For the Lord reviled not [at] all in hardship and
temptation unutterable.

70 For Fire hath this property that it reduces a thing
till finally it is not.

For all the filth of wicked of men shall be done away
by fire in Eternity.

For the furnace itself shall come up at the last accord-
ing to Abraham's vision.

For the Convex of Heaven shall work about on that
great event.

For the ANTARTICK POLE is not yet but shall answer in
the Consummation.

XI

1 For the devil hath most power in winter, because
darkness prevails.

For the Longing of Women is the operation of the
Devil upon their conceptions.

For the marking of their children is from the same
cause both of which are to be parried by prayer.

For the laws of King James the first against Witch-
craft were wise, had it been of man to make laws.

5 For there are witchces and wizards even now who are
spoken to by their familiars.

For the visitation of their familiars is prevented by
the Lord's incarnation.

For to conceive with intense diligence against one's
neighbour is a branch of witchcraft.

For to use pollution, exact and cross things and at the
same time to think against a man is the crime
direct.

For prayer with musick is good for persons so
exacted upon.

10 For before the NATIVITY is the dead of the winter and
after it the quick.

For the sin against the HOLY GHOST is INGRATITUDE.

For stuff'd guts make no musick; strain them strong
    and you shall have sweet melody.

For the SHADOW is of death, which is the Devil, who
    can make false and faint images of the works of
    Almighty God.

For every man beareth death about him ever since the
    transgression of Adam, but in perfect light there is
    no shadow.

For all Wrath is Fire, which the adversary blows   15
    upon and exasperates.

For SHADOW is a fair word from God, which is not
    returnable till the furnace comes up.

For the ECLIPSE is of the adversary—blessed be the
    name of Jesus for Whisson of Trinity.

For the shadow is his and the penumbra is his and his
    the perplexity of the phenomenon.

For the eclipses happen at times when the light is
    defective.

For the more the light is defective, the more the   20
    powers of darkness prevail.

For deficiences happen by the luminaries crossing one
    another.

For the SUN is an intelligence and an angel of the
    human form.

For the MOON is an intelligence and an angel in shape
    like a woman.

For they are together in the spirit every night like
    man and wife.

For Justice is infinitely beneath Mercy in nature and   25
    office.

For the Devil himself may be just in accusation and
    punishment.

For HELL is without eternity from the presence of
    Almighty God.

For Volcanos & burning mountains are where the
    adversary hath most power.

For the angel GRATITUDE is my wife—God bring me to her or her to me.

30 For the propagation of light is quick as the divine Conception.

For FROST is damp & unwholsome air candied to fall to the best advantage.

For I am the Lord's News-Writer—the scribe-evangelist—Widow Mitchel, Gun & Grange bless the Lord Jesus.

For Adversity above all other is to be deserted of the grace of God.

For in the divine Idea this Eternity is compleat & the Word is a making many more.

35 For there is a forlorn hope ev'n for impenitent sinners because the furnace itself must be the crown of Eternity.

For my hope is beyond Eternity in the bosom of God my saviour.

For by the grace of God I am the Reviver of ADORATION amongst ENGLISH-MEN.

For beeing deserted is to have desert in the sight of God and intitles one to the Lord's merit.

For things that are not in the sight of men are thro' God of infinite concern.

40 For envious men have exceeding subtlety quippe qui invideant.

For avaricious men are exceeding subtle like the soul seperated from the body.

For their attention is on a sinking object which perishes.

For they can go beyond the children of light in matters of their own misery.

For Snow is the dew candied and cherishes.

45 For TIMES and SEASONS are the Lord's—Man is no CHRONOLOGER.

For there is a CIRCULATION of the SAP in all vegetables.

For SOOT is the dross of Fire.

284

For the CLAPPING of the hands is naught unless it be
    to the glory of God.

For God will descend in visible glory when men
    begin to applaud him.

For all STAGE-Playing is Hypocrisy and the Devil is   50
    the master of their revels.

For the INNATATION of corpuscles is solved by the
    Goldbeater's hammer—God be gracious to Chris-
    topher Peacock and to all my God-Children.

For the PRECESSION of the Equinoxes is improving
    nature—something being gained every where for
    the glory of God perpetually.

For the souls of the departed are embodied in clouds
    and purged by the Sun.

For the LONGITUDE may be discovered by attending
    the motions of the Sun. Way 2d.

For you must consider the Sun as dodging, which he   55
    does to parry observation.

For he must be taken with an Astrolabe, & con-
    siderd respecting the point he left.

For you must do this upon your knees and that will
    secure your point.

For I bless God that I dwell within the sound of Suc-
    cess, and that it is well with ENGLAND this blessed
    day. NATIVITY of our LORD N.S. 1759.

For a Man is to be looked upon in that which he
    excells as on a prospect.

For there be twelve cardinal virtues—three to the   60
    East Greatness, Valour, Piety.

For there be three to the West—Goodness, Purity &
    Sublimity.

For there be three to the North—Meditation, Happi-
    ness, Strength.

For there be three to the South—Constancy,
    Pleasantry and Wisdom.

For the Argument A PRIORI is GOD in every man's
    CONSCIENCE.

65 For the Argument A POSTERIORI is God before every
   man's eyes.

   For the Four and Twenty Elders of the Revelation
   are Four and Twenty Eternities.

   For their Four and Twenty Crowns are their respec-
   tive Consummations.

XII

1 For a CHARACTER is the votes of the Worldlings, but
   the seal is of Almighty GOD alone.

   For there is no musick in flats & sharps which are not
   in God's natural key.

   For where Accusation takes the place of encourage-
   ment a man of Genius is driven to act the vices of
   a fool.

   For the Devil can set a house on fire, when the in-
   habitants find combustibles.

5 For the old account of time is the true—Decr. 28th
   1759–60——

   For Faith as a grain of mustard seed is to believe, as
   I do, that an Eternity is such in respect to the
   power and magnitude of Almighty God.

   For a DREAM is a good thing from GOD.

   For there is a dream from the adversary which is
   terror.

   For the phenomenon of dreaming is not of one solu-
   tion, but many.

10 For Eternity is like a grain of mustard as a growing
   body & improving spirit.

   For the malignancy of fire is oweing to the Devil's
   hiding of light, till it became visible darkness.

   For the Circle may be SQARED by swelling and flatten-
   ing.

   For the Life of God is in the body of man and his
   spirit in the Soul.

   For there was no rain in Paradise because of the deli-
   cate construction of the spiritual herbs and flowers.

For the Planet Mercury is the WORD DISCERNMENT.   15

For the Scotchman seeks for truth at the bottom of a
well, the Englishman in the Heavn of Heavens.

For the Planet Venus is the WORD PRUDENCE or provi-
dence.

For GOD nevertheless is an extravagant BEING and
generous unto loss.

For there is no profit in the generation of man and
the loss of millions is not worth God's tear.

For is the twelfth day of the MILLENIUM of the   20
MILLENNIUM foretold by the prophets give the glory
to God ONE THOUSAND SEVEN HUNDRED AND
SIXTY------.

For the Planet Mars is the word FORTITUDE.

For to worship naked in the Rain is the bravest thing
for the refreshing & purifying the body.

For the Planet Jupiter is the WORD DISPENSATION.

For Tully says to be generous you must be first just,
but the voice of Christ is distribute at all events.

For Kittim is the father of the Pygmies, God be   25
gracious to Pigg his family.

For the Soul is divisible & a portion of the Spirit may
be cut off from one & applied to another.

For NEW BREAD is the most wholesome especially if it
be leaven'd with honey.

For a NEW SONG also is best, if it be to the glory of
God, & taken with the food like the psalms.

For the Planet Saturn is the word TEMPERANCE or
PATIENCE.

For Jacob's Ladder are the steps of the Earth gradu-   30
ated hence to Paradice and thence to the throne of
God.

For a good wish is well but a faithful prayer is an
eternal benefit.

For SPICA VIRGINIS is the star that appeared to the
wise men in the East and directed their way before
it was yet insphered.

For an IDEA is the mental vision of an object.

For Lock supposes that an human creature, at a given time may be an atheist i.e. without God, by the folly of his doctrine concerning innate ideas.

35 For it is not lawful to sell poyson in England any more than it is in Venice, the Lord restrain both the finder and receiver.

For the ACCENTS are the invention of the Moabites, who learning the GREEK tongue marked the words after their own vicious pronuntiation.

For the GAULS (the now-French and original Moabites) after they were subdued by Cæsar became such Grecians at Rome.

For the Gaullic manuscripts fell into the hands of the inventors of printing.

For all the inventions of man, which are good, are the communications of Almighty God.

40 For all the stars have satellites, which are terms under their respective words.

For tiger is a word and his satellites are Griffin, Storgis, Cat and others.

For my talent is to give an impression upon words by punching, that when the reader casts his eye upon 'em, he takes up the image from the mould which I have made.

For JOB was the son of Issachar and patience is the child of strength.

For the Names of the DAYS, as they now stand, are foolish & abominable.

45 For the Days are the First, Second, Third, Fourth, Fifth, Sixth and Seventh.

For the names of the months are false—the Hebrew appellatives are of God.

For the Time of the Lord's temptation was in early youth and imminent danger.

For an equivocal generation is a generation and no generation.

XIII

Let Matthan rejoice with the Shark, who is supported   1
by multitudes of small value.

Let Jacob rejoice with the Gold Fish, who is an eye-
trap.

Let Jairus rejoice with the Silver Fish, who is bright
& lively.

Let Lazarus rejoice with Torpedo, who chills the life
of the assailant through his staff.

Let Mary Magdalen rejoice with the Place, whose   5
goodness & purity are of the Lord's making.

Let Simon the leper rejoice with the Eel-pout, who is
a rarity on account of his subtlety.

Let Alpheus rejoice with the Whiting, whom God
hath blessed in multitudes & his days are as the
days of PURIM.

Let Onesimus rejoice with the Cod—blessed be the
name of the Lord Jesus for a miraculous draught
of men.

Let Joses rejoice with the Sturgeon, who saw his
maker in the body and obtained grace.

Let Theophilus rejoice with the Folio, who hath   10
teeth, like the teeth of a saw.

Let Bartimeus rejoice with the Quaviver—God be
gracious to the eyes of him, who prayeth for the
blind.

Let CHRISTOPHER, who is Simon of Cyrene, rejoice
with the Rough—God be gracious to the CAM & to
DAVID CAM & his seed for ever.

Let Timeus rejoice with the Ling—God keep the
English Sailors clear of French bribery.

Let Salome rejoice with the Mermaid, who hath the
countenance & a portion of human reason.

Let Zacharias rejoice with the Gudgeon, who im-   15
proves in his growth till he is mistaken.

Let Campanus rejoice with the Lobster—God be
gracious to all the CAMPBELLS especially John.

Let Martha rejoice with the Skallop—the Lord revive
the exercise and excellence of the Needle.

Let Mary rejoice with the Carp—the ponds of Fair-
lawn and the garden bless for the master.

Let Zebedee rejoice with the Tench—God accept the
good Son for his parents also.

20 Let Joseph of Arimathea rejoice with the Barbel—a
good coffin and a tomb-stone without grudging?

Let Elizabeth rejoice with the Crab—it is good, at
times, to go back.

Let Simeon rejoice with the Oyster, who hath the life
without locomotion.

Let Jona rejoice with the Wilk—Wilks, Wilkie, and
Wilkinson bless the name of the Lord Jesus.

Let Nicodemus rejoice with the Muscle, for so he
hath provided for the poor.

25 Let Gamaliel rejoice with the Cockle   I will rejoice
in the remembrance of mercy.

Let Agabus rejoice with the Smelt —The Lord make
me serviceable to the HOWARDS.

Let Rhoda rejoice with the Sea-Cat, who is
pleasantry and purity.

Let Elmodam rejoice with the Chubb, who is wary of
the bait & thrives in his circumspection.

Let Jorim rejoice with the Roach—God bless my
throat & keep me from things stranggled.

30 Let Addi rejoice with the Dace—It is good to angle
with meditation.

Let Luke rejoice with the Trout—Blessed be Jesus in
Aa, in Dee and in Isis.

Let Cosam rejoice with the Perch, who is a little
tyrant, because he is not liable to that, which he
inflicts.

Let Levi rejoice with the Pike—God be merciful to all
dumb creatures in respect of pain.

Let Melchi rejoice with the Char, who cheweth the
cud.

Let Joanna rejoice with the Anchovy—I beheld and   35
  lo! a great multitude!

Let Neri rejoice with the Keeling Fish, who is also
  called the Stock Fish.

Let Janna rejoice with the Pilchard—the Lord restore
  the seed of Abishai.

Let Esli rejoice with the Soal [Seal], who is flat and
  spackles for the increase of motion.

Let Nagge rejoice with the Perriwinkle—'for the rain
  it raineth every day'.

Let Anna rejoice with the Porpus, who is a joyous fish 40
  and of good omen.

Let Phanuel rejoice with the Shrimp, which is the
  children's fishery.

Let Chuza rejoice with the Sea-Bear, who is full of
  sagacity and prank.

Let Susanna rejoice with the Lamprey, who is an eel
  with a title.

Let Candace rejoice with the Craw-fish—How hath
  the Christian minister renowned the Queen.

Let the Eunuch rejoice with the Thorn-Back—It is   45
  good to be discovered reading the BIBLE.

Let Simon the Pharisee rejoice with the Grigg—the
  Lord bring up Issachar and Dan.

Let Simon the converted Sorcerer rejoice with the
  Dab quoth Daniel.

Let Joanna, of the Lord's line, rejoice with the Min-
  now, who is multiplied against the oppressor.

Let Jonas rejoice with the Sea-Devil, who hath a good
  name from his Maker.

Let Alexander rejoice with the Tunny—the worse the   50
  time the better the eternity.

Let Rufus rejoice with the Needle-fish, who is very
  good in his element.

Let Matthat rejoice with the Trumpet-fish—God
  revive the blowing of the TRUMPETS.

Let Mary, the mother of James, rejoice with the Sea-
Mouse, it is good to be at peace.

Let Prochorus rejoice with Epodes, who is a kind of
fish with Ovid who is at peace in the Lord.

55 Let Timotheus rejoice with the Dolphin, who is of
benevolence.

Let Nicanor rejoice with the Skeat—Blessed be the
name of the Lord Jesus in fish and in the Shew-
bread, which ought to be continually on the altar,
now more than ever, and the want of it is the
Abomination of Desolation spoken of by Daniel.

Let Timon rejoice with Crusion—The Shew-Bread in
the first place is gratitude to God to shew who is
bread whence it is, and that there is enough and to
spare.

Let Parmenas rejoice with the Mixon—secondly it is
to prevent the last extremity, for it is lawful that
rejected hunger may take it.

Let Dorcas rejoice with Dracunculus—blessed be the
name of the Lord Jesus in the Grotto.

60 Let Tychicus rejoice with Scolopendra, who quits
himself of the hook by voiding his intrails.

Let Trophimus rejoice with the Sea-Horse, who
shoud have been to Tychicus the father of York-
shiremen.

Let Tryphena rejoice with Fluta—Saturday is the
Sabbath for the mouth of God hath spoken it.

Let Tryphosa rejoice with Acarne—With such pre-
paration the Lord's Jubile is better kept.

Let Simon the Tanner rejoice with Alausa—Five days
are sufficient for the purposes of husbandry.

65 Let Simeon Niger rejoice with the Loach—The
blacks are the seed of Cain.

Let Lucius rejoice with Corias—Some of Cain's seed
was preserved in the loins of Ham at the flood.

Let Manaen rejoice with Donax. My DEGREE is good
even here, in the Lord I have a better.

292

Let Sergius Paulus rejoice with Dentex—Blessed be
the name Jesus for my teeth.

Let Silas rejoice with the Cabot the philosophy of the
times evn now is vain deceit.

Let Barsabas rejoice with Cammarus—Newton is   70
ignorant for if a man consult not the WORD how
should he understand the WORK?——

Let Lydia rejoice with Attilus—Blessed be the name
of him which eat the fish & honey comb.

XIV

Let Jason rejoice with Alopecias, who is subtlety   1
without offence.

Let Dionysius rejoice with Alabes who is peculiar to
the Nile.

Let Damaris rejoice with Anthias—The fountain of
the Nile is known to the Eastern people who drink
it.

Let Apollos rejoice with Astacus, but St. Paul is the
Agent for England.

Let Justus rejoice with Crispus in a Salmon-Trout—   5
the Lord look on the soul of Richard Atwood.

Let Crispus rejoice with Leviathan—God be gracious
to the soul of HOBBES, who was no atheist, but a
servant of Christ, and died in the Lord—I wronged
him God forgive me.

Let Aquila rejoice with Beemoth who is Enoch no
fish but a stupendous creeping Thing.

Let Priscilla rejoice with Cythera. As earth increases
by Beemoth so the sea likewise enlarges.

Let Tyrannus rejoice with Cephalus who hath a great
head.

Let Gaius rejoice with the Water Tortoise—Paul &   10
Tychicus were in England with Agricola my father.

Let Aristarchus rejoice with Cynoglossus—The Lord
was at Glastonbury in the body and blessed the
thorn.

Let Alexander rejoice with the Sea-Urchin. The Lord
was at Bristol & blessed the waters there.

Let Sopater rejoice with Elacate—The waters of Bath
were blessed by St. Matthias.

Let Secundus rejoice with Echeneis who is the sea-
lamprey.

15 Let Eutychus rejoice with Cnide—Fish and honey-
comb are blessed to eat after a recovery.

Let Mnason rejoice with Vulvula a sort of fish—
Good words are of God, the cant from the
Devil.

Let Claudius Lysias rejoice with Coracinus who is
black and peculiar to Nile.

Let Bernice rejoice with Corophium which is a kind
of crab.

Let Phebe rejoice with Echinometra who is a beau-
tiful shellfish red & green.

20 Let Epenetus rejoice with Erythrinus who is red with
a white belly.

Let Andronicus rejoice with Esox, the Lax, a great
fish of the Rhine.

Let Junia rejoice with the Faber-Fish—Broil fish &
honeycomb may be taken for the sacrament.

Let Amplias rejoice with Garus, who is a kind of
Lobster.

Let Urbane rejoice with Glanis, who is a crafty fish
who bites away the bait & saves himself.

25 Let Stachys rejoice with Glauciscus, who is good for
Women's milk.

Let Apelles rejoice with Glaucus—behold the seed of
the brave & ingenious how they are saved!

Let Aristobulus rejoice with Glycymerides who is
pure and sweet.

Let Herodion rejoice with Holothuria which are
prickly fishes.

Let Narcissus rejoice with Hordeia I will magnify the
Lord who multiplied the fish.

Let Persis rejoice with Liparis I will magnify the   30
Lord who multiplied the barley loaves.

Let Rufus rejoice with Icthyocolla of whose skin a
water-glue is made.

Let Asyncritus rejoice with Labrus who is a voracious
fish.

Let Phlegon rejoice with the Sea-Lizard— Bless Jesus
THOMAS BOWLBY & all the seed of Reuben.

Let Hermas rejoice with Lamyrus who is of things
creeping in the sea.

Let Patrobas rejoice with Lepas, all shells are   35
precious.

Let Hermes rejoice with Lepus, who is a venomous
fish.

Let Philologus rejoice with Ligarius—shells are all
parries to the adversary.

Let Julia rejoice with the Sleeve-Fish—Blessed be
Jesus for all the TAYLERS.

Let Nereus rejoice with the Calamary—God give
success to our fleets.

Let Olympas rejoice with the Sea-Lantern, which   40
glows upon the waters.

Let Sosipater rejoice with Cornuta. There are fish for
the Sea-Night Birds that glow at bottom.

Let Lucius rejoice with the Cackrel Fish. God be
gracious to I Mr. FLETCHER who has my tackling.

Let Tertius rejoice with Maia which is a kind of crab.

Let Erastis rejoice with Melandry which is the largest
Tunny.

Let Quartus rejoice with Mena. God be gracious to   45
the immortal soul of poor Carte, who was barbar-
ously & cowardly murder'd—the Lord prevent the
dealers in clandestine death.

Let Sosthenes rejoice with the Winkle—all shells like
the parts of the body are good kept for those parts.

Let Chloe rejoice with the Limpin—There is a way to
the terrestrial Paradise upon the knees.

Let Carpus rejoice with the Frog-Fish —A man can-
not die upon his knees.

Let Stephanas rejoice with Mormyra who is a fish of
divers colours.

50 Let Fortunatus rejoice with the Burret—it is good to
be born when things are crossed.

Let Lois rejoice with the Angel-Fish—There is a fish
that swims in the fluid Empyrean.

Let Achaicus rejoice with the Fat-Back—The Lord
invites his fishers to the WEST INDIES.

Let Sylvanus rejoice with the Black-Fish—Oliver
Cromwell himself was the murderer in the Mask.

Let Titus rejoice with Mys—O Tite si quid ego
adjuero curam ve levasso!

55 Let Euodias rejoice with Myrcus—There is a per-
fumed fish I will offer him for a sweet savour to the
Lord.

Let Syntyche rejoice with Myax—There are shells in
the earth which were left by the FLOOD.

Let Clement rejoice with Ophidion—There are shells
again in earth at sympathy with those in sea.

Let Epaphroditus rejoice with Ophthalmias—The
Lord increase the Cambridge collection of fossils.

Let Epaphras rejoice with Orphus—God be gracious
to the immortal soul of Dr. Woodward.

60 Let Justus rejoice with Pagrus —God be gracious to
the immortal soul of Dr. Middleton.

Let Nymphas rejoice with Pagurus—God bless
Charles Mason & all Trinity College.

Let Archippus rejoice with Nerita whose shell swim-
meth.

Let Eunice rejoice with Oculata who is of the Lizard
kind.

Let Onesephorus rejoice with Orca, who is a great
fish.

65 Let Eubulus rejoice with Ostrum the scarlet God be
gracious to Gordon & Groat.

Let Pudens rejoice with Polypus—The Lord restore
my virgin!

Let Linus rejoice with Ozæna who is a kind of
Polype—God be gracious to Lyne & Anguish.

Let Claudia rejoice with Pascer—the purest creatures
minister to wantoness by unthankfulness.

Let Artemas rejoice with Pastinaca who is a fish with
a sting.

Let Zemas rejoice with Pecten—The Lord obliterate   70
the laws of man!

Let Philemon rejoice with Pelagia—The laws & judge-
ment are impudence & blindness.

Let Apphia rejoice with Pelamis—The Lord Jesus is
man's judgement.

Let Demetrius rejoice with Peloris, who is greatest of
Shell-Fishes.

Let Antipas rejoice with Pentadactylus—A papist
hath no sentiment God bless CHURCHILL.

XV

For putrifying matter nevertheless will yeild up its life   1
in diverse creatures and combinations of creatures.

For a TOAD can dwell in the centre of a stone, because
—there are stone whose constituent life is of those
creatures.

For a Toad hath by means of his eye the most
beautiful prospects of any other animal to make
himamends for his distance from his Creator in
Glory.

For FAT is the fruit of benevolence, therefore it was
the Lord's in the Mosaic sacrifices.

For the very particular laws of Moses are the deter-   5
minations of CASES that fell under his cognizance.

For the Devil can make the shadow thicker by
candlelight by reason of his powr over malignant
fire.

For the Romans clipped their words in the Augustan
thro idleness and effeminacy and paid foreign
actors for speaking them out.

For when the weight and the powr are equivalent the
prop is of none effect.

For shaving of the beard was an invention of the
people of Sodam to make men look like women.

10 For the ends of the world are the accomplishment of
great events, and the consummation of periods.

For ignorance is a sin because illumination is to be
obtained by prayer.

For Preferment is not from the East, West or South,
but from the North, where Satan, has most power.

For the ministers of the Devil set the hewer of wood
over the head of God's free Man.

For this inverting God's good order, edifice and edi-
fication, and appointing place, where the Lord has
not appointed.

15 For the Ethiopian question is already solved in that
the Blacks are the children of Cain.

For the phenomenon of the horizontal moon is the
truth—she appears bigger in the horizon because
she actually is so.

For it was said of old 'can the Ethiopian change his
skin?' The Lord has answerd the question by his
merit & death he shall—.

For the moon is magnified in the horizon by
Almighty God, and so is the Sun.

For she has done her days-work and the blessing of
God upon her, and she communicates with the
earth.

20 For when she rises she has been strengthned by the
Sun, who cherishes her by night.

For man is born to trouble in the body, as the sparks
fly upwards in the spirit.

For man is between the pinchers while his soul is
shaping and purifying.

For the ENGLISH are the seed of Abraham and work
up to him by Joab, David, and Naphtali. God be
gracious to us this day. General Fast March 14th
1760.

For the Romans and the English are one people the
children of the brave man who died at the altar
praying for his posterity, whose death was the
type of our Saviour's.

For the WELCH are the children of Mephibosheth and   25
Ziba with a mixture of David in the Jones's.

For the Scotch are the children of Doeg with a mix-
ture of Cush the Benjamite, whence their innate
antipathy to the English.

For the IRISH are the children of Shimei and Cush
with a mixture of something lower—the Lord
raise them!

For the FRENCH are Moabites even the children of
Lot.

For the DUTCH are the children of Gog.

For the Poles are the children of Magog.   30

For the Italians are the children of Samuel & are the
same as the Grecians.

For the Spaniards are the children of Abishai Joab's
brother, hence is the goodwill between the two
nations.

For the Portuguese are the children of Ammon—God
be gracious to Lisbon and send good angels
amongst them!

For the Hottentots are the children of Gog, with a
Black mixture.

For the Russians are the Children of Ishmael.   35

For the Turks are the children of Esaw, which is
Edom.

For the Wallachians are the children of Huz. God be
gracious to Elizabeth Hughes, as she was.

For the Germans are the children of the Philistins
even the seed of Anak.

For the Prussians are the children of Goliah—but the
present, whom God bless this hour, is a Campbell
of the seed of Phinees.

40 For the Hanoverians are Hittites of the seed of Uriah.
God save the King.

For the Hessians are Philistines with a mixture of
Judah.

For the Saxons are Benjamites, men of great subtlety
& Marshal Saxe was direct from Benjamin.

XVI

1 For the Danes are of the children of Zabulon.
For the Venetians are the children of Mark and
Romans.

For the Swiss are Philistins of a particular family.
God be gracious to Jonathan Tyers his family and
to all the people at Vaux Hall.

For the Sardinians are of the seed of David—The
Lord forward the Reformation amongst the good
seed first.

5 For the Mogul's people are the children of Phut.
For the old Greeks and the Italians are one people,
which are blessed in the gift of Musick by reason
of the song of Hannah and the care of Samuel with
regard to divine melody.

For the Germans and the Dutch are the children of
the Goths and Vandals who did a good in destruc-
tion of books written by heathen Free Thinkers
against God.

For there are Americans of the children of Toi.
For the Laplanders are the children of Gomer.

10 For the Phenomena of the Diving Bell are solved
right in the schools.

For NEW BREAD is the most wholesome—God be
gracious to Baker.

For the English are the children of Joab, Captain of
the host of Israel, who was the greatest man in the
world to GIVE and to ATCHIEVE.

For TEA is a blessed plant and of excellent virtue. God
give the Physicians more skill and honesty!

For nutmeg is exceeding wholesome and cherishing,
neither does it hurt the liver.

For The Lightning before death is God's illumination 15
in the spirit for preparation and for warning.

For Lavender Cotton is exceeding good for the teeth.
God be gracious to Windsmore.

For the Fern is exceeding good & pleasant to rub the
teeth.

For a strong preparation of Mandragora is good for
the gout.

For the Bark was a communication from God and is
sovereign.

For the method of curing an ague by terror is 20
exaction.

For Exaction is the most accursed of all things, be-
cause it brought the Lord to the cross, his betrayers
& murderers being such from their exaction.

For an Ague is the terror of the body, when the bless-
ing of God is witheld for a season.

For benevolence is the best remedy in the first place
and the bark in the second.

For, when the nation is at war, it is better to abstain
from the punishment of criminals, especially, every
act of human vengeance being a check to the grace
of God.

For the letter ל which signifies GOD by himself is on 25
the fibre of some leaf in every Tree.

For ל is the grain of the human heart & on the net-
work of the skin.

For ל is in the veins of all stones both precious and
common.

For ל is upon every hair both of man and beast.

For ל is in the grain of wood.
30 For ל is in the ore of all metals.
For ל is on the scales of all fish.
For ל is on the petals of all flowers.
For ל is upon on [*sic*] all shells.
For ל is in the constituent particles of air.
35 For ל is on the mite of the earth.
For ל is in the water yea in every drop.
For ל is in the incomprehensible ingredients of fire.
For ל is in the stars the sun and in the Moon.
For ל is upon the Sapphire Vault.
40 For the doubling of flowers is the improvement of the
   gardners talent.
For the flowers are great blessings.
For the Lord made a Nosegay in the medow with his
   disciples & preached upon the lily.
For the angels of God took it out of his hand and
   carried it to the Height.
For a man cannot have publick spirit, who is void of
   private benevolence.
45 For there is no Height in which there are not flowers.
For flowers have great virtues for all the senses.
For the flower glorifies God and the root parries the
   adversary.
For the flowers have their angels even the words of
   God's Creation.
For the warp & woof of flowers are worked by per-
   petual moving spirits.
50 For flowers are good both for the living and the dead.
For there is a language of flowers.
For there is a sound reasoning upon all flowers.
For elegant phrases are nothing but flowers.
For flowers are peculiarly the poetry of Christ.
55 For flowers are medicinal.
For flowers are musical in ocular harmony.
For the right names of flowers are yet in heaven.
   God make gardners better nomenclators.

For the Poorman's nosegay is an introduction to a
    Prince.

For it were better for the SERVICE, if only select psalms
    were read.

For the Lamentations of Jeremiah, Songs from other   60
    scriptures, and parts of Esdras might be taken to
    supply the quantity.

XVII

For A is the beginning of learning and the door of   1
    heaven.

For B is a creature busy and bustling.

For C is a sense quick and penetrating.

For D is depth.

For E is eternity —such is the power of the English   5
    letters taken singly.

For F is faith.

For G is God--whom I pray to be gracious to
    Livemore my fellow prisoner.

For H is not a letter, but a spirit—Benedicatur Jesus
    Christus, sic spirem!

For I is identity. God be gracious to Henry Hatsell.

For K is king.   10

For L is love, God in every language.

For M is musick and Hebrew כ is the direct figure of
    God's harp.

For N is new.

For O is open.

For P is power.   15

For Q is quick.

For R is right.

For S is soul.

For T is truth. God be gracious to Jermyn Pratt and
    to Harriote his Sister.

For U is unity, and his right name is Uve to work it   20
    double.

For W is word.

For X is hope—consisting of two check G—God be
gracious to Anne Hope.

For Y is yea. God be gracious to Bennet and his
family!

For Z is zeal.

25 For in the education of children it is necessary to
watch the words, which they pronounce with diffi-
culty, for such are against them in their conse-
quences.

For A is awe, if pronounced full. Stand in awe and
sin not.

For B pronounced in the animal is bey importing
authority.

For C pronounced hard is ke importing to shut.

For D pronounced full is day.

30 For E is east particularly when formed little e with his
eye.

For F in its secondary meaning is fair.

For G in a secondary sense is good.

For H is heave.

For I is the organ of vision.

35 For K is keep.

For L is light, and ♭ is the line of beauty.

For M is meet.

For N is nay.

For O is over.

40 For P is peace.

For Q is quarter.

For R is rain, or thus reign, or thus rein.

For S is save.

For T is take.

45 For V is veil.

For W is world.

For X beginneth not, but connects and continues.

For Y is young—the Lord direct me in the better way
going on in the Fifth year of my jeopardy June ye
17th N.S. 1760. God be gracious to Dr. YOUNG.

For Z is zest. God give us all a relish of our duty.

For Action & Speaking are one according to God and 50
the Ancients.

For the approaches of Death are by illumination.

For a man cannot have Publick Spirit, who is void of
private benevolence.

For the order of Alamoth is first three, second six,
third eighteen, fourth fifty four, and then the whole
band.

For the order of Sheminith is first ten, second twenty,
third thirty & then the whole band.

For the first entrance into Heaven is by complement. 55

For Flowers can see, and Pope's Carnations knew
him.

For the devil works upon damps and lowth and
causes agues.

For Ignorance is a sin because illumination is to be
had by prayer.

For many a genius being lost at the plough is a
false thought, the divine providence is a better
manager.

For a man's idleness is the fruit of the adversary's 60
diligence.

For diligence is the gift of God, as well as other good
things.

For it is a good NOTHING in one's own eyes and in
the eyes of fools.

For æra in its primitive sense is but a weed amongst
corn.

For there is no knowing of times & seasons, in sub-
mitting them to God stands the Christian's
Chronology.

For Jacob's brown sheep wore the Golden the fleece. 65

For Shaving of the face was the invention of the
Sodomites to make men look like women.

For God has given us a language of monosyllables to
prevent our clipping.

305

For a toad enjoys a finer prospect than another
    creature to compensate his lack.
        Tho' toad I am the object of man's hate
70   Yet better am I than a reprobate,
                who has the worst of prospects.

XVIII

1 For there are stones, whose constituent particles are
    little toads.

For the spiritual musick is as follows.

For there is the thunder-stop, which is the voice of
    God direct.

For the rest of the stops are by their rhimes.

5 For the trumpet rhimes are sound bound, soar more
    and the like.

For the Shawn rhimes are lawn fawn moon boon
    and the like.

For the harp rhimes are sing ring, string & the like.

For the cymbal rhimes are bell well toll soul & the like.

For the flute rhimes are tooth youth suit mute & the
    like.

10 For the dulcimer rhimes are grace place beat heat &
    the like.

For the Clarinet rhimes are clean seen and the like.

For the Bassoon rhimes are pass, class and the like.
    God be gracious to Baumgarden.

For the dulcimer are rather van fan & the like and
    grace place &c are of the bassoon.

For beat heat, weep peep &c are of the pipe.

15 For every word has it marrow in the English tongue
    for order and for delight.

For the dissyllables such as able, table &c are the
    fiddle rhimes.

For all dissyllables and some trissyllables are fiddle
    rhimes.

For the relations of words are in pairs first.

For the relations of words are sometimes in opposi-
tions.

For the relations of words are according to their   20
distances from the pair.

For there be twelve cardinal virtues the gifts of the
twelve sons of Jacob.

For Reuben is Great. God be gracious to Lord
Falmouth.

For Simeon is Valiant. God be gracious to the Duke
of Somerset.

For Levi is Pious. God be gracious to the Bishop of
London.

For Judah is Good. God be gracious to Lord   25
Granville.

For Dan is Clean—neat, dextrous, apt, active, com-
pact. God be gracious to Draper.

For Naphtali is sublime—God be gracious to
Chesterfield.

For Gad is Contemplative—God be gracious to Lord
Northampton.

For Ashur is Happy—God be gracious to George
Bowes.

For Issachar is strong—God be gracious to the Duke   30
of Dorsett.

For Zabulon is Constant—God be gracious to Lord
Bath.

For Joseph is Pleasant—God be gracious to Lord
Bolingbroke.

For Benjamin is Wise—God be gracious to Honey-
wood.

For all Foundation is from God depending.

For the two Universities are the eyes of England.   35

For Cambridge is the right and the brightest.

For Pembroke Hall was founded more in the Lord
than any College in Cambridge.

For mustard is the proper food of birds & men are
bound to cultivate it for their use.

For they that study the works of God are peculiarly
assisted by his Spirit.

40 For all the creatures mentiond by Pliny are some-
where or other extant to the glory of God.

For Rye is food rather for fowls than men.

For Rye-bread is not taken with thankfulness.

For the lack of Rye may be supplied by Spelt.

For languages work into one another by their bear-
ings.

45 For the power of some animal is predominant in every
language.

For the power and spirit of a CAT is in the Greek.

For the sound of a cat is in the most useful preposi-
tion $\varkappa\alpha\tau'$ $\varepsilon\upsilon\chi\eta\nu$.

For the pleasantry of a cat at pranks is in the lan-
guage ten thousand times over.

For JACK UPON PRANCK is in the performance of $\pi\varepsilon\rho\iota$
together or seperate.

50 For Clapperclaw is in the grappling of the words
upon one another in all the modes of versification.

For the sleekness of a Cat is in his $\alpha\gamma\lambda\alpha\iota\eta\varphi\iota$.

For the Greek is thrown from heaven and falls upon
its feet.

For the Greek when distracted from the lines is
sooner restored to rank & rallied into some form
than any other.

For the purring of a Cat is his $T\rho\upsilon\zeta\varepsilon\iota$.

55 For his cry is in $o\upsilon\alpha\iota$, which I am sorry for.

For the Mouse (Mus) prevails in the Latin.

For edi-mus, bibi-mus, vivi-mus—ore-mus.

For the Mouse is a creature of great personal valour.

For—this is a true case—Cat takes female mouse
from the company of male—male mouse will not
depart, but stands threatning & daring.

60 For this is as much as to challenge, if you will let her
go, I will engage you, as prodigious a creature as
you are.

308

For the Mouse is of an hospitable disposition.

For bravery & hospitality were said & done by the
Romans rather than others.

For two creatures the Bull & the Dog prevail in the
English.

For all the words ending in ble are in the creature.
Invisi-ble Incomprehensi-ble, ineffa-ble, A-ble.

XIX

For the Greek & Latin are not dead languages, but   1
taken up & accepted for the sake of him that spake
them.

For can is (canis) is cause & effect a dog.

For the English, is concise & strong. Dog & Bull
again.

For Newton's notion of colours is $\alpha\lambda o\gamma o\varsigma$ unphilo-
sophical.

For the colours are spiritual.   5

For WHITE is the first and the best.

For there are many intermediate colours before you
come to SILVER.

For the next colour is a lively GREY.

For the next colour is BLUE.

For the next is GREEN of which there are ten thousand 10
distinct sorts.

For the next is YELLOW which is more excellent than
red, tho Newton makes red the prime. God be
gracious to John Delap.

For RED is the next working round the Orange.

For Red is of sundry sorts till it deepens to BLACK.

For black blooms and it is PURPLE.

For purple works off to BROWN which is of ten   15
thousand acceptable shades.

For the next is PALE. God be gracious to William
Whitehead.

For pale works about to White again.

NOW that colour is spiritual appears inasmuch as the
blessing of God upon all things descends in colour.

For the blessing of health upon the human face is in
colour.

20 For the blessing of God upon purity is in the Virgin's
blushes.

For the blessing of God in colour is on him that keeps
his virgin.

For I saw a blush in Staindrop Church, which was of
God's own colouring.

For it was the benevolence of a virgin shewn to me
before the whole congregation.

For the blessing of God upon the grass is in shades of
Green visible to a nice observer as they light upon
the surface of the earth.

25 For the blessing of God unto perfection in all bloom
& fruit is by colouring.

For from hence something in the spirit may be taken
off by painters.

For Painting is a species of idolatry, tho' not so gross
as statuary.

For it is not good to look with earning upon any
dead work.

For by so doing something is lost in the spirit &
given from life to death.

30 For BULL in the first place is the word of Almighty
God.

For he is a creature of infinite magnitude in the height.

For there is the model of every beast of the field in
the height.

For they are blessed intelligences & all angels of the
living God.

For there are many words under Bull.

35 For Bul the Month is under it.

For Sea is under Bull.

For Brook is under Bull. God be gracious to Lord
Bolinbroke.

For Rock is under Bull.

For Bullfinch is under Bull. God be gracious to the
Duke of Cleveland.

For God, which always keeps his work in view has   40
painted a Bullfinch in the heart of a stone. God be
gracious to Gosling and Canterbury.

For the Bluecap is under Bull.

For the Humming Bird is under Bull.

For Beetle is under Bull.

For Toad is under bull.

For Frog is under Bull, which he has a delight to look 45
at.

For the Pheasant-eyed Pink is under Bull. Blessed
Jesus RANK EL.

For Bugloss is under Bull.

For Bugle is under Bull.

For Oxeye is under Bull.

For Fire is under Bull.   50

For I will consider my Cat Jeoffry.

For he is the servant of the Living God, duly and
daily serving him.

For at the first glance of the glory of God in the East
he worships in his way.

For is this done by wreathing his body seven times
round with elegant quickness.

For then he leaps up to catch the musk, which is the 55
blessing of God upon his prayer.

For he rolls upon prank to work it in.

For having done duty and received blessing he begins
to consider himself.

For this he performs in ten degrees.

For first he looks upon his fore-paws to see if they are
clean.

For secondly he kicks up behind to clear away there.   60

311

XX

1 For thirdly he works it upon stretch with the fore
paws extended.

For fourthly he sharpens his paws by wood.

For fifthly he washes himself.

For sixthly he rolls upon wash.

5 For Seventhly he fleas himself, that he may not be
interrupted upon the beat.

For Eighthly he rubs himself against a post.

For Ninthly he looks up for his instructions.

For Tenthly he goes in quest of food.

For having consider'd God and himself he will con-
sider his neighbour.

10 For if he meets another cat he will kiss her in kind-
ness.

For when he takes his prey he plays with it to give it
chance.

For one mouse in seven escapes by his dallying.

For when his day's work is done his business more
properly begins.

For keeps the Lord's watch in the night against the
adversary.

15 For he counteracts the powers of darkness by his
electrical skin & glaring eyes.

For he counteracts the Devil, who is death, by brisk-
ing about the life.

For in his morning orisons he loves the sun and the
sun loves him.

For he is of the tribe of Tiger.

For the Cherub Cat is a term of the Angel Tiger.

20 For he has the subtlety and hissing of a serpent,
which in goodness he suppresses.

For he will not do destruction, if he is well-fed,
neither will he spit without provocation.

For he purrs in thankfulness, when God tells him
he's a good Cat.

For he is an instrument for the children to learn
    benevolence upon.
For every house is incompleat without him & a
    blessing is lacking in the spirit.
For the Lord commanded Moses concerning the cats   25
    at the departure of the Children of Israel from
    Egypt.
For every family had one cat at least in the bag.
For the English Cats are the best in Europe.
For he is the cleanest in the use of his fore-paws of
    any quadrupede.
For the dexterity of his defence is an instance of the
    love of God to him exceedingly.
For he is the quickest tò his mark of any creature.   30
For he is tenacious of his point.
For he is a mixture of gravity and waggery.
For he knows that God is his Saviour.
For there is nothing sweeter than his peace when at
    rest.
For there is nothing brisker than his life when in   35
    motion.
For he is of the Lord's poor and so indeed is he
    called by benevolence perpetually—Poor Jeoffry!
    poor Jeoffry! the rat has bit thy throat.
For I bless the name of the Lord Jesus that Jeoffry is
    better.
For the divine spirit comes about his body to sustain
    it in compleat cat.
For his tongue is exceeding pure so that it has in
    purity what it wants in musick.
For he is docile and can learn certain things.   40
For he can set up with gravity which is patience
    upon approbation.
For he can fetch and carry, which is patience in
    employment.
For he can jump over a stick which is patience upon
    proof positive.

For he can spraggle upon waggle at the word of
command.

45 For he can jump from an eminence into his master's
bosom.

For he can catch the cork and toss it again.

For he is hated by the hypocrite and miser.

For the former is affraid of detection.

For the latter refuses the charge.

50 For he camels his back to bear the first notion of
business.

For he is good to think on, if a man would express
himself neatly.

For he made a great figure in Egypt for his signal
services.

For he killed the Icneumon-rat very pernicious by
land.

For his ears are so acute that they sting again.

55 For from this proceeds the passing quickness of his
attention.

For by stroaking of him I have found out electricity.

For I perceived God's light about him both wax and
fire.

For the Electrical fire is the spiritual substance, which
God sends from heaven to sustain the bodies both
of man and beast.

For God has blessed him in the variety of his move-
ments.

60 For, tho he cannot fly, he is an excellent clamberer.

For his motions upon the face of the earth are more
than any other quadrupede.

For he can tread to all the measures upon the musick.

For he can swim for life.

For he can creep.

XXI

Let Ramah rejoice with Cochineal. 1

Let Gaba rejoice with the Prickly Pear, which the
Cochineal feeds on.

Let Nebo rejoice with the Myrtle-leaved Sumach as
with the Skirrel Jub. 2d.

Let Magbish rejoice with the Sage-Tree Phlomis as
with the Goatsbeard Jub. 2d.

Let Hashum rejoice with Moon-Trefoil. 5

Let Netophah rejoice with Cow-wheat.

Let Chepirah rejoice with Millet.

Let Beeroth rejoice with Sea-Buckthorn.

Let Kirjath-arim rejoice with Cacalianthemum.

Let Hadid rejoice with Capsicum Guiney Pepper. 10

Let Senach rejoice with Bean Cape.

Let Kadmiel rejoice with Hemp-Agrimony.

Let Shobai rejoice with Arbor Molle.

Let Hatita rejoice with Millefolium Yarrow.

Let Ziha rejoice with Mitellia. 15

Let Hasupha rejoice with Turky Balm.

Let Hattil rejoice with Xeranthemum.

Let Bilshan rejoice with the Leek. David for ever!
God bless the Welch March 1st 1761. N.S.

Let Sotai rejoice with the Mountain Ebony.

Let Sophereth rejoice with White Hellebore. 20

Let Darkon rejoice with the Melon-Thistle.

Let Jaalah rejoice with Moly wild garlick.

Let Ami rejoice with the Bladder Sena in season or
out of season bless the name of the Lord.

Let Pochereth rejoice with Fleabane.

Let Keros rejoice with Tree Germander. 25

Let Padon rejoice with Tamnus Black Briony.

Let Mizpar rejoice with Stickadore.

Let Baanah rejoice with Napus the French Turnip.

Let Reelaiah rejoice with the Sea-Cabbage.

Let Parosh rejoice with Cacabalus Chickweed. 30

Let Hagab rejoice with Serpyllum Mother of Thyme.
Hosanna to the memory of Q. Anne. March 8th.
NS 1761.

Let Shalmai rejoice with Meadow Rue.—E
God be gracious to old Windsmore.

Let Habaiah rejoice with Asteriscus yellow Starwort.

Let Tel-harsa rejoice with Aparine Clivers.

35 Let Rehoboam rejoice with Polium Montanum. God
give grace to the Young King.

Let Hanan rejoice with Poley of Crete.

Let Sheshbazzar rejoice with Polygonatum Solomon's
seal.

Let Zeboim rejoice with Bastard Dittany.

Let The Queen of Sheba rejoice with Bulapathon
Herb Patience.

40 Let Cyrus rejoice with Baccharis Plowman's Spike-
nard. God be gracious to Warburton.

Let Lebanah rejoice with the Golden Wingged Fly-
catcher a Mexican Small Bird of Passage.

Let Hagabah rejoice with Orchis. Blessed be the name
of the Lord Jesus for my seed in eternity.

Let Siaha rejoice with the Razor-Fish. God be
gracious to John Bird and his wife.

Let Artaxerxes rejoice with Vanelloes. Palm Sunday
1761. The Lord strengthen me.

45 Let Bishlam rejoice with the Cotton-bush.

Let Mithridath rejoice with Balsam of Tolu.

Let Tabeel rejoice with the Carob-Tree.

Let Ariel rejoice with Balsam of Peru, which sweats
from a tree, that flowers like the Foxglove.

Let Ebed rejoice with Balsam of Gilead. God be
gracious to Stede.

50 Let Jarib rejoice with Balsam of Capivi. The Lord
strengthen my reins.

Let Shimshai rejoice with Stelis Missletoe on Fir.

Let Joiarib rejoice with Veronica Fluellen or Speed-
well.

Let Tatnai rejoice with the Barbadoes Wild Olive.

Let Ezra rejoice with the Reed—The Lord Jesus make musick of it. Good Friday 1761.

Let Josiphiah rejoice with Tower-Mustard. God be   55 gracious to Durham School.

Let Shether-boznai rejoice with Turnera. End of Lent 1761. No. 5.

Let Jozadak rejoice with Stephanitis a vine growing naturally into chaplets.

Let Jozabad rejoice with the Lily Daffodil. Easter Day 22d. March 1761.

Let Telem rejoice with Hart's Penny-royal.

Let Abdi rejoice with Winter-green. God be gracious   60 to Abdy.

Let Binnui rejoice with Spotted Lungwort or Couslip of Jerusalem. God give blessing with it.

Let Aziza rejoice with the Day Lily.

Let Zabbai rejoice with Buckshorn Plaintain Coronopus.

Let Ramoth rejoice with Persicaria.

Let Athlai rejoice with Bastard Marjoram.   65

Let Uel rejoice with Lysimachia Loose-strife which drinks of the brook by the way.

Let Kelaiah rejoice with Hermannia.

Let Elasah rejoice with Olibanum White or Male Frankinsense from an Arabian tree, good against Catarrhs and Spitting blood from which Christ Jesus deliver me.

Let Adna rejoice with Gum Opopanax from the wounded root of a species of panace Heracleum a tall plant growing to be two or three yards high with many large wings of a yellowish green—good for old coughs and asthmas.

Let Bedeiah rejoice with Gum-Sagapenum flowing   70 from a species of Terula which grows in Media. Lord have mercy on my breast.

Let Ishijah rejoice with Sago gotten from the inward
    pith of the bread-tree. The Lord Jesus strengthen
    my whole body.

Let Chelal rejoice with Apios Virginian Liquorice
    Vetch.

Let Miamin rejoice with Mezereon. God be gracious
    to Polly and Bess and all Canbury.

Let Zebida rejoice with Tormentil good for hæmor-
    rhages in the mouth even so Lord Jesus.

75 Let Shemaria rejoice with Riciasides.

Let Jadan rejoice with Flixweed.

Let Shimeon rejoice with Squills.

Let Sheal rejoice with Scorpioides. God be gracious
    to Legg.

Let Ramiah rejoice with Water-Germander.

80 Let Jeriah rejoice with Viper's Grass.

XXII

1 Let Machnadebai rejoice with the Mink, a beast.

Let Meremoth rejoice with the Golden Titmouse of
    Surinam.

Let Mattenai rejoice with Hatchet Vetch.

Let Chelluh rejoice with Horehound.

5 Let Iaasau rejoice with Bird's foot.

Let Maadai rejoice with Golden Rod.

Let Sharai rejoice with Honey-flower.

Let Shasai rejoice with Smyrnium.

Let Hananiah the son of an apothecary rejoice with
    Bdellium.

10 Let Hassenaah rejoice with the White Beet. God be
    gracious to Hasse and all musicians.

Let Hachaliah rejoice with Muscus Arboreus.

Let Sanballat rejoice with Ground Moss found some-
    times on human skulls.

Let Col-hozeh rejoice with Myrobalans, Bellerica,
    Chebula, Citrina, Emblica & Indica.

Let Meah rejoice with Variæ, a kind of streaked
panther. April 8th praise the name of the Lord.
Let Eliashib rejoice with Shepherd's Purse.   15
Let Azbuk rejoice with Valerianella Corn Sallet.
Let Geshem (which is Rain) rejoice with Kneeholm.
Blessed be the name of the Lord Jesus for Rain and
his family and for the plenteous rain this day.
April 9th 1761. NS.
Let Bavai rejoice with Calceolus Ladies slipper.
Let Henadiad rejoice with Cacalianthemum.
Let Shallun rejoice with Mullein Tapsus barbatus   20
good for the breast.
Let Ophel rejoice with Camara.
Let Meshezabeel rejoice with Stephanomelis. Old
April bless the name of the Lord Jesus.
Let Zadok the son of Baana rejoice with Viburnum.
Let Vaniah rejoice with Pug in a pinner. God be
gracious to house of Vane especially Anne.
Let Besodeiah rejoice with the Nettle.   25
Let Melatiah rejoice with Adonis Bird's eye.
Let Jadon rejoice with Borrage.
Let Palal rejoice with the female Balsamime. God be
gracious to my wife.
Let Ezer rejoice with Basella Climbing Nightshade.
Let Uzai rejoice with Meadow Sweet.   30
Let Zalaph rejoice with Rose-bay.
Let Halohesh rejoice with Ambrosia, that bears a
fruit like a club.
Let Malchiah Son of Rechab rejoice with the Rose-
colour'd flowring Rush.
Let Sia rejoice with Argemone Prickly Poppy.
Let Lebana rejoice with Amaranthoides Globe   35
Amaranth.
Let Rephaiah the Son of Hur rejoice with the Berry-
bearing Angelica.
Let Harhaiah of the Goldsmiths rejoice with Segul-
lum, the earth that detects the mine.

319

Let Harumaph rejoice with the Upright Honeysuckle.
Let Hashabniah rejoice with the Water Melon. Blessed
be the manuscripts of Almighty God.
40 Let Phaseah rejoice with the Cassioberry Bush.
Let Nephishesim rejoice with Cannacorus Indian
Reed.
Let Tamah rejoice with Cainito Star-Apple—God be
praised for this Eleventh of April o.s. in which I
enter into the Fortieth year of my age. Blessed,
Blessed, Blessed.
Let Siloah rejoice with Guidonia with a Rose-
Colour'd-Flower.
Let Benjamin a Rebuilder of Jerusalem rejoice with
the Rock-Rose. Newton, bless!
45 Let Malchijah Son of Harim rejoice with Crysan-
themoides.
Let Besai rejoice with Hesperis Queen's Gilly-Flow'r.
Let Perida rejoice with Podded Fumitory.
Let Tabbaoth rejoice with Goldy Locks. God be
merciful to my wife.
Let Bakbuk rejoice with Soft Thistle.
50 Let Hodevah rejoice with Coronilla.
Let Tobiah rejoice with Crotolaria. God be praised
for his infinite goodness & mercy.
Let Mehetabeel rejoice with Hæmanthus the Blood
Flower. Blessed be the name of the Blood of the
Lord Jesus.
Let Bazlith rejoice with the Horned Poppy.
Let Hagaba rejoice with the Turnsole. God be gra-
cious to Cutting.
55 Let Shalmai rejoice with Lycopersicum Love-apple.
God be gracious to Dunn.
Let Arah rejoice with Fritillaria the Chequer'd Tulip.
Let Raamiah rejoice with the Double Sweetscented
Pione.
Let Hashub Son of Pahath-moab rejoice with the
French Honeysuckle.

Let Ananiah rejoice with the Corn-Flag.

Let Nahamani rejoice with the May-apple. God give   60
me fruit to this month.

Let Mispereth rejoice with the Ring Parrakeet.

Let Nehum rejoice with the Artichoke.

Let Ginnithon rejoice with the Bottle Flower.

Let Zidkijah rejoice with Mulberry Blight. God be
gracious to Gum my fellow Prisoner.

Let Malluch rejoice with Methonica Superb Lily.   65

Let Jeremiah rejoice with Hemlock, which is good in
outward application.

Let Bilgai rejoice with Tamalapatra Indian Leaf.

Let Maaziah rejoice with Chick Pease. God be gra-
cious to Harris White 5th of May 1761.

Let Kelita rejoice with Xiphion the Bulbous Iris.

Let Pelaiah rejoice with Cloud-Berries. God be gra-   70
cious to Peele and Ferry.

Let Azaniah rejoice with the Water Lily.

Let Rehob rejoice with Caucalis Bastard Parsley.

Let Sherebiah rejoice with Nigella, that bears a white
flower.

Let Benina rejoice with Heart-Pear. God be gracious
to George Bening.

Let Bunni rejoice with Bulbine leaves like leek purple   75
flower.

Let Zatthu rejoice with the Wild Service.

Let Hiskijah rejoice with the Dwarf American Sun-
Flower.

Let Azzur rejoice with the Globe-Thistle.

Let Hariph rejoice with Summer Savoury.

Let Nebai rejoice with the Wild Cucumber.   80

Let Magpiash rejoice with the Musk.

Let Hezir rejoice with Scorpion Sena.

XXIII

1 For H is a spirit and therefore he is God.
For I is person and therefore he is God.
For K is king and therefore he is God.
For L is love and therefore he is God.
5 For M is musick and therefore he is God.
For N is novelty and therefore he is God.
For O is over and therefore he is God.
For P is power and therefore he is God.
For Q is quick and therefore he is God.
10 For R is right and therefore he is God.
For S is soul and therefore he is God.
For T is truth and therefore he is God.
For U is union and therefore he is God.
For W is worth and therefore he is God.
15 For X has the pow'r of three and therefore he is God.
For Y is yea and therefore he is God.
For Z is zeal and therefore he is God, whom I pray to
be gracious to the Widow Davis and Davis the
bookseller.
For Christ being A and Ω is all the intermediate
letters without doubt.
For there is a mystery in numbers.
20 For One is perfect and good being at unity in himself.
For Two is the most imperfect of all numbers.
For every thing infinitely perfect is Three.
For the Devil is two being without God.
For he is an evil spirit male and female.
25 For he is called the Duce by foolish invocation on
that account.
For Three is the simplest and best of all numbers.
For Four is good being square.
For Five is not so good in itself but works well in
combination.
For Five is not so good in itself as it consists of two
and three.

For Six is very good consisting of twice three.   30

For Seven is very good consisting of two compleat
   numbers.

For Eight is good for the same reason and propitious
   to me Eighth of March 1761 hallelujah.

For Nine is a number very good and harmonious.

For Cipher is a note of augmentation very good.

For innumerable ciphers will amount to something.   35

For the mind of man cannot bear a tedious accumu-
   lation of nothings without effect.

For infinite upon infinite they make a chain.

For the last link is from man very nothing ascending
   to the first Christ the Lord of All.

For the vowell is the female spirit in the Hebrew
   consonant.

For there are more letters in all languages not com-   40
   municated.

For there are some that have the power of sentences.
   O rare thirteenth of march 1761.

For St. Paul was caught up into the third heavens.

For there he heard certain words which it was not
   possible for him to understand.

For they were constructed by uncommunicated
   letters.

For they are signs of speech too precious to be com-   45
   municated for ever.

For after ה there follows another letter of the Hebrew
   tongue.

For his name is Wau and his figure is thus

For the Æolians knew something of him in the spirit,
   but could not put him down.

For the figures were first communicated to Esau.
   God be gracious to Musgrave.

For he was blest as a merchant.   50

For the blessing of Jacob was in the spirit and Esau's
   for temporal thrift.

For the story of Orpheus is of the truth.

For there was such a person a cunning player on the
  harp.

For he was a believer in the true God and assisted in
  the spirit.

55 For he playd upon the harp in the spirit by breathing
  upon the strings.

For this will affect every thing that is sustained by the
  spirit even every thing in nature.

For it is the business of a man gifted in the word to
  prophecy good.

For it will be better for England and all the world in a
  season, as I prophecy this day.

For I prophecy that they will obey the motions of the
  spirit descended upon them as at this day.

60 For they have seen the glory of God already come
  down upon the trees.

For I prophecy that it will descend upon their heads
  also.

For I prophecy that the praise of God will be in every
  man's mouth in the Publick streets.

For I prophecy that there will be Publick worship in
  the cross ways and fields.

For I prophecy that the general salutation will be.
  The Lord Jesus prosper you. I wish you good luck
  in the name of the Lord Jesus.

65 For I prophecy that there will be more mercy for
  criminals.

For I prophecy that there will be less mischief con-
  cerning women.

For I prophecy that they will be cooped up and kept
  under due controul.

For I prophecy that there will be full churches and
  empty play-houses.

For I prophecy that they will learn to take pleasure in
  glorifying God with great cheerfulness.

70 For I prophecy that they will observe the Rubrick
  with regard to days of Fasting & Abstinence.

For I prophecy that the clergy in particular will set a
better example.

For I prophecy that they will not dare to imprison a
brother or sister for debt.

For I prophecy that hospitality and temperance will
revive.

For I prophecy that men will be much stronger in the
body.

For I prophecy that the gout, and consumptions will   75
be curable.

For I prophecy that man will be as good as a Lupine.

For the Lupine professes his Saviour in Grain.

For the very Hebrew letter is fairly graven upon his
seed.

For with diligence the whole Hebrew Alphabet may
be found in a parcel of his seed.

For this is a stupendous evidence of the communicat-   80
ing God in externals.

XXIV

For I prophecy that they will call the days by better   1
names.

For the Lord's day is the first.

For the following is the second.

For so of the others untill the seventh.

For the seventh day is the Sabbath according the   5
word of God direct for ever and ever.

For I prophecy that the King will have grace to put
the crown upon the altar.

For I prophecy that the name of King in England
will be given to Christ alone.

For I prophecy that men will live to a much greater
age, this ripens apace God be praised.

For I prophecy that they will grow taller and stronger.

For degeneracy has done a great deal more than is in   10
general imagined.

For men in David's time were ten feet high in
general.

For they had degenerated also from the strength of
their fathers.

For I prophecy that players and mimes will not be
named amongst us.

For I prophecy in the favour of dancing which in
mutual benevolence is for the glory of God.

15 For I prophecy that the exactions of Moab will soon
be at an end.

For the Moabites even the French are in their chas-
tisement for humiliation.

For I prophecy that the Reformation will make way
in France when Moab is made meek by being well
drubbed by the English.

For I prophecy that the Reformation will make great
way by means of the Venetians.

For the Venetian will know that the Englishman is his
brother.

20 For the Liturgy will obtain in all languages.

For England is the head and not the tail.

For England is the head of Europe in the spirit.

For Spain, Portugal and France are the heart.

For Holland and Germany are the middle.

25 For Italy is one of the legs.

For I prophecy that there will not be a meeting house
within two miles of a church.

For I prophecy that schismaticks will be detected.

For I prophecy that men will learn the use of their
knees.

For every thing that can be done in that posture
(upon the knees) is better so done than otherwise.

30 For I prophecy that they will understand the blessing
and virtue of the rain.

For rain is exceedingly good for the human body.

For it is good therefore to have flat roofs to the
houses, as of old.

For it is good to let the rain come upon the naked
   body unto purity and refreshment.
For I prophecy that they will respect decency in all
   points.
For they will do it in conceit, word, and motion.   35
For they will go forth afield.
For the Devil can work upon stagnating filth to a
   very great degree.
For I prophecy that we shall have our horns again.
For in the day of David Man as yet had a glorious
   horn upon his forehead.
For this horn was a bright substance in colour & con- 40
   sistence as the nail of the hand.
For it was broad, thick and strong so as to serve for
   defence as well as ornament.
For it brightend to the Glory of God, which came
   upon the human face at morning prayer.
For it was largest and brightest in the best men.
For it was taken away all at once from all of them.
For this was done in the divine contempt of a general 45
   pusillanimity.
For this happened in a season after their return from
   the Babylonish captivity.
For their spirits were broke and their manhood
   impaird by foreign vices for exaction.
For I prophecy that the English will recover their
   horns the first.
For I prophecy that all the nations in the world will
   do the like in turn.
For I prophecy that all Englishmen will wear their   50
   beards again.
For a beard is a good step to a horn.
For when men get their horns again, they will delight
   to go uncovered.
For it is not good to wear any thing upon the head.
For a man should put no obstacle between his head
   and the blessing of Almighty God.

327

55 For a hat was an abomination of the heathen. Lord
    have mercy upon the Quakers.

For the ceiling of the house is an obstacle and there-
    fore we pray on the house-top.

For the head will be liable to less disorders on the
    recovery of it's horn.

For the horn on the forehead is a tower upon an arch.

For it is a strong munition against the adversary, who
    is sickness & death.

60 For it is instrumental in subjecting the woman.

For the insolence of the woman has increased ever
    since Man has been crest-fallen.

For they have turned the horn into scoff and derision
    without ceasing.

For we are amerced of God, who has his horn.

For we are amerced of the blessed angels, who have
    their horns.

65 For when they get their horns again they will put
    them upon the altar.

For they give great occasion for mirth and musick.

For our Blessed Saviour had not his horn upon the
    face of the earth.

For this was in meekness & condescension to the
    infirmities of human nature at that time.

For at his second coming his horn will be exalted in
    glory.

70 For his horn is the horn of Salvation.

For Christ Jesus has exalted my voice to his own
    glory.

For he has answered me in the air as with a horn from
    Heaven to the ears of many people.

For the horn is of plenty.

For this has been the sense of all ages.

75 For Man and Earth suffer together.

For when Man was amerced of his horn, earth lost
    part of her fertility.

For the art of Agriculture is improving.

328

For this is evident in flowers.

For [it] is more especially manifest in double flowers.

For earth will get it up again by the blessing of God   80
on the industry of man.

For the horn is of plenty because of milk & honey.

For I pray God be gracious to the Bees and the Beeves
this day.

XXV

Let Dew, house of Dew rejoice with Xanthenes a   1
precious stone of an amber colour.

Let Round, house of Round rejoice with Myrmeeites
a gem having an Emmet in it.

Let New, house of New rejoice with Nasamonites a
gem of a sanguine colour with black veins.

Let Hook, house of Hook rejoice with Sarda a Corne-
lian—blessed be the name of the Lord Jesus by
hook.

Let Crook, house of Crook rejoice with Ophites black   5
spotted marble—Blessed be the name of the Lord
Jesus by crook. The Lord enable me to shift.

Let Lime, house of Lime rejoice with Sandareses a
kind of gem in Pliny's list.

Let Linnet, house of Linnet rejoice with Tanos, which
is a mean sort of emerald.

Let Hind, house of Hind rejoice with Pæderos Opal—
God be gracious to Mrs. Hind, that lived at
Canbury.

Let Tyrrel, house of Tyrrel rejoice with Sardius Lapis
an Onyx of a black colour. God speed Hawke's
Fleet.

Let Moss, house of Moss rejoice with the Pearl-   10
Oyster behold how God has consider'd for him that
lacketh.

Let Ross, house of Ross rejoice with the Great
Flabber Dabber Flat Clapping Fish with hands.
Vide Anson's Voyage & Psalm 98th, ix.

Let Fisher, house of Fisher rejoice with Sandastros
kind of burning stone with gold drops in the body
of it. God be gracious to Fisher of Cambridge & to
all of his name & kindred.

Let Fuller, house of Fuller rejoice with Perileucos a
precious stone with a white thread descending from
its face to the bottom.

Let Thorpe, house of Thorpe rejoice with Xystios an
ordinary stone of the Jasper-kind.

15 Let Alban, house of Alban rejoice with Scorpites a
precious stone in some degree of the creatures.

Let Wand, house of Wand rejoice with Synochitis a
gem supposed by Pliny to have certain magical
effects.

Let Freeman, house of Freeman rejoice with Carci-
nias a precious stone the colour of a sea-crab.
The Lord raise the landed interest.

Let Quince, house of Quince rejoice with Onychi-
puncta a gem of the jasper kind.

Let Manly, house of Manly rejoice with the Booby a
tropical bird.

20 Let Fage, house of Fage rejoice with the Fiddlefish.
Blessed be the name of the Lord Jesus in the fish's
mouth.

Let Benning, house of Benning rejoice with the Sea-
Egg. Lord have mercy on the soul of Benning's wife.

Let Singleton, house of Singleton rejoice with the
Hog-Plump. Lord have mercy on the soul of Lord
Vane.

Let Thickness, house of Thickness rejoice with The
Papah a fruit found at Chequetan.

Let Heartly, house of Heartly rejoice with the Drum-
mer-Fish. God be gracious to Heartly of Christ, to
Marsh, Hingeston & Bill.

25 Let Sizer, house of Sizer rejoice with Trichros a pre-
cious stone black at bottom, white atop and blood-
red in the middle.

Let Chetwind, house of Chetwind rejoice with Ham-
mocrysos, a gem with gold sands on it.

Let Branch, house of Branch rejoice with Hæmatites
--Blessed be the name of the Lord Jesus THE
BRANCH.

Let Dongworth, house of Dongworth rejoice with
Rhymay the Bread-fruit. God be gracious to the
immortal soul of Richard Dongworth.

Let Randall, house of Randall rejoice with Guavoes.
God give Randall success.

Let Osborne, house of Osborne rejoice with Lithi-　　30
zontes a sort of carbuncle. God be gracious to the
Duke of Leeds & his family.

Let Oldcastle, house of Oldcastle rejoice with Leu-
copthalmos. God put it in heart of King to repair
& beautify Dover Castle.

Let Beeson, house of Beeson rejoice with Pyropus,
carbuncle opal. God be gracious to Masters of
Yoke's Place.

XXVI

Let Salmon, house of Salmon rejoice with Sapinos a　　1
kind of Amethyst.

Let Crutenden, house of Crutenden rejoice with
Veneris Gemma a kind of amethyst.

Let Bridges, house of Bridges rejoice with Jasponyx,
which is the Jasper-onyx.

Let Lane, house of Lane rejoice with Myrmecias a
precious stone with little knots in it.

Let Cope, house of Cope rejoice with Centipedes.　　5
God give me strength to cope with all my adver-
saries.

Let Sutton, house of Sutton rejoice with Cholos a
gem of the Emerald kind.

Let Pelham, house of Pelham rejoice with Callimus in
Taphiusio one stone in the body of another. God
bless the Duke of Newcastle.

Let Holles, house of Holles rejoice with Pyriasis a
black stone that burns·by friction. The Lord kindle
amongst Englishmen a sense of their name.

Let Lister, house of Lister rejoice with Craterites a
very hard stone. The Lord hear my prayer even as I
attend unto his commandments.

10 Let Ash, house of Ash rejoice with Callaica a green
gem. God be gracious to Miss Leroche my fellow
traveler from Calais.

Let Baily, house of Baily rejoice with Catopyrites of
Cappadocia. God be gracious to the immortal soul
of Lewes Baily author of the Practice of Piety.

Let Glover, house of Glover rejoice with Capnites a
kind of Jasper blessed be the memory of Glover
the martyr.

Let Egerton, house of Egerton rejoice with Sphragis
green but not pellucid.

Let Reading, house of Reading rejoice with Synodon-
tites found in the fish Synodontes. 27th July N.S.
1762. Lord Jesus have mercy on my soul.

15 Let Bolton, house of Bolton rejoice with Polygram-
mos, a kind of Jasper with white streaks.

Let Paulet, house of Paulet rejoice with Chalcites, a
precious stone of the colour of Brass.

Let Stapleton, house of Stapleton rejoice with Scythis
a precious stone the Lord rebuild the old houses of
England.

Let Newdigate, house of Newdigate rejoice with San-
daserion a stone in India like Green Oil.

Let Knightly, house of Knightly rejoice with Zorony-
sios a gem supposed by the ancients to have magical
effects. Star-word-herb-gem.

20 Let Fellows, house of Fellows rejoice with Syrites a
gem found in a Wolf's bladder.

Let Ascham, house of Ascham rejoice with Thyitis a
precious stone remarkably hard. God be gracious
to Bennet.

Let Mowbray, house of Mowbray rejoice with The
Black & Blue Creeper a beautiful small bird of
Brazil.

Let Aldrich, house of Aldrich rejoice with the Trin-
calo or Tricolor, a leaf without a flower or the
flower of a leaf.

Let Culmer, house of Culmer rejoice with Phloginos a
gem of a fire-colour.

Let Catesby, house of Catesby rejoice with Cerites a 25
precious stone, like wax.

Let Atterbury, house of Atterbury rejoice with
Eurotias a black stone with the appearance of
mould on it.

Let Hoare, house of Hoare rejoice with Crysopis a
precious stone of a gold-colour. God be gracious to
John Rust.

Let Fane, house of Fane rejoice with Chalcedonius
Lapis a sort of onyx called a Chalcedony.

Let Lorman, house of Lorman rejoice with Chera-
mites, a sort of precious stone.

Let Flexney, house of Flexney rejoice with Triop- 30
thalmos. God be gracious to Churchill, Loyd and
especially to Sheels.

Let Gavel, house of Gavel rejoice with Phlogites a
precious stone of a various flame-colour.

Let Hederick, house of Hederick rejoice with Pyritis a
precious stone which held in the hand will burn it;
this is fixed fire.

XXVII

Let Pleasant, house of Pleasant rejoice with The 1
Carrier Fish. God be gracious to Dame Fysh.

Let Tayler, house of Tayler rejoice with the Flying
Mole. God keep him from the poor man's
garden. God be gracious to William Tayler Sen &
Junr.

Let Grieve, house of Grieve rejoice with Orites, a
   precious stone perfectly round. Blessed be the name
   of the Man of Melancholy for Jacob Grieve.

Let Bowes, house of Bowes rejoice with the Dog Fly.
   Lord have mercy upon me & support me in all my
   plagues & temptations.

5 Let Alberton, house of Alberton rejoice with Paneros
   a precious stone good against barrenness.

Let Morgan, house of Morgan rejoice with Prasius
   Lapis of a Leek-green colour.

Let Powell, house of Powell rejoice with Synochitis a
   precious stone abused by the ancient sorcerers.

Let Howell, house of Howell rejoice with Ostracias a
   gem like an oyster.

Let Close, house of Close rejoice with Chalcophonos
   a gem sounding like brass. O all ye gems of the mine
   bless ye the Lord, praise him & magnify him for ever.

10 Let Johnson, house of Johnson rejoice with Omphalo-
   carpa a kind of bur. God be gracious to Samuel
   Johnson.

Let Hopgood, house of Hopgood rejoice with
   Nepenthes an herb which infused in wine drives
   away sadness—very likely.

Let Hopwood, house of Hopwood rejoice with Aspa-
   lathus the Rose of Jerusalem.

Let Benson, house of Benson rejoice with Sea-Rag-
   wort or Powder'd Bean. Lord have mercy on the
   soul of Dr. Benson Bsp. of Glouscester.

Let Marvel, house of Marvel rejoice with Brya a little
   shrub like birch.

15 Let Hull, house of Hull rejoice with Subis a bird
   called the Spight which breaks the Eagle's eggs.

Let Mason, house of Mason rejoice with Suberies the
   Capitol Cork Tree. Lord be merciful to William
   Mason.

Let Fountain, house of Fountain rejoice with Syriacus
   Rephanus a sweet kind of Radish.

Let Scroop, house of Scroop rejoice with Fig-Wine—
Palmi primarium vinum. Not so—Palmi-primum is
the word.

Let Hollingstead, house of Hollingstead rejoice with
Sissitietæris herb of good fellowship. Praise the
name of the Lord September 1762.

Let Moyle, house of Moyle rejoice with Phlox a   20
flame-colourd flower without smell, tentanda via
est. Via, veritas, vita sunt Christus.

Let Mount, house of Mount rejoice with Anthera a
flowering herb. The Lord lift me up.

Let Dowers, house of Dowers rejoice with The
American Nonpareil a beautiful small bird.

Let Cudworth, house of Cudworth rejoice with the
Indian Iaca Tree, which bears large clusters of fruit
like apples.

Let Cuthbert, house of Cuthbert rejoice with Phyllan-
drian a good herb growing in marshes. Lord have
mercy on the soul of Cornelius Harrison.

Let Chillingworth, house of Chillingworth rejoice   25
with Polygonoides an herb with leaves like laurel
long & thick good against serpents.

Let Conworth, house of Conworth rejoice with
Nenuphar a kind of water Lily.

Let Ransom, house of Ransom rejoice with Isidos
Plocamos a sea shrub of the Coral kind, or rather
like Coral.

Let Ponder, house of Ponder rejoice with Polion an
herb, whose leaves are white in the morning, purple
at noon, & blue in the evening.

Let Woodward, house of Woodward rejoice with
Nerium the Rose-Laurel—God make the professor-
ship of fossils in Cambridge a useful thing.

Let Spincks, house of Spincks rejoice with Struthio-   30
mela a little sort of Quinces—The Lord Jesus pray
for me.

Let Peacock, house of Peacock rejoice with Engalac-
ton an herb good to breed milk.

Let Nason, house of Nason rejoice with Errhinum a
medicine to clear the nose.

XXVIII

1 Let Bold, house of Bold rejoice with the Hop-Horn-
beam. God send me a neighbour this September.

Let Spriggings, house of Spriggings rejoice with Eon
the Tree of which Argo was built.

Let Bear, house of Bear rejoice with Gelotophyllis an
herb which drank in wine & myrrh causes excess of
laughter.

Let Sloper, house of Sloper rejoice with Gelotophye
another laughing plant.

5 Let Tollfree, house of Tollfree rejoice with Fern of
Trees—Lord stave off evil this day.

Let Clare, house of Clare rejoice with Galeotes a kind
of Lizard at enmity with serpents. Lord receive the
soul of Dr. Wilcox Master of Clare Hall.

Let Wilmot, house of Wilmot rejoice with Epipetros
an herb coming up spontaneous (of the seed of the
earth) but never flowers.

Let Anstey, house of Anstey rejoice with Eumeces a
kind of balm. Lord have mercy on Christopher
Anstey & his kinswoman.

Let Ruston, house of Ruston rejoice with Fulviana
Herba, ab inventore good to provoke urine. Lord
have mercy upon Roger Pratt & his family.

10 Let Atwood, house of Atwood rejoice with Rhodora
with leaves like a nettle and flower like a rose. God
bless all benefactors of Pembroke Hall.

Let Shield, house of Shield rejoice with Reseda herb
dissolving swelling, and imposthumes.

Let Atkins, house of Atkins rejoice with Salicastrum
Wild Wine upon willows & osiers.

Let Pearson, house of Pearson rejoice with the
American Aloe. I pray for the soul of Frances
Burton.

Let Hough, house of Hough rejoice with Pegasus The
Flying Horse. There be millions of them in the air.
God bless the memories of Bsp. Hough & of Peter.

Let Evelyn, house of Evelyn rejoice with Phu a   15
Plinian shrub sweet-scented. I pray God for trees
enough in the posterities.

Let Wing, house of Wing rejoice with Phlomos a sort
of Rush. I give the glory to God, thro Christ, for
taking the Havannah. Septr. 30th 1762.

Let Chace, house of Chace rejoice with Papyrus. God
be gracious to Sr Richard & family.

Let Pulteney, house of Pulteney rejoice with Tragion,
a shrub like Juniper.

Let Abdy, house of Abdy rejoice with Ecbolia a medi-
cine to fetch a dead child out of the womb. God
give me to bless for Gulstone & Halford.

Let Hoadley, house of Hoadley rejoice with Dryos   20
Hyphear which is the Oak-Missletoe.

Let Free, house of Free rejoice with Thya a kind of
Wild Cypress.

Let Pink, house of Pink rejoice with Trigonium herb
used in garlands—the Lord succeed my pink
borders.

Let Somner, house of Somner rejoice with the Blue
Daisie. God be gracious to my neighbour & his
family this day. 7th Octr. 1762.

Let Race, house of Race rejoice with Osiritis Dogs-
head. God be praised for the eighth of October
1762.

Let Trowell, house of Trowell rejoice with Teachites   25
kind of sweet rush.

Let Tilson, house of Tilson rejoice with Teramnos a
kind of weed. Lord have mercy on the soul of
Tilson Fellow of Pembroke Hall.

Let Loom, house of Loom rejoice with Calocasia, an
Egyptian Bean of whose leaves they made cups &
pots.

Let Knock, house of Knock rejoice with Condurden
which bears red flowers in July & worn about the
neck is good for scrophulous cases.

Let Case, house of Case rejoice with Coctanum a
Syrian Fig. The Lord care [cure?] my cough.

30 Let Tomlyn, house of Tomlyn rejoice with Tetralix a
kind of herb.

Let Bason, house of Bason rejoice with Thelypteris
which is Sea-Fern.

Let Joslyn, house of Joslyn rejoice with Cotonea a
Venetian herb.

XXIX

1 Let Mace, house of Mace rejoice with Adipsos a
kind of green Palm with the smell of a quince.

Let Potts, house of Potts rejoice with Ulex a herb like
rosemary with a quality of attracting gold.

Let Bedingfield, house of Bedingfield rejoice with
Zygia, which is a kind of maple.

Let Tough, house of Tough rejoice with Accipitrina.
N.B. The hawk beat the raven St. Luke's day
1762.

5 Let Balsam, house of Balsam rejoice with Chenomy-
con an herb the sight of which terrifies a goose.
Lord have mercy on William Hunter his family.

Let Graves, house of Graves rejoice with Cinnaris the
Stag's antidote the persecuted Christian is as the
hunted stag.

Let Tombs, house of Tombs rejoice with Acesis Water
Sage. God be gracious to Christopher Charles
Tombs.

Let Addy, house of Addy rejoice with Crysippea a
kind of herb so called from the discoverer.

Let Jump, house of Jump rejoice with Zoster a Sea-
shrub. Blessed be the name of Christ for the Anni-
versary of the Battle of Agincourt 1762.

Let Bracegirdle, house of Bracegirdle rejoice with   10
Xiris a kind of herb with sharp leaves.

Let Girdlestone, house of Girdlestone rejoice with
Crysocarpum a kind of Ivy.

Let Homer, house of Homer rejoice with Cinnabar
which makes a red colour.

Let Lenox, house of Lenox rejoice with Achnas the
Wild Pear Tree. God be gracious to the Duke of
Richmond.

Let Altham, house of Altham rejoice with the Ever-
lasting Apple-Tree.

Let Travell, house of Travell rejoice with Ciborium   15
The Egyptian Bean.

Let Tyers, house of Tyers rejoice with Ægilops a kind
of bulbous root. God give goodwill to Jonathan
Tyers and his family this day. All Saints. N.S.
1762.

Let Clever, house of Clever rejoice with Calathiana a
sort of Autumnal flower.

Let Bones, house of Bones rejoice with The Red-
Crested Black and Blue Bird of Surinam.

Let Pownall, house of Pownall rejoice with the
Murrion a creature of the Beaver kind.

Let Fig, house of Fig rejoice with Fleawort. The Lord 20
magnify the idea of Smart singing hymns on this
day in the eyes of the whole University of Cam-
bridge. Novr. 5th. 1762. N.S.

Let Codrington, house of Codrington rejoice with
Thelyphonon an herb whose root kills scorpions.

Let Butler, house of Butler rejoice with Theombrotios
a Persian herb. God be gracious to the immortal
Soul of the Duke of Ormond.

Let Bodley, house of Bodley rejoice with Tetragna-
thius a creature of the Spider kind.

Let Acton, house of Acton rejoice with Theangelis
    an herb used by the Ancients for magical
    purposes.

25 Let Peckwater, house of Peckwater rejoice with Tetti-
    gonia a small kind of Grasshopper.

Let Sheldon, house of Sheldon rejoice with Teucrion
    an herb like Germander.

Let Brecknock, house of Brecknock rejoice with
    Thalassegle an herb. God be merciful to Timothy
    Brecknock.

Let Plank, house of Plank rejoice with the Sea Pur-
    slain—God be gracious to Thomas Rosoman and
    family.

Let Goosetree, house of Goosetree rejoice with
    Hippophaes a kind of teazle used in the dressing of
    cloth. God exalt the Soul of Captain Goosetree.

30 Let Baimbridge, house of Baimbridge rejoice with
    Hippophæstum of the same kind. Horses should be
    clock'd in winter.—Bambridge praise the name of
    the Lord.

Let Metcalf, house of Metcalf rejoice with Holcus
    Wall-Barley—God give grace to my adversaries
    to ask council of Abel.

Let Graner, house of Graner rejoice with Hircules
    Bastard Nard. The Lord English Granier and his
    family.

Let Cape, house of Cape rejoice with Orgament an
    herb.

XXX

1 Let Oram, house of Oram rejoice with Helus an herb
    like unto Orgament.

Let Sykes, house of Sykes rejoice with Hadrobolum a
    kind of sweet gum.

Let Plumer, house of Plumer rejoice with Hastula
    Regia an herb resembling a spear.

THE MS. OF JUBILATE AGNO

Page xxix, lines 20–33

Let Digby, house of Digby rejoice with Glycyrhiza
Sweetroot. God be gracious to Sr Digby Legard his
Son and family.

5 Let Otway, house of Otway rejoice with Hippice an
herb which being held in an horse's mouth keeps
him from hunger.

Let Cecil, house of Cecil rejoice with Gnaphalium an
herb bleached by nature white & soft for the
purpose of flax. God bless Lord Salisbury.

Let Rogers, house of Rogers rejoice with Hypelates a
kind of Laurel—God be gracious to Rogers &
Spilsbury with their families.

Let Cambden, house of Cambden rejoice with Glis-
chromargos a kind of white marl.

Let Conduit, house of Conduit rejoice with Graecula
a kind of Rose. God be gracious to the immortal
Soul of Sr Isaac Newton.

10 Let Hands, house of Hands rejoice with Hadro-
sphaerum kind of Spikenard with broad leaves.

Let Snipe, house of Snipe rejoice with Haemotimon a
kind of red glass. Blessed be the name of Jesus for
the 29th of Nov^r.

Let Aylesworth, house of Aylesworth rejoice with
Glinon which is a kind of Maple.

Let Aisley, house of Aisley, rejoice with Halicastrum
which is a kind of bread corn.

Let Ready, house of Ready rejoice with Junco The
Reed Sparrow. blessed be the name of Christ Jesus
Voice & Instrument.

15 Let Bland, house of Bland rejoice with Lacta a kind
of Cassia. God be gracious to Bland of Durham &
the Widow George.

Let Abington, house of Abington rejoice with Lea a
kind of Colewort praise him upon the sound of the
trumpet.

Let Adcock, house of Adcock rejoice with Lada a
shrub, which has gummy leaves.

Let Snow, house of Snow rejoice with Hysginum a
    plant dying Scarlet.
Let Wardell, house of Wardell rejoice with Leiostreum
    a smooth oyster. God give grace to the black trum-
    peter & have mercy on the soul of Scipio.
Let Herring, house of Herring rejoice with Iberica a   20
    kind of herb. blessed be the name of the Lord
    Jesus for Miss Herring.
Let Dolben, house of Dolben rejoice with Irio
    Winter Cresses, Rock Gentle or Rock Gallant.
Let Oakley, house of Oakley rejoice with the Skink a
    little amphibious creature found upon Nile.
Let Owen, house of Owen rejoice with the Shag-
    green a beast from which the skin so called is
    taken.
Let Twist, house of Twist rejoice with Neottophora
    a little creature that carries its young upon its
    back.
Let Constant, house of Constant rejoice with the   25
    Musk-Goat. I bless God for two visions of Anne
    Hope's being in charity with me.
Let Amos, house of Amos rejoice with The Avosetta
    a bird found at Rome.
Let Humphreys, house of Humphreys rejoice with
    The Beard manica a curious bird.
Let Busby, house of Busby rejoice with The Ganser a
    bird. God prosper Westminster-School.
Let Alured, house of Alured rejoice with the Book-
    Spider—I refer the people of both Universitys to
    the Bible for their morality.
Let Lidgate, house of Lidgate rejoice with the Flam-   30
    mant a curious large bird on the coast of Cuba.
    God make us amends for the restoration of the
    Havannah.
Let Cunningham, house of Cunningham rejoice with
    The Bohemian Jay. I pray for Peace between the
    K. of Prussia & Empress Queen.

Let Thornhill, house of Thornhill rejoice with The
    Albicore, a Sea-Bird. God be gracious to Hogarth
    his wife. Blessed be the name of the Lord Jesus at
    Adgecomb.

Let Dawn, house of Dawn rejoice with The Frigate
    Bird which is found upon the coasts of India.

XXXI

1 Let Horton, house of Horton rejoice with Birdlime.
    Blessed be the name of the Lord Jesus against the
    destruction of Small Birds.

Let Arne, house of Arne rejoice with The Jay of
    Bengal. God be gracious to Arne his wife to
    Michael & Charles Burney.

Let Westbrooke, house of Westbrooke rejoice with
    the Quail of Bengal. God be gracious to the people
    of Maidstone.

Let Allcock, house of Allcock rejoice with The King
    of the Wavows a strange fowl. I pray for the whole
    University of Cambridge especially Jesus College
    this blessed day.

5 Let Audley, house of Audley rejoice with The Green
    Crown Bird. The Lord help on with the hymns.

Let Bloom, house of Bloom rejoice with Hecatompus
    a fish with an hundred feet.

Let Beacon, house of Beacon rejoice with Amadavad
    a fine bird in the East Indies.

Let Blomer, house of Blomer rejoice with Halimus a
    Shrub to hedge with. Lord have mercy upon poor
    labourers this bitter frost Decr. 29 N.S. 1762.

Let Merrick, house of Merrick rejoice with Lageus a
    kind of Grape. God all-sufficient bless & forward
    the Psalmist in the Lord Jesus.

10 Let Appleby, house of Appleby rejoice with
    Laburnum a shrub whose blossom is disliked by
    bees.

Let Waite, house of Waite rejoice with the Shittah-
Tree—blessed be the name of the Lord Jesus for
the musicians & dancers this holiday-time.

Let Stedman, house of Stedman rejoice with Jacobæa
St. James's Wort. God be merciful to the house of
Stuart.

Let Poet, house of Poet rejoice with Hedrychum a
kind of ointment of a sweet smelling savour. God
speed the New Year thro' Christ 1763.

Let Jesse, house of Jesse rejoice with the Lawrey a
kind of bird. God forward my version of the
psalms thro' Jesus Christ our Lord.

Let Clemison, house of Clemison rejoice with Helia a   15
kind of Ivy. God be praised for the vision of the
Redcap & packet.

Let Crockatt, house of Crockatt rejoice with Embo-
line an Asiatic Shrub with small leaves an antidote.
I pray for the soul of Crockatt the bookseller the
first to put me upon a version of the Psalms.

Let Oakley, house of Oakley rejoice with Haliphæus a
tree with such bitter fruit that nothing but swine
will touch it.

Let Preacher, house of Preacher rejoice with Helvella
a small sort of cabbage. God be merciful to the
immortal soul of Stephen Preacher.

Let Heron, house of Heron rejoice with the Junal-
Tree on which the Cochineal feeds.

Let Kitcat, house of Kitcat rejoice with Copec the   20
Pitch-Stone. Janry 8th 1763 Hallelujah.

Let Gisbourne, house of Gisbourne rejoice with Iso-
cinnamon an herb of a sweet smelling savour.

Let Poor, house of Poor rejoice with Iasione a kind of
Withwind. Lord have mercy on the poor this hard
weather.—Jan. 10th 1763.

Let Eccles, house Eccles rejoice with Heptapleuros a
kind of Plantaine. I pray for a musician or
musicians to set the new psalms.

Let Moseley, house of Moseley rejoice with Spruce
——I bless God for Old Foundation Day at Pemb.
Hall.

25 Let Pass, house of Pass rejoice with Salt—The Lord
pass the last year's accounts in my conscience, thro'
the merits of Jesus Christ. New Year by Old Stile
1763.

Let Forward, house of Forward rejoice with Immus-
sulus a kind of bird the Lord forward my transla-
tion of the psalms this year.

Let Quarme, house of Quarme rejoice with Thyosiris
yellow Succory. I pray God bless all my Subscribers.

Let Larkin, house of Larkin rejoice with Long-wort
or Torch-herb—God give me good riddance of my
present grievances.

Let Halford, house of Halford rejoice with Siren a
musical bird. God consider thou me for the base-
ness of those I have served very highly.

30 Let Ayerst, house of Ayerst rejoice with the Wild
Beet—God be gracious to Smith, Cousins, Austin,
Cam & Kingsley & Kirleside.

Let Decker, house of Decker rejoice with Sirpe a
Cyrenian plant yielding an oderiferous juice.

Let Cust, house of Cust rejoice with Margaris a date
like unto a pearl.

Let Usher, house of Usher rejoice with Condurdon
an herb with a red flower worn about the neck for
the scurvy.

Let Slingsby, house of Slingsby rejoice with Midas a
little worm breeding in beans.

35 Let Farmer, house of Farmer rejoice with Merios an
herb growing at Meroe leaf like lettuce & good for
dropsy.

XXXII

Let Affleck, house of Affleck rejoice with The Box-   1
thorn. Blessed be the name of the Lord Jesus
Emanuel.

Let Arnold, house of Arnold rejoice with Leuco-
graphis a simple good against spitting of blood.

Let Morris, house of Morris rejoice with Lepidium a
Simple of the Cress kind.

Let Crane, house of Crane rejoice with Libanotis an
herb that smells like Frankinsense.

Let Arden, house of Arden rejoice with Mew an herb   5
with the stalk & leaves like Anise.

Let Joram, house of Joram rejoice with Meliphylla
Balm. Gentle God be gracious to John Sherrat.

Let Odwell, house of Odwell rejoice with Lappago
Maiden Lips. Blessed be the name of Jesus in
singularities & singular mercies.

Let Odney, house of Odney rejoice with Canaria a
simple called Hound's-grass.

A Song to David

Contents. Invocation, ver. 1, 2, 3.—The excellence and
lustre of David's character in twelve points of view,
ver. 4; proved from the history of his life, to ver. 17.
—He consecrates his genius for consolation and
edification.—The subjects he made choice of—the
Supreme Being—angels; men of renown; the works
of nature in all directions, either particularly or
collectively considered, to ver. 27.—He obtains
power over infernal spirits, and the malignity of his
enemies; wins the heart of Michal, to ver. 30.—
Shews that the pillars of knowledge are the monu-
ments of God's works in the first week, to ver. 38.—
An exercise upon the decalogue, from ver. 40 to 49.
—The transcendent virtue of praise and adoration,
ver. 50 and 51.—An exercise upon the seasons, and
the right use of them, ver. 52 to 64.—An exercise
upon the senses, and how to subdue them, from
ver. 65 to 71.—An amplification in five degrees,
which is wrought up to this conclusion, That the
best poet who ever lived was thought worthy of the
highest honour which possibly can be conceived, *as
the Saviour of the world was ascribed to his house,
and called his son in the body.*

Christopher Smart.

I

O Thou, that sit'st upon a throne,
With harp of high majestic tone,
   To praise the King of kings;
And voice of heaven-ascending swell,
Which, while its deeper notes excell,
   Clear, as a clarion, rings:

II

To bless each valley, grove, and coast,
And charm the cherubs to the post
    Of gratitude in throngs;
To *keep* the days on Zion's Mount,
And send the year to his account,
    With dances and with songs:

III

O Servant of God's holiest charge,
The minister of praise at large,
    Which thou mayst now receive;
From thy blest mansion hail and hear,
From topmost eminence appear
    To this the wreath I weave.

IV

Great, valiant, pious, good, and clean,
Sublime, contemplative, serene,
    Strong, constant, pleasant, wise!
Bright effluence of exceeding grace;
Best man!—the swiftness and the race,
    The peril, and the prize!

V

Great—from the lustre of his crown,
From Samuel's horn and God's renown,
    Which is the people's voice;
For all the host, from rear to van,
Applauded and embraced the man—
    The man of God's own choice.

VI

Valiant—the word and up he rose—
The fight—he triumphed o'er the foes,
    Whom God's just laws abhor;

And, arm'd in gallant faith, he took
Against the boaster, from the brook,
   The weapons of the war.

VII

Pious—magnificent and grand;
'Twas he the famous temple plan'd,
   (The seraph in his soul:)
Foremost to give the Lord his dues,
Foremost to bless the welcome news,
   And foremost to condole.

VIII

Good—from Jehudah's genuine vein,
From God's best nature good in grain,
   His aspect and his heart;
To pity, to forgive, to save,
Witness En-gedi's conscious cave,
   And Shimei's blunted dart.

IX

Clean—if perpetual prayer be pure,
And love, which could itself innure
   To fasting and to fear—
Clean in his gestures, hands, and feet,
To smite the lyre, the dance compleat,
   To play the sword and spear.

X

Sublime—invention ever young,
Of vast conception, tow'ring tongue,
   To God the eternal theme;
Notes from yon exaltations caught,
Unrival'd royalty of thought,
   O'er meaner strains supreme.

XI

Contemplative—on God to fix
His musings, and above the six
 The sabbath-day he blest;
'Twas then his thoughts self-conquest prun'd,
And heavenly melancholy tun'd,
 To bless and bear the rest.

XII

Serene—to sow the seeds of peace,
Remembring, when he watchd the fleece,
 How sweetly Kidron purld—
To further knowledge, silence vice,
And plant perpetual paradise,
 When God had calmed the world.

XIII

Strong—in the Lord, who could defy
Satan, and all his powers that lie
 In sempiternal night;
And hell, and horror, and despair
Were as the lion and the bear
 To his undaunted might.

XIV

Constant—in love to God, THE TRUTH,
Age, manhood, infancy, and youth—
 To Jonathan his friend
Constant, beyond the verge of death;
And Ziba, and Mephibosheth,
 His endless fame attend.

XV

Pleasant—and various as the year;
Man, soul, and angel, without peer,
 Priest, champion, sage and boy;

351

In armour, or in ephod clad,
His pomp, his piety was glad;
  Majestic was his joy.

XVI

Wise—in recovery from his fall,
Whence rose his eminence o'er all,
  Of all the most revil'd;
The light of Israel in his ways,
Wise are his precepts, prayer and praise
  And counsel to his child.

XVII

His muse, bright angel of his verse,
Gives balm for all the thorns that pierce,
  For all the pangs that rage;
Blest light, still gaining on the gloom,
The more than Michal of his bloom,
  The Abishag of his age.

XVIII

He sung of God—the mighty source
Of all things—the stupendous force
  On which all strength depends;
From whose right arm, beneath whose eyes,
All period, pow'r, and enterprize
  Commences, reigns, and ends.

XIX

Angels—their ministry and meed,
Which to and fro with blessings speed,
  Or with their citterns wait;
Where Michael with his millions bows,
Where dwells the seraph and his spouse,
  The cherub and her mate.

XX

Of man—the semblance and effect
Of God and Love—the Saint elect
   For infinite applause—
To rule the land, and briny broad,
To be laborious in his laud,
   And heroes in his cause.

XXI

The world—the clustring spheres he made,
The glorious light, the soothing shade,
   Dale, champaign, grove, and hill;
The multitudinous abyss,
Where secrecy remains in bliss,
   And wisdom hides her skill.

XXII

Trees, plants, and flow'rs—of virtuous root;
Gem yielding blossom, yielding fruit,
   Choice gums and precious balm;
Bless ye the nosegay in the vale,
And with the sweetness of the gale
   Enrich the thankful psalm.

XXIII

Of fowl—e'en ev'ry beak and wing
Which chear the winter, hail the spring,
   That live in peace or prey;
They that make music, or that mock,
The quail, the brave domestic cock,
   The raven, swan, and jay.

XXIV

Of fishes—ev'ry size and shape,
Which nature frames of light escape,
   Devouring man to shun:

353

The shells are in the wealthy deep,
The shoals upon the surface leap,
   And love the glancing sun.

XXV

Of beasts—the beaver plods his task;
While the sleek tigers roll and bask,
   Nor yet the shades arouse;
Her cave the mining coney scoops;
Where o'er the mead the mountain stoops,
   The kids exult and brouse.

XXVI

Of gems—their virtue and their price,
Which hid in earth from man's device,
   Their darts of lustre sheathe;
The jasper of the master's stamp,
The topaz blazing like a lamp
   Among the mines beneath.

XXVII

Blest was the tenderness he felt
When to his graceful harp he knelt,
   And did for audience call;
When satan with his hand he quell'd,
And in serene suspence he held
   The frantic throes of Saul.

XXVIII

His furious foes no more malign'd
As he such melody divin'd,
   And sense and soul detain'd;
Now striking strong, now soothing soft,
He sent the godly sounds aloft,
   Or in delight refrain'd.

354

XXIX

When up to heaven his thoughts he pil'd
From fervent lips fair Michal smil'd,
  As blush to blush she stood;
And chose herself the queen, and gave
Her utmost from her heart, 'so brave,
  And plays his hymns so good'.

XXX

The pillars of the Lord are seven,
Which stand from earth to topmost heav'n;
  His wisdom drew the plan;
His WORD accomplished the design,
From brightest gem to deepest mine,
  From CHRIST enthron'd to man.

XXXI

Alpha, the cause of causes, first
In station, fountain, whence the burst
  Of light, and blaze of day;
Whence bold attempt, and brave advance,
Have motion, life, and ordinance,
  And heaven itself its stay.

XXXII

Gamma supports the glorious arch
On which angelic legions march,
  And is with sapphires pav'd;
Thence the fleet clouds are sent adrift,
And thence the painted folds, that lift
  The crimson veil, are wav'd.

XXXIII

Eta with living sculpture breathes,
With verdant carvings, flow'ry wreaths,
  Of never-wasting bloom;

In strong relief his goodly base
All instruments of labour grace,
   The trowel, spade, and loom.

XXXIV

Next Theta stands to the Supreme—
Who formed, in number, sign, and scheme,
   Th' illustrious lights that are;
And one address'd his saffron robe,
And one, clad in a silver globe,
   Held rule with ev'ry star.

XXXV

Iota's tuned to choral hymns
Of those that fly, while he that swims
   In thankful safety lurks;
And foot, and chapitre, and niche,
The various histories enrich
   Of God's recorded works.

XXXVI

Sigma presents the social droves
With him that solitary roves,
   And man of all the chief;
Fair on whose face, and stately frame,
Did God impress his hallow'd name,
   For ocular belief.

XXXVII

OMEGA! GREATEST and the BEST,
Stands sacred to the day of rest,
   For gratitude and thought;
Which blessed the world upon his pole,
And gave the universe his goal,
   And clos'd th' infernal draught.

XXXVIII

O DAVID, scholar of the Lord!
Such is thy science, whence reward
    And infinite degree;
O strength, O sweetness, lasting ripe!
God's harp thy symbol, and thy type
    The lion and the bee!

XXXIX

There is but One who ne'er rebell'd,
But One by passion unimpell'd,
    By pleasures unintice't;
He from himself his semblance sent,
Grand object of his own content,
    And saw the God in CHRIST.

XL

Tell them, I am, JEHOVA said
To MOSES; while earth heard in dread,
    And, smitten to the heart,
At once above, beneath, around,
All Nature, without voice or sound,
    Replied, 'O Lord, THOU ART.'

XLI

Thou art—to give and to confirm,
For each his talent and his term;
    All flesh thy bounties share:
Thou shalt not call thy brother fool:
The porches of the Christian school
    Are meekness, peace, and pray'r.

XLII

Open, and naked of offence,
Man's made of mercy, soul, and sense;
    God armed the snail and wilk;

357

Be good to him that pulls thy plough;
Due food and care, due rest, allow
  For her that yields thee milk.

XLIII

Rise up before the hoary head,
And God's benign commandment dread,
  Which says thou shalt not die:
'Not as I will, but as Thou wilt',
Prayed He, whose conscience knew no guilt;
  With Whose bless'd pattern vie.

XLIV

Use all thy passions!—love is thine,
And joy, and jealousy divine;
  Thine hope's eternal fort,
And care thy leisure to disturb,
With fear concupiscence to curb,
  And rapture to transport.

XLV

Act simply, as occasion asks;
Put mellow wine in season'd casks;
  Till not with ass and bull:
Remember thy baptismal bond;
Keep from commixtures foul and fond,
  Nor work thy flax with wool.

XLVI

Distribute: pay the Lord his tithe,
And make the widow's heart-strings blithe;
  Resort with those that weep:
As you from all and each expect,
For all and each thy love direct,
  And render as you reap.

XLVII

The slander and its bearer spurn,
And propagating praise sojourn
    To make thy welcome last;
Turn from Old Adam to the New;
By hope futurity pursue;
    Look upwards to the past.

XLVIII

Controul thine eye, salute success,
Honour the wiser, happier bless,
    And for their neighbour feel;
Grutch not of mammon and his leaven,
Work emulation up to heaven
    By knowledge and by zeal.

XLIX

O DAVID, highest in the list
Of worthies, on God's ways insist,
    The genuine word repeat:
Vain are the documents of men,
And vain the flourish of the pen
    That keeps the fool's conceit.

L

PRAISE above all—for praise prevails;
Heap up the measure, load the scales,
    And good to goodness add:
The generous soul her saviour aids,
But peevish obloquy degrades;
    The Lord is great and glad.

LI

For ADORATION all the ranks
Of angels yield eternal thanks,
    And DAVID in the midst;

359

With God's good poor, which, last and least
In man's esteem, thou to thy feast,
   O blessed bridegroom, bidst.

LII

For ADORATION seasons change,
And order, truth, and beauty range,
   Adjust, attract, and fill:
The grass the polyanthus cheques;
And polish'd porphyry reflects,
   By the descending rill.

LIII

Rich almonds colour to the prime
For ADORATION; tendrils climb,
   And fruit-trees pledge their gems;
And Ivis, with her gorgeous vest,
Builds for her eggs her cunning nest,
   And bell-flowers bow their stems.

LIV

With vinous syrup cedars spout;
From rocks pure honey gushing out,
   For ADORATION springs:
All scenes of painting croud the map
Of nature; to the mermaid's pap
   The scaled infant clings.

LV

The spotted ounce and playsome cubs
Run rustling 'mongst the flow'ring shrubs,
   And lizards feed the moss;
For ADORATION beasts embark,
While waves upholding halcyon's ark
   No longer roar and toss.

LVI

While Israel sits beneath his fig,
With coral root and amber sprig
　　The wean'd advent'rer sports;
Where to the palm the jasmin cleaves,
For ADORATION 'mongst the leaves
　　The gale his peace reports.

LVII

Increasing days their reign exalt,
Nor in the pink and mottled vault
　　The opposing spirits tilt;
And, by the coasting reader spied,
The silverlings and crusions glide
　　For ADORATION gilt.

LVIII

For ADORATION rip'ning canes,
And cocoa's purest milk detains
　　The western pilgrim's staff;
Where rain in clasping boughs inclos'd,
And vines with oranges dispos'd,
　　Embow'r the social laugh.

LIX

Now labour his reward receives,
For ADORATION counts his sheaves,
　　To peace, her bounteous prince;
The nectarine his strong tint imbibes,
And apples of ten thousand tribes,
　　And quick peculiar quince.

LX

The wealthy crops of whit'ning rice,
'Mongst thyine woods and groves of spice,
　　For ADORATION grow;

And, marshall'd in the fenced land,
The peaches and pomegranates stand,
  Where wild carnations blow.

LXI

The laurels with the winter strive;
The crocus burnishes alive
  Upon the snow-clad earth:
For ADORATION myrtles stay
To keep the garden from dismay,
  And bless the sight from dearth.

LXII

The pheasant shows his pompous neck;
And ermine, jealous of a speck,
  With fear eludes offence:
The sable, with his glossy pride,
For ADORATION is descried,
  Where frosts the waves condense.

LXIII

The chearful holly, pensive yew,
And holy thorn, their trim renew;
  The squirrel hoards his nuts:
All creatures batten o'er their stores,
And careful nature all her doors
  For ADORATION shuts.

LXIV

For ADORATION, DAVID's Psalms
Lift up the heart to deeds of alms;
  And he, who kneels and chants,
Prevails his passions to controul,
Finds meat and med'cine to the soul,
  Which for translation pants.

LXV

For ADORATION, beyond match,
The scholar bulfinch aims to catch
    The soft flute's iv'ry touch;
And, careless, on the hazel spray,
The daring redbreast keeps at bay
    The damsel's greedy clutch.

LXVI

For ADORATION, in the skies,
The Lord's philosopher espies
    The Dog, the Ram, and Rose;
The planet's ring, Orion's sword;
Nor is his greatness less ador'd
    In the vile worm that glows.

LXVII

For ADORATION on the strings
The western breezes work their wings,
    The captive ear to sooth.—
Hark! 'tis a voice—how still, and small—
That makes the cataracts to fall,
    Or bids the sea be smooth!

LXVIII

For ADORATION, incense comes
From bezoar, and Arabian gums,
    And on the civet's furr:
But as for prayer, or e're it faints,
Far better is the breath of saints
    Than galbanum or myrrh.

LXIX

For ADORATION from the down
Of dam'sins to th' anana's crown,
    God sends to tempt the taste;

363

And while the luscious zest invites,
The sense, that in the scene delights,
  Commands desire be chaste.

LXX

For ADORATION, all the paths
Of grace are open, all the baths,
  Of purity refresh;
And all the rays of glory beam
To deck the man of God's esteem,
  Who triumphs o'er the flesh.

LXXI

For ADORATION, in the dome
Of CHRIST, the sparrow's find an home;
  And on his olives perch:
The swallow also dwells with thee,
O man of God's humility,
  Within his Saviour CHURCH.

LXXII

Sweet is the dew that falls betimes,
And drops upon the leafy limes;
  Sweet, Hermon's fragrant air:
Sweet is the lilly's silver bell,
And sweet the wakeful tapers smell
  That watch for early pray'r.

LXXIII

Sweet the young nurse, with love intense,
Which smiles o'er sleeping innocence;
  Sweet when the lost arrive:
Sweet the musician's ardour beats,
While his vague mind's in quest of sweets,
  The choicest flow'rs to hive.

LXXIV

Sweeter, in all the strains of love,
The language of thy turtle dove,
　　Pair'd to thy swelling chord;
Sweeter, with every grace endu'd,
The glory of thy gratitude,
　　Respir'd unto the Lord.

LXXV

Strong is the horse upon his speed;
Strong in pursuit the rapid glede,
　　Which makes at once his game:
Strong the tall ostrich on the ground;
Strong through the turbulent profound
　　Shoots xiphias to his aim.

LXXVI

Strong is the lion—like a coal
His eyeball—like a bastion's mole
　　His chest against the foes:
Strong, the gier-eagle on his sail,
Strong against tide, th' enormous whale
　　Emerges as he goes.

LXXVII

But stronger still, in earth and air,
And in the sea, the man of pray'r,
　　And far beneath the tide;
And in the seat to faith assign'd,
Where ask is have, where seek is find,
　　Where knock is open wide.

LXXVIII

Beauteous the fleet before the gale;
Beauteous the multitudes in mail,
　　Ranked arms and crested heads:

Beauteous the garden's umbrage mild,
Walk, water, meditated wild,
    And all the bloomy beds.

LXXIX

Beauteous the moon full on the lawn;
And beauteous, when the veil's withdrawn,
    The virgin to her spouse:
Beauteous the temple, deck'd and fill'd,
When to the heav'n of heav'ns they build
    Their heart-directed vows.

LXXX

Beauteous, yea beauteous more than these,
The shepherd king upon his knees,
    For his momentous trust;
With wish of infinite conceit,
For man, beast, mute, the small and great,
    And prostrate dust to dust.

LXXXI

Precious the bounteous widow's mite;
And precious, for extream delight,
    The largess from the churl:
Precious the ruby's blushing blaze,
And alba's blest imperial rays,
    And pure cerulean pearl.

LXXXII

Precious the penitential tear;
And precious is the sigh sincere;
    Acceptable to God:
And precious are the winning flow'rs,
In gladsome Israel's feast of bow'rs,
    Bound on the hallow'd sod.

LXXXIII

More precious that diviner part
Of David, even the Lord's own heart,
  Great, beautiful, and new:
In all things where it was intent,
In all extreams, in each event,
  Proof—answ'ring true to true.

LXXXIV

Glorious the sun in mid career;
Glorious th' assembled fires appear;
  Glorious the comet's train:
Glorious the trumpet and alarm;
Glorious th' almighty stretched-out arm;
  Glorious th' enraptur'd main:

LXXXV

Glorious the northern lights a-stream;
Glorious the song, when God's the theme;
  Glorious the thunder's roar:
Glorious hosannah from the den;
Glorious the catholic amen;
  Glorious the martyr's gore:

LXXXVI

Glorious,—more glorious, is the crown
Of Him that brought salvation down,
  By meekness, called thy Son:
Thou at stupendous truth believ'd;—
And now the matchless deed's atchiev'd,
  DETERMINED, DARED, and DONE.

NOTES

NOTES

Page 5. *To the King*. Printed among other tributes from senior members of the University on the return of George II to England.

Page 9. *Lord Barnard*. Henry Vane, father of Anne Vane (Smart's playmate at Raby Castle), succeeded to the title in 1753. When he was created Earl of Darlington Smart dedicated to him his Seatonian Prize poem *On the Eternity of the Supreme Being*, and addressed another ode to him on his becoming Paymaster to the Forces. It may be that Smart owed this member of the Vane family a particular debt for the continuation of his pension after the death of the Duchess of Cleveland.

Page 10. *Cleveland*. Henrietta, first Duchess of Cleveland, mother-in-law to Henry Vane (see above). She had given Smart a pension of £40 when he went up to Cambridge in 1739. See also the epitaph *On the Duchess of Cleveland*, p. 35.

Page 10. *Hope*. Anne Vane, Smart's childhood love, and perhaps his lifelong passion. If the story told by Mrs. Le Noir (Smart's daughter) is true, the pair tried to elope from Raby Castle when Smart was thirteen. Also according to Mrs. Le Noir, Anne Vane was the 'Ethelinda' of the poem on p. 198, said to have been written at about the same time. Anne Vane married first Charles Hope Weir, and it was probably for this marriage that Smart wrote his *Epithalamium* (p. 199); her second husband was George Monson. Smart mentions her (as Anne Hope) many times in *Jubilate Agno*.

Page 13. *Admiral Sir George Pocock*. Captured Havannah in 1762. See note on *Jubilate Agno*, p. 380. *And they whose offspring*. 'Alluding to the

Admiral's noble benefaction to the Sons of the Clergy' (Smart).

Page 16. *General Draper*. See note on *Jubilate Agno*, p. 377. *Thou chose*. 'Alluding to the famous copy of verses written by Draper at Eton' (Smart). *Matross*. An assistant gunner.

Page 22. *Kingsley*. See note on *Jubilate Agno*, p. 380.

Page 23. *Lady Hussey Delaval*. The wife of Edward Hussey Delaval, scientist and fellow of Pembroke.

Page 35. *Henrietta, Duchess of Cleveland*. See note on *Ode to Lord Barnard*, p. 375.

Page 35. *Henry Fielding*. There is nothing to show that Smart knew Fielding personally, but he took his side in the 'Paper War' (see note on the *Hilliad*, p. 372) and clearly had great admiration for him.

Page 36. *James Sheeles*. See note on *Jubilate Agno*, p. 379.

Page 37. *Duke of Argyle*. See note on *Jubilate Agno*, p. 378.

Page 73. *blazon*. 1791 has 'blaze on', followed by Chalmers, &c.

Page 78. *Reason and Imagination*. The first 26 lines and the last 22 appear only in *Poems*, 1763: they were not printed by Hunter in 1791, and may well have been a late addition by Smart. The style is certainly that of Smart's later years.

Page 81. *Kenrick*. If this is the William Kenrick who attacked Smart in *Kapelion* and in the pamphlet 'The Magazines blown up' (? 1750) it is no mean tribute to Smart's powers of forgiveness. The best account of the early quarrel is in Ainsworth and Noyes, *Christopher Smart*.

Page 88. *On Taking &c*. The allusions are to the Ode of Horace mentioned. *Nor is King's chapel ...* Regali situ pyramidum altius. *Shall time ...* Quod non innumerabilis | Annorum series ... possit

diruere. *Till to the church* ... dum Capitolium |
scandet cum tacita virgine pontifex. *Then with Æolian*
... princeps Æolium carmen ad Italos | deduxisse
modos. *For Horace* ... sume superbiam | quaesitam
meritis. *My head* ... et mihi Delphica | lauro cinge
volens, Melpomene comam.

Page 90. *Prologue &c.* Smart's play, *The Grateful
Fair, or a Trip to Cambridge*, was performed in Pem-
broke in 1747. Only the Prologue and the Soliloquy
seem to be extant. The plot is given in Chalmer's 'Life
of Smart' (*English Poets*, vol. 16): Sheridan may have
borrowed from it for his *Trip to Scarborough*. The
'Harriot' mentioned is probably Harriet Pratt of
Downham: see 'Lovely Harriote' and *Jubilate Agno*.

Page 92. *Mr. Garrick &c.* This piece was no doubt
one of the turns in the Old Woman's Oratory, a vaude-
ville show devised by Newbery and Smart to advertise
Newbery's publications. It was put on at the New
Theatre, Haymarket, in December 1751. The pro-
gramme of the first performance, from the *London
Daily Advertiser*, 2nd December 1751, is given in the
Introduction, p. xxiii. For *Garrick and Barry* see
D.N.B., s.n. 'Barry'. They were the managers and
stars of the two rival London theatres, Drury Lane
and Covent Garden (1750).

Page 93. *On seeing the incomparable Mons. Timber-
toe &c.* From an advertisement for the Old Woman's
Oratory: signed Lewis Lun—one of Smart's pseu-
donyms.

Page 94. *An Occasional Prologue and Epilogue to
Othello.* This show was put on at Drury Lane in
March 1751, before an audience which included the
Prince and Princess of Wales. One of the actors was
John Blake Delaval, whom Smart had tutored at
Cambridge. For criticism of the performance and of
Smart's connexion with it, see the *Gentleman's Maga-
zine*, vol. xxi.

Page 98. *Epilogue &c.* At the conclusion of *The Conscious Lovers* given at the Theatre Royal, in aid of the Middlesex Hospital.

Page 102. *Harriot.* The original version (*London Magazine*, 1748) had 'Delia'. See 'Lovely Harriote', etc., and note on Jermyn Pratt, *Jubilate Agno*, p. 378.

Page 115. *Mecaenas.* So spelt in the *Midwife.* A free paraphrase of Hor., *Od.*, I, i.

Page 123. *Timolus.* Cf. Ovid, *Metamorphoses*, xi, 217 ff. Ovid uses the form 'Tmolus', but Smart's spelling is found in Pliny.

Page 142. *The Hop Garden.* For 'Georgics' of a similar type see Philips's *Cyder* and Dyer's *Fleece.* Page 143. *Madum.* Maidstone. Page 150. *If thou, O Philips.* 'Mr. John Philips, author of Cider, a poem' (Smart). Page 155. *Theophilus.* 'Mr. Theophilus Wheeler of Christ Church, Cambridge' (Smart). See Venn, *Alumni Cantabrigienses*, s.n. 'Wheeler'. Page 156. *Mariane.* 'The author's youngest sister' (Smart).

Page 169. *The Hilliad.* The object of this satire was the self-styled Sir John Hill, pamphleteer, botanist and would-be member of the Royal Society. He had attacked Smart through his two papers, the *Inspector* and the *Impertinent.* For a brief account of this quarrel, and of the 'Paper War' between Hill and Fielding, see D'Israeli *Miscellanies of Literature*, s.à. 'Quarrels of Authors'. Fuller details are given in *D.N.B.*, s.n. 'Hill', and in Botting, *Christopher Smart in London.* The elaborate 'Prolegomena' and 'Notes Variorum', of which only a selection is printed here, were modelled on those of Pope's *Dunciad.* Smart may have had the help of Arthur Murphy in compiling them.

Page 176. (*Notes Variorum*) *Oratory-Right-Reason-Chapel.* 'Orator' John Henley held his 'Oratory' (a mixture of enthusiastic preaching and farce) in Lincoln's Inn Fields on Sundays and Wednesdays (see

Pope's *Dunciad*, ed. J. R. Sutherland, pp. 173, 4 n., and elsewhere). Smart's note is a parody of Henley's style.

Page 178. *When privately &c.* Cf. Hor., *Od.*, I, x, 9 ff.

Page 179. (*Notes Variorum*) *Diamond in an Aethiop's ear.* Cf. *Romeo and Juliet*, I, v. 'Diamond' was the name of Hill's mistress. A *Smartead* was actually published, though Hill may not have been the author.

Page 187. *Miss H—— P——t.* Presumably Harriot Pratt, as in the following poem. The grounds for assigning this to Smart are the initials in the title, the fact that Smart contributed to the *Museum* (there is another poem by him in this issue) and the style which strongly suggests Smart.

Page 188. *Lovely Harriote.* See note on Jermyn Pratt, *Jubilate Agno*, p. 378.

Page 190. *Miss H——.* See previous notes. This poem gives the name 'Harriot', and is signed 'S'.

Page 192. *With a Pocket Book.* From a manuscript letter of Mrs. Le Noir, Smart's daughter. The recipient of the pocket book was Smart's sister (probably Margaret).

Page 192. *Miss A——n.* 'Addison'(?). Smart's tutor at Cambridge was Leonard Addison, and this lady may have been a connexion. But there is no evidence apart from the terminals of the name.

Page 197. *Kitty Bennet.* See note on *Jubilate Agno*, p. 378.

Page 199. *Ethelinda.* See note on Anne Hope, p. 375.

Page 199. *Epithalamium.* Probably written for the wedding of Anne Vane to George Hope Weir. See the note on the previous poem.

Page 202. *The Lass with the Golden Locks.* This, and the following three poems, concern Anna Maria Carnan, stepdaughter to Smart's publisher, John Newbery. She was married to Smart in 1753.

Page 204. *Miss S—— P——e*. Unidentified; perhaps a Reading friend of Miss Carnan (see previous note).

Page 207. *Mr. T. B.* Possibly Thomas Bowlby, for whom see note on *Jubilate Agno*, p. 378; but there is nothing but the initials to support this.

Page 211. *John Sherratt*. It is clear from this poem that Smart regarded Sherratt as being instrumental in getting him released from confinement. He is mentioned again in *Jubilate Agno*, p. 347, but apart from a depreciatory reference in the *Critical Review* (vol. cvi, p. 72), I have been unable to find any other allusio.. to him.

Page 211. *Rolt*. Historian and poet whose style hardly deserves this encomium. He was Smart's partner in a contract which the two men signed with the bookseller Gardner in 1756, to write exclusively for the *Universal Visiter*. Johnson used this contract as a stick to beat the booksellers, but it has been shown that the document was in fact quite reasonable (see Mr. Stuart Piggott's article in *The Times Literary Supplement*, 13 July 1929, p. 247). Although the contract was for ninety-nine years, any partner to it might withdraw without difficulty. Rolt may also have helped Smart in the Old Woman's Oratory.

Page 221. *Webster*. For William Webster, Warburton's opponent in religious controversy, see *D.N.B.*, s.n. 'Webster'.

Page 223. *On the Eternity &c.* This is the first of the Seatonian Prize poems. The prize was first offered in 1750 for a work dealing with 'one or other of the perfections or attributes of the Supreme Being'. The value of the prize was about £30 in Smart's day: he won it in 1750 with this poem and in 1751, 1752, 1754 and 1755 with the poems which follow. It was a condition of his being allowed to keep his name on the College books after he had left Cambridge that he should compete for the poem.

Page 244. *Hymn to the Supreme Being*. This poem is dedicated in a prefatory letter to Dr. James, inventor of the famous 'Fever Powder' for which Newbery was the sole agent.

Page 244. *When Israel's ruler*. See *Isaiah* xxxviii. The king is Hezekiah, not Saul, as some commentators in their search for premonitions of *A Song to David* would have it.

Page 249. *Jubilate Agno*. The text here printed is that of Mr. W. F. Stead, whose edition of Smart's manuscript was published by Jonathan Cape in 1939, under the title *Rejoice in the Lamb*. I have adopted many of Mr. Stead's emendations silently, and, since this is not primarily a critical edition, have omitted his diacritics. For the benefit of those who wish to refer to the manuscript readings and to Mr. Stead's excellent notes I have retained the pagination and line numbering of his text. Notes taken either verbatim or substantially from Mr. Stead are marked [St.].

Page 265. (VI. 71.) *John Dore*. An inmate of St. Luke's asylum and of Bedlam; probably a fellow-inmate with Smart. [St.]

Page 266. (VII. 7.) *Family bickerings*. This seems to indicate that Smart was at home when he wrote this. Stead (q.v.) dates this passage as 'probably not later than March 1760'.

Page 266. (VII. 19.) *Colonel Draper*. See *Ode to General Draper*, p. 16. Draper held a fellowship at King's while Smart was at Cambridge. He served in the army in India, captured Manilla in 1762, and presented the standards to his college. He subscribed for forty copies of Smart's *Psalms*.

Page 267. (VII. 23.) *Staindrop Moor*. Adjacent to Raby Castle, the home of Anne Vane, to whom this is an indirect allusion. See also pp. 304, 310, and notes on *Ode to Lord Barnard*, p. 375.

Page 267. (VII. 25.) *Thomas Hall*. A child of excep-

C.S.—I   377   EE

tional stature who seems to have been put on show near Cambridge. [St.] Cf. *G.M.*, xv (1745).

Page 270. (VIII. 5.) *Canbury*. Canonbury House, Islington, where Smart lived after his marriage. It housed several of Newbery's authors, among them Goldsmith.

Page 274. (IX. 8.) *pillars*. See *A Song to David*, st. xxx.

Page 279. (X. 22.) *Benjamin Hallett*. A child musician who took the part of Cupid in the Old Woman's Oratory: see Introduction, p. xxiii.

Page 289. (XIII. 16.) *Campbells*. (?) John Campbell, Duke of Argyle. See the *Epitaph* on p. 37. This epitaph, at least, does not refer to the Campbell mentioned in Stead's note.

Page 290. (XIII. 26.) *Howard*. Samuel Howard, organist of St. Clement Dane's, who set some of Smart's Psalms to music (Ainsworth and Noyes).

Page 295. (XIV. 33.) *Thomas Bowlby*. At Durham School with Smart and later at Trinity Hall, Cambridge. See Venn, *Alumni Cantabrigienses*. Possibly the recipient of 'To my Worthy Friend Mr. T. B', p. 207.

Page 300. (XVI. 3.) *Tyers*. Proprietor of Vauxhall Gardens, where several settings of Smart's poems were performed.

Page 302. (XVI. 40.) *flowers*. See Boswell, *Life*, vol. i, p. 397, 'He [Smart] digs in the garden', and later in this poem, 'my pink borders', p. 337.

Page 302. (XVII. 19.) *Jermyn Pratt*. Of Downham in Norfolk: he was at Cambridge with Smart. His sister, Harriot Pratt, was 'a lady for whom our author had entertained a long and unsuccessful passion' (Hunter, *Memoir*). She is the subject of the 'Harriote' poems, pp. 187–191.

Page 304. (XVII. 23.) *Bennet*. James Bennet, master of Hoddesden Grammar School (see Boswell, *Life* vol. i, p. 464 n.). Kitty Bennet (see p. 197) was presumably his daughter.

Page 304. (XVII. 48.) *The fifth year*. This places the beginning of Smart's confinement in 1756. [St.] See Stead's *Introduction* and note, *ad. loc.*

Page 307. (XVIII. 21 ff.) Cf. *A Song to David*, st. iv ff.

Page 315. (XXI. 4.) *Jub*. Jubilate. [St.]

Page 320. (XXII. 48.) *Goldy Locks*. Smart's wife; see p. 202 and note.

Page 321. (XXII. 70.) *Peele*. John Peele, fellow of Pembroke 1743, came to Smart's help when he was being pursued by his creditors in 1747 (see *Correspondence of Thomas Gray*, ed. Tovey, i. 291 f.). The unidentified Ferry perhaps performed the same office. [St.]

Page 322. (XXIII. 17.) *Davis the bookseller*. Possibly the Thomas Davies who introduced Boswell to Johnson, and who sold *PSO* 1763. [St.]

Page 326. (XXIV. 18.) *that the Reformation &c*. The quarrel between the Papacy and the Venetian Republic was a subject of topical interest. Stead cites Walpole's *Letters* appositely. This is one of the many pieces of evidence that Smart in confinement was up to date in current affairs.

Page 332. (XXVI. 11.) *Lewis Baily*. Author of *The Practice of Piety*. See *D.N.B.* s.n. 'Bayly'.

Page 333. (XXVI. 28.) *Fane*. Another form of Vane. [St.]

Page 333. (XXVI. 30.) *Flexney &c*. The publisher of Smart's *Psalms*. *Sheels*. Probably the James Sheeles of the *Epitaph* on p. 36.

Page 334. (XXVII. 7.) *Powell*. Presumably the recipient of the verse letter on p. 206.

Page 334. (XXVII. 13.) *Dr. Benson*. Canon of Durham in 1724. Smart may have known him at that time. [St.]

Page 334. (XXVII. 16.) *William Mason.* Gray's friend, the recipient of his acid comments on Smart's behaviour. Like Gray, he (somewhat peevishly) befriended Smart on more than one occasion. Smart praises both men as poets in one of the *Fables*: there is no reason for assuming, as most people do, that this praise is insincere.

Page 336. (XXVIII. 6.) *Dr. Wilcox.* As Master of Clare College, Cambridge, he had awarded Smart the Seatonian Prize on five occasions.

Page 337. (XXVIII. 16.) *Havannah.* Captured by Admiral Sir George Pocock in 1762. See also XXX. 30, and the 'Ode' on p. 13.

Page 340. (XXIX. 28.) *Rosoman.* Proprietor of Sadlers Wells, and one of the witnesses to Smart's contract with Gardner to write for *The Universal Visiter.* See note on Rolt, p. 374.

Page 340. (XXIX. 32.) *English.* 'Naturalise.' [St.]

Page 344. (XXXI. 2.) *Arne &c.* Thomas Arne, 1710–78, see Grove, *Dictionary of Music. Charles Burney* studied under Arne: he was one of Smart's kindest and most persistent friends. See the *Early Diary of Madame D'Arblay,* i. 28, and elsewhere.

Page 346. (XXXI. 25.) 'This is the latest date in the MS.; Smart was probably set at liberty at about this time.' [St.]

Page 346. (XXXII. 30.) *Kingsley.* Lieutenant-General, commander of 'Kingsley's Grenadiers', the heroes of Minden, and originators of Minden Roses. See also 'On ... Kingsley at Minden', p. 22.

Page 347. (XXXII. 6.) *John Sherrat.* See 'Epistle to John Sherratt', p. 211, and note, *ad loc.*

Page 348. *A Song to David.* This poem was excluded by Hunter as showing 'melancholy proofs of Smart's recent estrangement of mind'. It was reprinted by Smart at the end of his *Psalms,* and not again until 1827. The text here given is that of the first edition (1763) in the library of Pembroke College. For the plan of the poem, see R. D. Havens, *The Structure of Smart's Song to David* in *Review of English Studies*, XV (April 1938).

The following notes are in part Smart's own, in part the editor's. Definitions are those of the *O.E.D.*

St. vi, 'the boaster'—Goliath

viii, *En-gedi*—1 Samuel xxiv.

xiv, *Ziba and Mephibosheth*—2 Samuel xvi. and xix.

xix, *citterns*—harps

xxi, *champaign*—level country

xxx, *Pillars*—the monuments of God's work in the first week (see Havens, *op. cit.*)

xlii, *wilk*—whelk

liii, *Ivis*—humming-bird

lv, *ounce*—leopard

lvii, *crusions*—carp

lx, *thyine*—sweet

lxvii, *on the strings*—*sc.* of the Æolian harp

lxviii, *bezoar*—a substance found in the stomachs of ruminants

Galbanum—gum-resin, used in incense

lxix, *anana*—a species of pineapple

lxxv, *glede*—hawk

xiphias—sword-fish

lxxvi, *gier-eagle*—eagle or vulture (cf. Deut. xiv.)

lxxviii, *umbrage*—shade

lxxxi, *alba*—alb or surplice

cerulean—blue.

For Product Safety Concerns and Information please contact our EU
representative GPSR@taylorandfrancis.com
Taylor & Francis Verlag GmbH, Kaufingerstraße 24, 80331 München, Germany